AF600283

LATINITY AND IDENTITY IN ANGLO-SAXON LITERATURE

Latinity and Identity in Anglo-Saxon Literature

EDITED BY REBECCA STEPHENSON
AND EMILY V. THORNBURY

UNIVERSITY OF TORONTO PRESS
Toronto Buffalo London

Toronto Buffalo London
www.utppublishing.com

ISBN 978-1-4426-3758-0

Library and Archives Canada Cataloguing in Publication

Latinity and identity in Anglo-Saxon literature/edited by Rebecca Stephenson and Emily V. Thornbury.

(Toronto Anglo-Saxon series)
Includes bibliographical references and index.
ISBN 978-1-4426-3758-0 (hardback)

1. English literature – Old English, ca. 450–1100 – History and criticism. 2. Identity (Philosophical concept) in literature. 3. Monasticism and religious orders in literature. 4. Latin literature – History and criticism. I. Thornbury, Emily Victoria, 1977–, editor II. Stephenson, Rebecca, 1975–, editor III. Series: Toronto Anglo-Saxon series

PR173.L38 2016 829'.09 C2016-901670-6

University of Toronto Press gratefully acknowledges the financial assistance of the Centre for Medieval Studies, University of Toronto in the publication of this book.

University of Toronto Press acknowledges the financial assistance to its publishing program of the Canada Council for the Arts and the Ontario Arts Council, an agency of the Government of Ontario.

Canada Council for the Arts Conseil des Arts du Canada

Funded by the Government of Canada Financé par le gouvernement du Canada | Canada

Contents

Acknowledgments

Collaborative projects such as these include the aid and generosity of countless people for each article in the volume, but we have space here to thank only a few. First, thc cditors gratcfully acknowledge the financial support awarded by their institutions, including travel grants from UC Berkeley's Committee on Research and the funds available from the Tommy and Mary Barham Endowed Professorship in English at the University of Louisiana at Monroe.

The 45th and 46th International Congress on Medieval Studies in Kalamazoo, Michigan, and the 2011 International Medieval Congress in Leeds provided wonderful venues in which these ideas were first presented as conference papers, discussed, and later blossomed into articles. We would also like to thank our anonymous readers for their suggestions, which helped us refine and nuance this volume. Finally, we would like to thank Suzanne Rancourt for her support for this project, and for shepherding this volume to completion.

Note on Translations

Unless otherwise specified, all translations are by the authors.

LATINITY AND IDENTITY IN ANGLO-SAXON LITERATURE

Introduction

Latin, after the collapse of the western Empire, was a language of choice; and though that choice may have seemed more inevitable in some places and periods than in others, it was always heavily laden with emotional and social meaning. We can understand a little of what it meant to choose Latin from descriptions of the alternative possibility: the opposite of the vernacular must be the language of the slavemaster, the foreigner, the cosmopolite; the opposite of the mother tongue, that of the father.[1] And all of these implications were indeed part of the legacy of Latin in the early Middle Ages. But reducing history and linguistic relations to a schematized Oedipal struggle interposes a distorted lens between the past and us. For many years – and sometimes still – medieval literature has been forced by post-medieval commentators into the highly ethically charged set of binary relations illustrated in the table:

Latin	**Vernacular**
Christian	Worldly
Authoritative	Subversive
Intellectual	Creative
Unitary	Multiple
Collective	Individual
Masculine	Feminine
Normative	Queer
Rigorous	Interesting

1 See Lewis and Short, *Latin Dictionary*, svv. *verna*, *vernaculus*, and *DMLBS*, sv. *vernaculus*. On the implied gender dynamics of Latin and vernaculars in Anglo-Saxon England, see most recently Karkov, "Mother's Tongue."

Which side of the table corresponded to *good* and which to *bad* has tended to hinge on the temperament and training of the readers and scholars involved.

Perhaps among the most important achievements of the last two generations of medievalists has been to show how badly these dichotomies mischaracterize both Latin *and* vernacular literature. On the vernacular side, the insights achieved through serious literary attention to devotional and sermon literature, translations, and the construction of authority (to name only a few examples) need not be rehearsed here, although they have transformed the contemporary study of Anglo-Saxon literature. Yet work on England's early Latin literature has been no less transformative, allowing us to understand this material as both literary art and part of a complex social phenomenon, not simply a set of sources for vernacular texts. This work is integrally part of a broader contemporary trend in recognizing the vibrancy and diversity of medieval Latin across Europe.[2] And so we come, in this volume, to a fresh consideration of what it meant to choose Latin in Anglo-Saxon England.

First, even to native speakers of a Germanic language, Latin did not manifest itself as a homogeneous, timeless, elemental substance. From the beginning of the period to the end, many kinds of Latin were available to the Anglo-Saxons, who then constructed other forms themselves.[3] For example, the letter that Aldhelm, abbot of Malmesbury, wrote sometime between 675 and 690 to Heahfrith, a former student just returned from Ireland, shows Aldhelm half-seriously playing with a kind of nationalized idea of Virgilius Maro's "Twelve Latinities," even if the reference he made to Virgilius's *Epitome* was facetious.[4] Aldhelm's letter displays a

2 As one important recent example, the essays in Hexter and Townsend, eds., *Oxford Handbook of Medieval Latin Literature*, engage with Latin along multiple axes, with a particular emphasis on variety across time and space, and Latin's intersections with social formations at the level of the group and of the individual.

3 See further Townsend, "Latinities," who demonstrates how the variety of later Anglo-Latin reveals "Latinity ... as a strategy of agency" (530) for individuals in varied social circumstances.

4 *Epistola ad Ehfridum*, in Ehwald, ed., *Aldhelmi Opera*, 486–94, esp. 494. (For analysis and translation of Aldhelm's letters, see Lapidge and Herren, *Prose Works*.) In his *Epitome* I (ed. Huemer, 5–6), the mysterious seventh-century philosopher-grammarian "Virgilius Maro" records the twelve kinds of Latin through their words for "fire": of which only one, *ignis*, is commonly known, even as the other eleven varieties of *latinitas inussitata* capture different aspects of fire's multifarious nature. Multiplicity was integral to Virgilius's understanding of wisdom: see Law, *Wisdom, Authority, and Grammar*, esp. 47–56.

hyperbolically alliterative and grandiose prose that both parodies Irish Latin and offers an even more spectacular English alternative. But he constructs the English version of Latinity as superior because it depended on the living voices of Mediterranean scholars sent directly from Papal Rome to Canterbury, namely Archbishop Theodore and Abbot Hadrian, who are credited with bringing Greek arcane vocabulary to Anglo-Saxon England.[5] Aldhelm was the first English author to include such esoteric and Greek-derived vocabulary, and by establishing his prose style as separate from the Irish tradition, he shows us that, even from the beginning of the period, Anglo-Latin authors were acutely conscious of style as a performance of affinities.

Aldhelm himself worked within a set of largely Continental, late antique literary paradigms, but the sensibility through which he filtered this material was unique, and came to be seen by his successors as distinctively English.[6] During Aldhelm's lifetime, and immediately after his death, his literary technique was evidently considered a recognizable personal attribute. Bede's well-known characterization of Aldhelm's language as *nitidus* "glittering" and his own quite different way of writing perhaps mark a certain ambivalence towards his already well-known predecessor.[7] But other contemporaries actively embraced Aldhelm's style. Of these, his student Æthilwald makes clearest the degree to which choice of literary form is a display of personal connection: in both prose and, especially, his rhythmic octosyllabic verse, Æthilwald's form is a hyperbolic version of all the most distinctive elements of his master's.[8] In his days as a West Saxon schoolmaster named Wynfrith, Boniface too embraced the most notable formal qualities of Aldhelm's verse, particularly the formulaic systems that likely stemmed from a shared background in oral poetry.[9] The Latin verse of Boniface and his disciple Lull – who had trained at Malmesbury before joining the mission to Germany – is intensely Aldhelmian in its diction and structure; use of their predecessor's poetic style seems to

5 Bischoff and Lapidge, *Biblical Commentaries.*

6 For Aldhelm's antecedents see Winterbottom, "Aldhelm's Prose Style." For his later reception, see (in this volume) Herren, "Boniface's Epistolary Prose Style."

7 See Szarmach, "Bede on Aldhelm"; Orchard, *Poetic Art*, 254–60; Thornbury, *Becoming a Poet*, 187–91.

8 Orchard, *Poetic Art*, 21–6; Miles, "*Carmina rhythmica.*"

9 Lapidge, "Aldhelm's Latin Poetry"; Orchard, *Poetic Art* and "Old Sources, New Resources."

have become, for the Anglo-Saxons on the Continent, a way of demonstrating a common purpose and a shared national origin.[10]

Yet Boniface was not simply a literary clone of his West Saxon forebear, as Michael W. Herren shows here in "Boniface's Epistolary Prose Style: The Letters to the English." Through a close study of a wide range of stylistic features – "alliteration, hyperbaton (including double hyperbaton), chiasmus, pleonasm (including the redundant genitive), rhyming cola, and abstruse lexical items" – Herren is able to tease out substantive differences between Aldhelm's style and Boniface's.[11] Most importantly, he demonstrates that Boniface adapts his style to connect with a particular audience, a feature which Aldhelm does not share. On the whole, the works Boniface wrote to leaders of the Church were more challenging than those he wrote to Anglo-Saxon kings or women. The responsiveness of his prose to the perceived needs of his audience shows that the Latinity of Boniface's letters is thus itself part of a dialogue, and tells us something about his understanding of the variegated English society he had left behind.

Latin style, then, was an almost infinitely malleable signifier of identity; and even distinctive, relatively unified styles (like Aldhelm's) were perceived as composed of separable, independently usable elements. Continued scholarly attention to the real multiplicity and complexity of Anglo-Latin styles, and their practitioners' self-consciousness in constructing and deploying them, will help us better understand literary affinity and development throughout the period. As one example, Alastair Campbell thought that Æthilwulf, in his poem *De abbatibus*, was relatively little indebted to the work of his near-contemporary and fellow Northumbrian Alcuin.[12] Lapidge, however, demonstrated that there were in fact substantial connections between the two poets' work; and in this volume, Emily V. Thornbury's "Æthilwulf *poeta*" further considers the influence of Alcuin's poetic persona on Æthilwulf's. As a rule, Anglo-Saxon authors did not call themselves poets (*scop* in Old English, or *vates* or *poeta* in Latin). Æthilwulf, however, broke with this convention and called himself *poeta* openly. In so doing, Æthilwulf follows the model of Alcuin and other poets of the court of Charlemagne, where newly rediscovered classical models had prompted authors to position themselves in the line of *vates* and *poetae* like Vergil and Tibullus. Yet Æthilwulf was working in a small

10 Thornbury, *Becoming a Poet*, 200–9.

11 Below, p. 21.

12 Campbell, *Æthelwulf: De abbatibus*, xlvi–xlvii.

monastery in Northumbria, not among other *vates* in Charlemagne's court, and his poem does not leave evidence of the kind of easy supportive relationship with his patron such as Alcuin enjoyed. Æthilwulf's construction of himself as *poeta* thus differed substantially both from native traditions and the Carolingian court culture from which he borrowed the title. However, by asserting his own authorship, Æthilwulf affirms his role in constructing and maintaining his monastery's history; and moreover, by directly referencing his role as *poeta*, he frees himself both from the historiographical tradition that precedes him and from dependence on episcopal patronage.

Æthilwulf's self-construction as a *poeta* is particularly interesting because it illustrates how an aspect of Alcuin's poetry which most likely read to contemporaries as modern, even exotic, could be integrated into a poetic persona that was otherwise deeply concerned with a historically conscious, rather inward-focused Northumbrian identity. Throughout the Anglo-Saxon period, we see many other instances in which Latinity is made to simultaneously signal both modernity and historical consciousness: the best-known instance of this is perhaps the "Aldhelm revival" that accompanied the tenth-century reform of many of the great Benedictine monasteries in the south. As Lapidge showed in his classic article on the "Hermeneutic Style," the peculiar Latin vocabulary characteristic of the monastic reformers and their students was largely created through intensive study of Aldhelm's writings and of glossaries derived from them.[13] Lapidge adopted the name of the "hermeneutic style" from Alistair Campbell, who seems to have so called it because of its practitioners' perceived dependence on Greek-Latin glossaries like the *Hermeneumata Pseudo-Dositheana*.[14] At the time Lapidge adopted the name "hermeneutic style," he was uncomfortable with it, suggesting that "glossematic" might be more appropriate to reflect the connection of the style to unusual words derived from glossaries. In 2005, Lapidge further considered the characteristics of this style of Latin, explaining that he was "naively bedazzled by

13 Lapidge, "Hermeneutic Style" and "Byrhtferth at Work." Rauer's chapter in this volume shows that the intensive use of Aldhelm glosses for the enrichment of literary registers was confined neither to the tenth century nor to Latin.

14 See Campbell, ed., *Chronicle of Æthelweard*, xlv–xlvi, who distinguishes between two kinds of Anglo-Latinity: the "classical," associated with Bede, and the "hermeneutic," associated with Aldhelm. See also Campbell, "Some Linguistic Features," 11–13, 17–19, and Lapidge, "Hermeneutic Style," 105–6.

the display of vocabulary which one encounters there," but "now I suspect that that perception needs modification: that the authors' principal aim was not obfuscation, but was their (misguided, perhaps) attempt to reach in their prose a high stylistic register."[15] In this article, he details seven categories of poeticism that could contribute to an elevated stylistic register,[16] but since he no longer felt the words were derived specifically from glosses, he refrained from using the word "hermeneutic" in that article and in all later publications.[17]

The lack of a term to describe this style of writing creates a significant lacuna in scholarship, since these were not idiosyncratic writers working by themselves. Rather they were a very specific group of authors working in the late tenth and early eleventh century, nearly all of whom bear some connection to the Benedictine Reform.[18] Even the two authors who were not Benedictine monks have significant monastic connections: Æthelweard wrote his Chronicle while a layman, but later retired to a Benedictine monastery, and the secular cleric known as "B" composed his Life of St Dunstan in this elevated style as part of his plea to Benedictine monks that he should be allowed to return to a reformed England. While there is a tremendous range in how individual writers apply the style – some preferring Grecisms, others neologisms, and still others polysyllabic adverbs[19] – it is definitely a distinctive style practised by a discrete group of people who have substantial connections to each other; in short, it is a literary and historical phenomenon. By eliminating the term "hermeneutic" without replacing it with something else, we find ourselves unable to discuss this style in a rigorous way, since it possesses a constellation of very specific features that are not shared in the same ways by texts from other periods, even when such writings aspire to elevated styles. Therefore, the editors

15 Lapidge, "Poeticism," 336.

16 See ibid., esp. 336–7. In the introduction to *Politics of Language*, Stephenson outlines a number of further characteristics of hermeneutic Latin, including complex syntax or word-order (such as hyperbaton), rhyme and other aural devices, and especially an insistence on *variatio* at the level of both word and phrase.

17 Particularly, he does not use the word in his *Lives of St. Oswald and St. Ecgwine* and in the *Early Lives of St. Dunstan* that he edited with Michael Winterbottom.

18 The discussion here is necessarily compressed. A full history of this style of Latin in England and its connections to the Continent can be found in the introduction to Stephenson's *Politics of Language*.

19 Lapidge, "Hermeneutic Style," 139.

and authors of this volume have chosen to retain the term "hermeneutic" because, ultimately, the coincidence of name between the hermeneutic style and hermeneutics as a practice seems to be fortuitous, pointing as it does towards a key function of the style. This esoteric register of Anglo-Latin served many immediate ends, as scholars have recently shown: Byrhtferth of Ramsey, for instance, used it to separate monastic sheep from secular goats,[20] while "B," who was Dunstan's former student as well as his biographer, used his knowledge of Aldhelm to placate English patrons.[21] In these cases, and others developed in this volume (especially by Stephenson, Fleming, and Davis-Secord), this register of Latin demands a particular kind of hermeneutic practice from its readers. To appreciate – or even to simply understand – this complex and Aldhelm-saturated strain of hermeneutic Anglo-Latin, a tenth-century reader would have to have been a particular kind of person: one who had studied at a reformed Benedictine foundation in England.

Reliance on Anglo-Latin models and sources thus gave the works of the tenth century a distinctive national character, even as the reformers looked to the Continent for new ways of structuring the Church and envisioning its relation to the world. Latin was a critical part of the Benedictine Reform not simply because it was the medium of international discourse, but because the structures that supported its learning, teaching, and use also enabled a wholesale reconstruction of the individual and, through the individual, the community. As Katherine O'Brien O'Keeffe has argued,

> the learning of Latin was the foundation on which the textual life of the community depended, and as such ... the learning of Latin in the first instance, and thereafter the learning and interpretation of other fundamental texts, constituted the indispensable building blocks of the textual identity of the members of the monastic community.[22]

The discipline that imparted Latinity – *grammatica* – was thus a kind of architect of the individual, forming body and mind into a total way of being.[23] It also laid the groundwork for an interpretative practice potentially

20 Stephenson, "Scapegoating the Secular Clergy" and (in this volume) "Saint Who?"

21 Lapidge, "B. and the *Vita S. Dunstani.*"

22 O'Brien O'Keeffe, *Stealing Obedience*, 110–11.

23 Irvine, *Making of Textual Culture*. On the violence associated with *grammatica*, see O'Brien O'Keeffe, *Stealing Obedience*, 121–3.

applicable to all literature, and, as Damian Fleming argues in this volume, to abstract ideas of language that left room for other *linguae sacrae* and even vernaculars.

Those who entered the heavenly city of the cloister were bound to accept a fundamental alteration in their most basic relations to language, yet monks were not merely passive recipients in this process of intellectual transformation. Not only must learning be willed in order to be effective, as O'Brien O'Keeffe has shown in *Stealing Obedience*, but, as Scott DeGregorio argues here in "*Interpretatio Monastica*: Biblical Commentary and the Forging of Monastic Identity in the Early Middle Ages," the practice of exegesis itself had for centuries offered many different models for self-formation. In his comparison of Bede's *On Ezra and Nehemiah* with Gregory's *Homilies on Ezekiel*, DeGregorio shows that the process of biblical commentary was also a process of identification, as exegetes came to speak through and for their subjects. In these commentaries on relatively peripheral biblical books, each author dramatizes the formation of both a coherent monastic identity and distinctive authorial personae. While Gregory envisions himself as a "visionary prophet," Bede sees himself as a "priestly reformer": each thus invokes a biblical mode as a means of relating to himself, his immediate community, and the world at large.

While Bede and Gregory were unusual in the degree to which each recognized and was willing to exploit the flexibility of apparently immutable disciplines like biblical exegesis and – in Bede's case – computus, the example of Byrhtferth of Ramsey demonstrates that a willingness to manipulate and exploit the learned tradition was not confined to doctors of the Church. In "Saint Who? Building Monastic Identity through Computistical Inquiry in Byrhtferth's *Vita S. Ecgwini*," Rebecca Stephenson shows that computus, in Byrhtferth's hands, became an almost infinitely flexible signifier for a specifically monastic learning. By the tenth century, almost nothing seems to have been known of the historical St Ecgwine of Evesham: making him, as Stephenson points out, "the perfect *tabula rasa*" for the inscription of an ideal identity. For Byrhtferth, computus, calendrics, number theory, and *grammatica* were effectively a single contiguous means of structuring the universe. But this structure was recognizable only to those educated in the form of Latinity that, in the late tenth century, was restricted to reformed Benedictine monasteries. With its elaborate, authorial textual apparatus and complex discussions of the meaning of numbers and dates, Byrhtferth's *Vita S. Ecgwini* encodes a panoply of symbols of monastic education. For him, a "perfect" number is one that enables the display of exegetical learning: as Stephenson shows, the elements of computus that Byrhtferth builds into his hagiography work primarily as signifiers of a monastic identity shared by Ramsey and Evesham. Like a sort of computistical Humpty Dumpty, Byrhtferth makes both words and numbers mean what *he* wants them to mean.

Yet even the most reverential participation in an authoritative tradition involves some transformation of the tradition itself. We see this perhaps most clearly in the cross-fertilization that took place as Latinate discourses like hagiography and grammar were filtered through English – transforming the vernacular in the process, as Christine Rauer demonstrates in "The *Old English Martyrology* and Anglo-Saxon Glosses." Through her index of the rare vocabulary in this pioneering work of ninth-century prose, Rauer shows that a great many of these words were either Latinate or derived from Latin glosses, particularly the Aldhelm glosses. The style of this Old English writer was heavily influenced by his Latin education, a feature that can also be seen in other ninth-century texts like the *Old English Bede*, Wærferth's translation of Gregory's *Dialogi*, and the *Old English Orosius*. Rauer's word study illustrates how closely connected Old English literature is to active engagement with Latin literature, and particularly to the curriculum authors. The importance of Aldhelm within this curriculum reinforces the distinctly English form this Latinity took. Rauer's work reminds us that the traffic between Anglo-Latin and Old English was two-way, as readers understood Latin texts through English glosses while expanding the bounds of English with exotic Latin vocabulary.

In "Hebrew Words and English Identity in Educational Texts of Ælfric and Byrhtferth," Damian Fleming turns to the writings of the Benedictine reformers to examine how Ælfric of Eynsham and Byrhtferth of Ramsey use Hebrew words within an already bilingual matrix to construct an identity for their respective audiences. In his Latin-English *Grammar*, Ælfric used Hebraisms commonly available in the New Testament as a way to move beyond Latin and English translation to a broader discussion of how languages operate. His contemporary Byrhtferth, however, used Hebraisms as part of a larger pursuit of unusual words that he incorporated into his distinctive prose style, the so-called hermeneutic style. Fleming sees the cultivation of Hebraisms to be yet another device that sets the Latinate monastic audience apart from their clerical counterparts, who probably did not have the same mastery of Latin. Therefore, the Hebrew language was used by two contemporary authors from monastic backgrounds to construct decidedly different identities for their Latinate audiences. Both Ælfric and Byrhtferth used a third term to break the Latin-English binary;

but while Ælfric's discussion of interjections worked to demonstrate that all languages had unique powers of expression (and thus that Latin, like Hebrew, was ultimately not so different from English), Byrhtferth's Hebraisms were calculated to fissure and stratify Latinity into esoteric and exoteric forms. Fleming's reading of Byrhtferth's *Enchiridion* dovetails with Stephenson's interpretation of the *Vita Ecgwini*, suggesting that Byrhtferth had a highly coherent intellectual persona.

Esoteric Latin, however, was not always intended as exclusionary. The remarkable poem "Centum concito" in Cambridge, University Library, Gg.5.35, attributed to Oswald the Younger of Ramsey, requests readers to scan it again backward, and thus to appreciate the skill that went into constructing retrograde verses that could be scanned in both directions. As Leslie Lockett shows in "Oswald's *uersus retrogradi*: A Forerunner of Post-Conquest Trends in Hexameter Composition," this poem and its companion in the manuscript were constructed according to an ingenious modular method that Oswald apparently devised himself. Although his verses resemble dactylic hexameters and pentameters – the pre-eminent forms in Anglo-Latin verse – they are actually a kind of compound metre assembled from self-contained metrical units. This conception of the metrical line as a set of smaller modules, rather than an organic unity, reflects Carolingian metrical theory, and resembles the practice of Continental poets like Odo of Cluny, whose original compound metres were often divided in the manuscript into their subcomponents. But the modular method of constructing hexameters became even more popular after the Conquest, when it was used to facilitate complex internal rhymes. Lockett thus shows Oswald of Ramsey to be both out of his time and place, and yet also of it. His verses, reflecting as they do Continental theory and practice, look abroad for their models, and foreshadow eleventh- and twelfth-century developments in poetry. At the same time, it was the hexameter and pentameter that Oswald chose to approximate in his retrograde lines, suggesting a desire to appeal to more conservative English-trained sensibilities as well.

Oswald's enthusiastic mastery and display of learning acquired abroad is particularly characteristic of Anglo-Latin from the tenth century onward. In "Sequences and Intellectual Identity at Winchester," Jonathan Davis-Secord demonstrates both the intellectual omnivorousness of liturgists in tenth-century Winchester and the ability of writers there to build grand innovations from a surprisingly small set of exempla. The Benedictine reformers – especially Æthelwold, bishop of Winchester – are usually connected with the culture of West Frankish monasteries, especially Corbie and Fleury. Davis-Secord, however, shows that many of the sequences composed for the newly reformed community at Winchester display the distinctive influence of the East Frankish liturgist Notker Balbulus, who favoured strictly isotonic rhythms. Given the relatively few examples of Notker's work known at Winchester, these texts must have been intensively studied by scholars closely attuned to prose rhythm. The sequences thus relate to an intellectual culture at Winchester that pervades several genres of writing. Davis-Secord connects the distinctive rhythms of Winchester sequences both with Ælfric's rhythmical prose and with hermeneutic Latin. While Ælfric's writing is often contrasted with that of the hermeneutic style, the sequences show concerns common to both styles of writing. Davis-Secord sees all three forms – hermeneutic, Ælfrician, and sequences – as arising from a specific Winchester intellectual culture, one open to eclectic foreign influences and alive to the affective power of rhythm in literature.

The number and variety of foreign influences on Anglo-Saxon literary culture increased in the course of the eleventh century; and though the remaking of libraries in the wake of the Norman Conquest would favour a narrative in which a closed, conservative English culture was forcibly modernized by the new regime,[24] this volume's essays argue that such an assumption distorts and oversimplifies the situation in late Anglo-Saxon England. Elizabeth M. Tyler's "German Imperial Bishops and Anglo-Saxon Literary Culture on the Eve of the Conquest: *The Cambridge Songs* and Leofric's Exeter Book" demands a reconsideration of the literary and courtly culture in this period. In particular, she considers how the Latin poetic manuscript called *The Cambridge Songs* relates to the themes, structure, and use of the vernacular Exeter Book, as it would have been read by Bishop Leofric of Exeter. Leofric is a striking and multifaceted figure: an Englishman trained in Lotharingia (probably at Liège, and thus in a French-speaking region), he was appointed bishop by Edward the Confessor, and died in 1072, having witnessed several charters of William the Conqueror. *The Cambridge Songs* are considered unusual since they are pre-Conquest material imported from Germany that seem to connect more closely with post-Conquest literary interests, including an emphasis on Statius's *Thebaid* and other works that became more popular in the late eleventh century. But while the foreign origin and eclectic, sometimes pagan contents of *The Cambridge Songs* often lead them to be bracketed or ignored by Anglo-Saxonists, by placing these poems in the context of their

24 See, e.g., Webber, *Scribes and Scholars*, and Thomson, "Norman Conquest."

manuscript – Cambridge, University Library, Gg.5.35, a vast omnibus of Latin poetry – and by comparison with the Exeter Book, Tyler is able to show that Anglo-Saxon England was quite receptive to this type of collection. Tyler carefully constructs the connections that Anglo-Saxon bishops like Leofric and his close colleague Ealdred of York would have had to both German and French courts, where classical literature was becoming newly fashionable. She also emphasizes that Harold and Tostig's conflict resembles that of Eteocles and Polynices, and therefore the Theban story may have been seen as topically interesting even before the Conquest. This chapter as a whole is an argument against a radical break at 1066 as England became French, but rather sees the late Anglo-Saxon period as one in which England's royal court has strong ties to European courts. In this context, many languages would have been privileged, and the concerns of the Exeter Book could have been easily set beside those of *The Cambridge Songs*, seeing English as yet another valuable mode of communication.

The foreign training of Bishops Leofric and Ealdred thus allowed them to act as bridge-figures between English and Continental models of literary culture as well as the episcopacy. In "Writing Community: Osbern and the Negotiations of Identity in the *Miracula S. Dunstani*," Katherine O'Brien O'Keeffe illuminates the work of another kind of bridge-figure in late eleventh-century Canterbury. In the *Miracula S. Dunstani*, Osbern uses the Latin language to build a common identity in the troubled post-Conquest community at Christ Church. Osbern lived between two worlds, as an Anglo-Saxon monk who was sent to Bec in Normandy to further his education but also as discipline for some unknown infraction. In this miracle collection, Osbern negotiates between his Anglo-Saxon identity and his Norman education. The chapter centres itself on the story of Ægelward, an English monk whose madness posed a serious threat to the authority of Lanfranc, the new Norman archbishop. O'Brien O'Keeffe reveals how Osbern's Latinity manages to finesse moments in Ægelward's story that might otherwise emphasize ethnic division. For instance, his demon's uncanny ability to understand the French spoken by his superiors – though the young brother had known nothing of the language in his normal state – was explained by Eadmer (writing some decades later), but omitted by Osbern. The universality of the Latin language is an important tool that Osbern employs to build an identity for the monastic community through the veneration of Dunstan: his text looks forward to a future when all *Angligenae* will be united under the protection of Canterbury's patron.

After the Conquest, much of the most characteristic Anglo-Latin writing fell from favour. Osbern, for instance, explicitly positions his *vita* of

Dunstan as a replacement for the tenth-century life written by "B" in "hermeneutic" Latin: in the "inflated style" ("suff[la]tum ... eloquentiae"), as Osbern put it.[25] In his account of Aldhelm, William of Malmesbury attempts to defend his patron's style against the scorn and neglect of modern readers:

> Sermones eius minus infundunt hilaritas quam uellent hi qui rerum incuriosi uerba trutinant: iudices inportuni, qui nesciant quod secundum mores gentium uarientur modi dictaminum. Denique Greci inuolute, Romane splendide, Angli pompatice dictare solent ... Quem [=Aldelmum] si perfecte legeris, et ex acumine Grecum putabis, et ex nitore Romanum iurabis, et ex pompa Anglum intelliges.[26]

> [His writings seem less amusing than is desired by those who, neglecting the content, weigh only the words: they are unqualified judges, who do not realize that modes of discourse vary according to national character. And so the Greeks commonly write in a complex style, the Romans illustriously, and the English with display ... If you read him properly, from his subtletly you will believe him a Greek, and from his polish judge him a Roman, and from his display you will know him as an Englishman.]

The correspondence William draws between style and nationality has an ethical force: not only does one *know* (as opposed to merely believe or judge) that Aldhelm is English, the implication seems to be that readers who consider themselves English ought to adopt some of Aldhelm's *pompa*. But though William's recuperative program saved some of Aldhelm's writings, it did not change post-Conquest style: Osbern, with his rejection of the *sufflatum*, was a harbinger of the new mode.

Yet as we have seen in this volume, Anglo-Latin was too complex a phenomenon to be strictly periodized. While Latin is often portrayed as a fossilized or atemporal phenomenon, it is perhaps better understood as inherently polychronic, with multiple layers of time operating simultaneously. This phenomenon is beautifully exemplified by CUL Gg.5.35: within this anthology, Tyler is able to identify productive connections between eleventh-century England and Germany, built partly on a foundation of

25 O'Brien O'Keeffe, "Writing Community," p. 208 below (and esp. note 26).

26 Winterbottom and Thomson, eds., *Gesta pontificum* V.196, 518–20.

classical epic, while Lockett shows that the tenth-century work of a French-trained Englishman anticipated eleventh- and twelfth-century poetic form. As a carefully structured collection of texts that originated across Europe and ranged in date from classical antiquity to only a few years before the book was assembled, CUL Gg.5.35 dramatizes the construction of a kind of unity that does not reject, or even minimize, multiplicity.

The intertwining themes in this volume suggest a number of important lines of future work. First, the tendency of English writers to selectively embrace contemporary Continental developments opens the door for a much broader and more complex understanding of the Anglo-Saxons' place in early medieval literary history. Davis-Secord, Lockett, and Thornbury all show how Anglo-Latin writers recognized and exploited novel developments – in liturgical prose rhythm, metrical theory, and poetic self-positioning respectively – in ways that imply a conscious choice among alternatives, rather than uncritical imitation. Even within what would seem to be a homogeneous set of influences, we see authors making choices, as Herren makes clear in his study of Boniface's stylistic relationship to Aldhelm. In all these studies, the use of fine-grained textual analysis has revealed previously unrecognized complexities in what had often been considered straightforward lines of literary affinity: similar attention to other Anglo-Latin works will no doubt help us better understand the Anglo-Saxons' relationship to their neighbours on the Continent, as well as in Ireland and Wales.

Whether or not Latin actually created the concept of a vernacular, it is certain that multilingualism was a pervasive aspect of early medieval literary culture; and, as several of the essays here show, the interconnection between languages had lasting effects. Rauer's study of the *Old English Martyrology* demonstrates the cross-fertilizing effect of English-Latin scholarship on English vocabulary, while Davis-Secord shows that writers trained in tenth-century Winchester brought a similar interest in prose rhythm to both Latin and Old English compositions. Moreover, breaking down a Latin/English binary was intellectually productive: Fleming finds that the addition of Hebrew allowed Ælfric to come to a deeper theoretical understanding of language, while it helped Byrhtferth differentiate multiple Latinities; Tyler, meanwhile, investigates the ways in which the apparently anomalous *Cambridge Songs*, which contain macaronic verse in German and Latin, resonated with late Anglo-Saxon culture. A broader understanding of Latinity, and its place *within* vernaculars, will help us better trace its historical contiguities and interactions with a largely vernacular-speaking culture as it helped form notions of national identity and difference.

Tyler's essay points to the under-studied vibrancy of clerical culture in Anglo-Saxon England. Yet this volume's contents also suggest that many facets of English monasticism are far from fully explored. The articles by DeGregorio and Stephenson, in particular, show us that even when monastic authors proclaimed themselves as adhering closely to authoritative structures, they were often re-creating those structures in their chosen images. Despite Bede's reverence for Gregory, he himself preferred Ezra as his own model for scholarly self-formation; while Byrhtferth's version of computus made numbers into infinitely malleable signifiers of monastic community. Textual scholarship, these articles demonstrate, was integral to the formation of the individual in a monastic setting; and, as O'Brien O'Keeffe shows, authors were also acutely aware of the power of texts to forge those individuals into a community. Modes like biblical commentary, computus, and hagiography were tools for the creation of the monastic self and community, and through them we can perceive how the Anglo-Saxons used Latin scholarship to shape and engage with an identity that put them at odds with the world. Moreover, the studies centred on the reformed Benedictine monasteries of the tenth century make particularly clear that Latinity itself was multiple and complex: through the study of the "hermeneutic" style, we can better see other instances in which linguistic differentiation was made to signify new kinds of identity.

The chronological and methodological variety of the studies in this volume points to the richness of Anglo-Latin literature *as* literature. Ranging across six centuries and multiple genres, the essays in *Latinity and Identity in Anglo-Saxon England* exemplify many ways in which these texts reflect light on medieval thought about individual and group identities, from international relations to inner consciousness. By approaching Anglo-Latinity as a dynamic and complex phenomenon rather than a static monolith, and recognizing its relation to vernaculars as interdependent rather than oppositional, the scholars represented here open new pathways to the study of early medieval literature and invite further exploration of the field.

Boniface's Epistolary Prose Style: The Letters to the English*

MICHAEL W. HERREN

We all know what style is, or think we do when we see or hear it. We know an Oscar de la Renta dress when it walks into a room, and we know when Glenn Gould, and not Angela Hewitt, is playing Bach when we switch on the radio. If we are asked, however, what makes style, what makes something unique and recognizable for what it is, our usual reply is that it is indefinable, that someone or something just has a certain "je ne sais quoi."

The components, or factors, that make up Latin prose style can be just as hard to identify. If you were to define Aldhelm's prose style[1] as having "long sentences, lots of clauses, hard words," you would be right, of course, but the same constellation of phrases could also describe any number of Latin writers from antiquity to the end of the Middle Ages (indeed, beyond). So we are pressed to be more precise, to look for details – not only in the choice of words and methods of their manufacture, but also, even more so, in their arrangement into visual patterns and sound effects. Latin prose style affects both eye and ear: we see it as patterns on a page, and we also hear it in the mind's ear. All of these patterns and sound effects

* References in this essay of the type I.A1, etc. are to be found in the appendix, printed at the end of the body of the paper. Page references for Boniface are to the edition of Rau, *Briefe des Bonifatius*; references to Aldhelm are to Ehwald, *Aldhelmi Opera*.

1 For the most comprehensive treatment available, see Winterbottom, "Aldhelm's Prose Style." For a study of the reception and influence of Aldhelm's style, see Lapidge, "Hermeneutic Style."

need to be identified and studied to see where, how, and even why they are employed. It is not really good enough to say that a particular writer uses alliteration. We need to know where it is employed, how frequently, and in what places in a sentence.

It has been asserted that Boniface's Latin style was strongly influenced by Aldhelm. When Paul Lehmann discovered Boniface's grammatical work *De octo partibus*, he was so taken by the resemblance of the style of the prologue to that of Aldhelm that he initially attributed the work to him.[2] As Andy Orchard has demonstrated, there is no doubt that Boniface had read Aldhelm's poetry and that his own poetic writings were deeply influenced by both the metrical and accentual forms of Aldhelm's verse.[3] As for Boniface's letters, it is clear that the author borrowed Aldhelmian formulae and phrases in the inscriptions to his letters as well as in the body of those texts.[4] Take, for example, Boniface's letter to Abbess Eadburg (no. 30), which he prefaces with "iam dudum spiritalis clientellae propinquitate conexae," which is nearly identical to Aldhelm's salutation to King Aldfrith, whom he address as "Acircius" with the words "mihique iam dudum spiritalis clientelae catenis conexo." The only substitution is the replacement of "catenis" by "propinquitate." The opening sentence of Boniface's letter to Nithard calls the recipient "inlustrem pubertatis tuae indolem," clearly echoing Aldhelm's "pulcherrimam pubertatis indolem" from the *Prosa de virg.*, p. 302.13. The phrase "naufragio periculose tempestatis" drawn from the same letter reflects "periculoso saeculi naufragio" from *Prosa de virg.*, p. 238.18. There are many more examples, including Aldhelm's familiar "vita comite," or "patrocinium praestante," which are scattered throughout Boniface's letters.

Frequency of quotation and repetition of formulaic phrases, however, is quite a different thing from stylistic influence. Some years ago the opening chords of Beethoven's Fifth Symphony – da-da-da-dah – were quoted in a rock number, but as far as I could tell, that was the extent of the master's

2 Lehmann, "Ein neuentdecktes Werk"; corrected in "Die Grammatik aus Aldhelms Kreise." Note that the ninth-century manuscript of this grammar, Trier, Stadtbibliothek, MS 1104 (fols. 91r–93r), has the following inscription: "Incipit prefatio Althelmi Anglorum episcopi ad Sigibertum de VIII partibus orationum."

3 Orchard, "After Aldhelm," 103–7, and *Poetic Art*, 64–7, 275–8.

4 For a list of Aldhelmian parallels in Boniface's poetry, see Orchard, "After Aldhelm," 103–7. For parallels in the letters, see the apparatus fontium of Tangl's edition for letters 9, 10, 33, 66, 75, 78, 86, and 91.

influence. The imitator of another's prose style must not merely quote, but also control the minutiae of his model's repertoire of techniques. The gross techniques consist in sentence and clause length and the use of hypotaxis, but it is the fine techniques that individuate an author. Word order is crucial to Latin style,[5] so we should examine such components as hyperbaton, double hyperbaton or interlocking word order, and chiasmus; we must not only note if they are employed, but also how frequently and where they are used. The same applies to the use of "sound effects" such as alliteration, assonance, and rhyming cola. A question we shall ask is, does alliteration assist or hinder the parsing of a sentence? Varieties of pleonasm also come into play. One such is the use of a present participle of a verb that is a synonym of the finite verb to which it is conjoined, such as Boniface's "amittentes perdent" in I.A1, line 7. A feature favoured by Aldhelm is the use of a redundant noun in the genitive case, e.g. "impedimentorum obstaculis" (literally: by the obstacles of impediments) or "garrulo verbositatis strepitu" (by the garrulous chatter of verbosity), both examples from III.B1. Unlike other uses of the genitive which qualify a related noun in order to add meaning, the redundant genitive adds nothing except a *flatus aeris* – all style and no content![6]

We cannot, however, forget words, for they too belong to style. Yet we have to be cautious here. The use of Greek words, for example, does not of itself individuate style, since the Greek element already present in the Latin language was augmented considerably under Christian influence.[7] We should look for Greek words not normally admitted into Latin, such as Aldhelm's "pantorum" for "pantōn" in I.B2, line 1, or for neologisms based on Greek.[8] Archaisms are also important markers. Even though writers of the seventh and eighth centuries may no longer have felt a word as an archaism, they still had to fetch the word out of a glossary of rare

5 The literature on Latin word order is vast. See the bibliography in Devine and Stephens, *Latin Word Order*, 611–30. This is a book for specialists of the subject. For helpful introductions see Ullman, "Latin Word-Order"; Marouzeau, *L'ordre des mots*; Leumann, Hofmann, and Szantyr, *Lateinische Grammatik* 2:685–99.

6 This particular stylistic use of the genitive is not treated by Bourgain, "Le génitif d'interprétation," doubtless for the reason that it does not really interpret or modify anything; it simply restates or reinforces.

7 Löfstedt, *Late Latin*, 88–119; Prinz, "Zum Einfluss des Griechischen"; for a survey of Greek in classical Latin, see Weise, *Die griechischen Wörter*.

8 For the absence of Greek-based neologisms in Aldhelm's writings, see Marenbon, "Les sources," 85.

lexica such as Festus's *De significatu verborum*. Word formation is also important. A fondness for diminutives or particular formations such as adjectives in *–osus*[9] or adverbs in *–tim* or *–iter* in place of the usual ending in *–e* also contributes to the creation of style.

In what follows I offer a comparison of the letters by Aldhelm and Boniface arranged by addressee,[10] beginning with students who were doubtless attached to these masters, and proceeding to abbesses, bishops, and kings. All of the addressees are resident in Britain, and all except one (King Geraint in the last example) are of Anglo-Saxon origin. This limitation is especially important in the case of Boniface, who employs a rather neutral formulaic style when addressing popes and other Continental potentates, but gives full rein to his more florid native style when writing to his countrymen, although he nuances his style for categories within that population. We shall first look at overall similarities and differences between the two letter writers, then compare them for adjustments made to style according to the status of the addressees. The main features to be examined are alliteration, hyperbaton (including double hyperbaton), chiasmus, pleonasm (including the redundant genitive), rhyming cola, and abstruse lexical items. There are other effects one could study, but that will have to await another occasion.

In listing examples of hyperbaton I have included those in which a noun (redundant or not) in the genitive case is inserted between a noun and its modifier. It has been argued recently that collocations of this type are normal and "do not interrupt the continuity of the phrase."[11] This may well be true of classical Latin, at least literary Latin, but such groupings, I believe, would have been challenging to eighth-century readers accustomed to the grouping noun + adjective + submodifier. I have therefore included them in the study.

There is nothing in the Bonifatian corpus to equal the sheer exuberance of the opening sentence of Aldhelm's letter no. 5, to Heahfrith. The oft-quoted opening sentence beginning with "Primitus pantorum procerum" contains a run of fifteen words alliterating in *p*, most of which also assonate

9 For a model article making optimum use of this feature of word-formation, see Niedermann, "Les dérivés en ōsus."

10 For previous work on Boniface's style as related to the recipients of the letters, see Orchard, "Old Sources, New Resources."

11 Powell, "Hyperbaton and Register in Cicero."

with the vowel *o*. The same ninety-word sentence also contains a run of five words alliterating in *t*: "torrentia tetrae tortionis in tartara trusit." This collocation is of special note, as one might be inclined to assume that an alliterative run is contained within a syntactical group. Such is not the case here. "Torrentia" is construed with "venena," while the adjacent "tetrae tortionis" confusingly modifies "tartara." As Carin Ruff's discussion of this passage has shown, "Alliteration also appears to be a distraction from the underlying structure ... of the sentence."[12] In the examples quoted here, Boniface's alliterative runs do not exceed three, and perhaps as a consequence there is no obstacle to parsing. None the less, Boniface's use of alliteration at times is fairly copious. In I.A1 (to Nithard) there are five examples of two-word alliteration in a sentence of forty-eight words, approximately half the length of the opening sentence of Aldhelm's Letter to Heahfrith. Note the nicely alliterative and rhythmical "limine latrat" in (b) line 2, followed by a different alliterative pattern in *t*, "tum tremebundi." In the same line Boniface rather tastefully avoids excessive alliteration by separating "divino" from "destituti." In the last sentence of the letter, I.A2, which runs to 112 words, thus longer than the opening sentence in the Letter to Heahfrith, there are only three examples, none of which is very striking. In the opening sentence of Boniface's first letter to Eadburg (*Ep*. 10) there is only one example, "patrocinium praestante," which is an Aldhelmian formula. Note, however, that Boniface substitutes "Deo" for Aldhelm's "Christo" in this phrase.[13]

The opening lines of the Letter to Heahfrith may contain the longest alliterative run in Aldhelm's works, but there are others of note: a run of four in I.B1 (to Wihtfrid), "fausta fraterna feliciter fruatur," and a run of five in II.B1 (to Hildelith), "studia scripturarum sagacissima sermonum serie." There Aldhelm sacrifices a final alliterative word to close the period in order to achieve the rhythmical rhyme with the previous colon: "claruerunt ... patuerunt."[14] More study will be needed to see if there are important differences in where each of these authors employs alliteration, but suffice it to say that a clear difference emerges between them in respect of the number of words in an alliterative run.

12 Ruff, "Perception of Difficulty," 174.

13 Aldhelm, *De virg.*, pp. 240.21, 300.8, 301.18; *Ep*. 4 (to Geraint), p. 482.7. All of Aldhelm's examples are construed with *Christo*.

14 This type of *Rheimprosa* is particularly marked in the sermons of Augustine; see Norden, *Die antike Kunstprosa*, 2:622.

A similar pattern emerges regarding the employment of hyperbaton. Once again "Heahfrith" wins the prize hands down: I count eight examples in the ninety words of the first sentence of the "Heahfrith Letter" (I.B2). There are only two examples in the closing sentence of the "Wihtfrith Letter" (I.B1), but that passage also contains a double hyperbaton: "flabra e climate olim septentrionali emergentia neglecto." According to the late and *regretté* François Kerlouégan, double hyperbaton, or interlocking word-order, is a shibboleth of Celtic Latinity. This feature is plentifully represented in Aldhelm's writings. Kerlouégan noted nine examples in the Letter to Heahfrith and twenty in the prose *De virginitate*.[15] Although I have not combed the entire collection of Boniface's letters, examples of double hyperbaton are rare. One occurs in the inscription of the Letter to Nithard (p. 25.1–2): "temporalis caducum auri munus." Another occurs in the same letter (p. 24.18): "veridicam psalmigraphi sententiam dicentis," a partial echo of *Prosa de virg.*, p. 298.6. However, apart from the Letter to Nithard, even single hyperbaton is relatively scarce. Early in his career it appears that Boniface enjoyed its employment, as he composed seven hyperbata in the first sentence quoted from the Letter to Nithard (I.A1), and four in the second passage (I.A2). We note two examples in the first letter to Eadburg (II.A1), written at about the same time as the letter to Nithard, ca. 716. But in a second letter to this nun written twenty years letter (II.A2) there are no examples, not only in the sample given here, but likewise in the rest of the albeit short letter. In the letter to Nothelm, archbishop of Canterbury (III.AI), we find only one example in a sentence of seventy-nine words; likewise, in a letter to Pehthelm of Whithorn, written in 735, there are three instances of single hyperbaton. But in a letter to Aethelbald, king of Mercia (IV.A1), written eleven years later, there are no examples. It is possible that Boniface's taste for this feature declined over time, but it is, perhaps, even likelier that he simplified his style when writing to kings.

Chiasmus is represented only patchily in the passages cited here. There are two adjacent examples in the first sentence of Boniface's Letter to Nithard: "Humillimis mediocritatis meae apicibus" followed immediately by "inlustrem pubertatis tuae indolem." Another in the same letter (I.A2): "humido terrenae cupiditatis pulvere." Interestingly, Boniface employs chiasmus in his later letter to Eadburg even where he omits hyperbaton: "solamine librorum sive vestimentorum adiuvamine" – note the three-syllable

15 Kerlouégan, "Une mode stylistique," 281–2.

end rhyme of the bookend words and the internal phrase coupled with internal alliteration of *v*. Likewise there is one example in the Letter to Nothelm (III.A1): "variis Germanicarum gentium tempestatum fluctibus." Not surprisingly, most of the examples from Aldhelm exhibit chiasmus. Indeed, when one turns to the *Prosa de virg.*, chiasmus occurs on almost every page, often in multiples. A blind *sortilegium* turned up the following examples on p. 244: p. 244.4 "singularis generosae virginitatis nobilitas"; p. 244.8 "inseparabili angelicae sodalitatis collegio"; p. 244.10 "opulenta ecclesiasticae segetis ubertate"; 244.21 "cetera argenti et electri stagnique metalla." The Bonifatian letters will require more study for this feature, but chiasmus appears to be a constant device of the saint's repertoire. We see it as late as 747 in a letter to Cudbehrt, archbishop of Canterbury, to whom Boniface wishes "optabilem in Christo intimae caritatis salutem" and hopes to be joined to him "aureo celestis amoris vinculo."

Examples of chiasmus sometimes reveal the feature that I term the "redundant genitive," that is, a single word or phrase in the genitive case that adds nothing to the meaning of the word or phrase to which it is attached. Take the just cited "inseparabili angelicae sodalitatis collegio" (in the inseparable society of angelic fellowship) – there is hardly any discernible difference between "sodalitas" and "collegium."

Slightly different syntactically is "singularis generosae virginitatis nobilitas" (the singular nobility of well-born virginity), where "generosa" is an exact synonym of "nobilis." The redundant genitive appears without chiasmus in other Bonifatian examples, as in the letter to Nithard (I.A2): "verae pulchritudinis venustatem" (the beauty of true pulchritude). From Aldhelm's letters (III.B1) we have "impedimentorum obstaculis" (the obstacles of impediments), and "garrulo verbositatis strepitu" (the garrulous chatter of verbosity). (What is verbosity if not garrulous chatter?) I suspect, though this remains to be proved, that while Aldhelm revelled in this conceit throughout his oeuvre, Boniface used it sparingly.

The largest concentration of rare lexical items in Boniface's letters occurs predictably in the Letter to Nithard: "aurilegi," "ambrones," "apo ton grammaton," "agiis," "cata," "Erebia," to which we might add the metaphorical use of the name "Pluto." With the exception of the strange "ambrones"[16] (gluttons *or* gluttonous), borrowed from Aldhelm, these

16 The uses of this unusual word appear to be confined to Britain; see citations beginning with Gildas in *DMLBS*, fascicule 1, p. 76. The same dictionary calls the word "a tribal name."

abstrusa are transparent. "Aurilegus" is made up of "aurum" and "lego," while "Erebia" is simply "Erebus" with an adjectival ending. Even the Greek words are very common ones, though not normally incorporated into the structure of a sentence as if they were Latin words. By contrast, Aldhelm's employment of Grecisms, archaisms, neologisms, and other rarities – a few of which we see in the opening of the Heahfrith Letter – permeates all his writing.

Some tentative conclusions: Boniface was intimately familiar with Aldhelm's writings and knew his entire range of stylistic turns and conceits. He poured these out on parchment in his letter to his student Nithard, written probably while he was still in England. In his letters written to Anglo-Saxons from the Continent we still see his use of these techniques, but they become rarer and more controlled. Boniface was also very conscious of his recipients. His replies to Abbess Eadburg are mostly unadorned and decidedly un-Aldhelmian. The same holds for his letters to Anglo-Saxon kings: Boniface apparently wanted to believe that these head-bashers, or at least their ministers, could have understood them if written plainly enough. When he wrote to English bishops and archbishops, however, the style once again becomes more elevated and more demanding of the reader, noticeably in the letters to Nothelm and Cudbehrt. Aldhelm wrote to please himself and to challenge his recipients. In contrast to Boniface, who appears to tone down (without dumbing down) his letters to women, Aldhelm expected as high a degree of literacy from Hildelith and her followers as he did from the male students he trained. With the exception of a short letter to a nun named Sigegyth (II.B2), he took no prisoners.

I have not presented here anything like a "scientific" selection of philological data. Instead, following "old school" methodology, I have sought out passages that appeared to me to be most suggestive of the two authors' styles. Clearly, much more needs to be done in the way of expanding the samples and refining the analysis. My intention was to give a sharper definition to the concept of Latin style that would enable both analysis and comparison. Even here, more criteria could be introduced. Clause length and prose rhythm come immediately to mind. Let the work begin![17]

17 I am very grateful to the anonymous readers of this volume for their helpful and perceptive comments on my essay.

Appendix

Latin text of Boniface's letters: R. Rau, *Briefe des Bonifatius, Willibalds Leben des Bonifatius* (Darmstadt, 1968).
Latin text of Aldhelm: R. Ehwald, MGH AA 15 (Berlin, 1919).
English translations of Aldhelm: M. Lapidge and M. Herren, *Aldhelm: The Prose Works (AprW)* (Cambridge, 1979; repr. Woodbridge, Suffolk, 2009).
English translations of Boniface by M. Herren.

Texts of Letters
Roman underlined = alliteration
Italics = pleonasm
Bolded roman = chiasmus
Bolded italics = hyperbaton

I. Letters to Students

I.A1. *Boniface, Ep. 9.2–7 pp. 24–6 (to Nithard):*

(a) Et hac de re universi aurilegi ambrones apo ton grammaton agiis *frustratis adflicti inservire excubiis* et *fragilia aranearum in cassum ceu flatum tenuem sive pulverem captantia tetendisse retia* dinoscuntur, qui cata psalmistam thesaurizant et ignorant cui congregent illa. [38 words] ... (b) Et dum exactrix invisi Plutonis, mors videlict, cruentatis crudeliter *frendens dentibus* in limine latrat, tum tremebundi et omni divino suffragio destituti, *animam* pariter pretiosam et fallacem gazam, cui avari die noctuque sollicite inserviebant, subito *amittentes perdent*, et exinde, *diabolicis rapti manibus,/ teterrima subeunt claustra /Erebia aeterna luituri supplicia.* (48 words)

Alliteration: cruentatis crudeliter, limine latrat, pariter pretiosum, tum tremebundi, pariter pretiosam
Pleonasm: amittentes perdent
Chiasmus: none
Hyperbaton: frustratis ... excubiis, fragilia ... retia, cruentatis ... dentibus, animam ... pretiosam, diabolicis ... manibus, teterrima ... claustra, aeterna ... supplicia
Lexica abstrusa: aurilegi, ambrones, apo ton grammaton, agiis, cata, Erebia
Figura etymologica (paronomasia): cruentatis crudeliter

[And concerning this matter all the gluttonous gold seekers (known) from the writings of Holy Scripture,[18] having been condemned to endure fruitless sleeplessness, are discerned to spread the fragile webs of spiders that capture to no purpose (things) like a thin breeze or dust, who, according to the psalmist, store up treasure and do not know for whom they collect such things. **(b)** And when the bill-collector of hated Pluto, death to wit, cruelly gnashing with bloodied teeth, barks at the threshold, then, trembling and deprived of all divine assistance, they shall suddenly release and lose their precious life and likewise the deceptive treasure, to which the greedy are so attentively submissive day and night, and from that time forth, seized by diabolical hands, they endure the most foul prison of Erebus to suffer eternal punishments.]

I.A2. *Ibid., p. 26.8–23:*

His autem omnibus absque scrupulo falsitatis ita se habentibus, ***precibus caritate interlitis*** obnixe flagitantibus te implorare procuro, ut, his ***universis veraciter perspectis***, resuscitare festines gratiam ingenii naturalis, que in te est, et liberalium litterarum scientiam et divini intellectus ***flagrantem spiritaliter ignem*** aquoso luto et **humido terrenae cupiditatis pulvere** non exstinguas, sed memor **psalmigraphi de beato viro sententiam proferentis** ... et Moysen in Deuteronomio ... "et meditaberis in ea diebus ac noctibus," omnibus non **profuturis aliarum rerum obstaculis** porro abolitis, studium sanctarum litterarum mentis intentione sequi nitaris, et inde gloriose ac *vere pulchritudinis venustatem* adquirere, id est divinam sapientiam, quae est splendidior auro, speciosior argento, ignitior carbunculo, candidior cristallo, pretiosior topazio, et secundum sanctionem ingeniosi contionatoris, "omne pretiosum non est ea dignum." (112 words not counting scriptural quotations)

Alliteration: liberalium litterarum, studium sanctarum, carbunculo candidior cristallo, secundum sanctionem
Pleonasm (*redundant genitive*): verae pulchritudinis venustatem

18 The phrase, if taken strictly according to the rules of classical Greek, would mean something like "far from the writings for holy men." But I do not think that this was Boniface's meaning.

Chiasmus: humido terrenae cupiditatis pulvere, profuturis aliarum rerum obstaculis
Hypberaton: precibus caritate interlitis, universis veraciter perspectis, flagrantem spiritaliter ignem, psalmigrafi … sententiam proferentis
Lexica abstrusa: psalmigrafi *for attested* psalmographi

[However, since all these things are so without the least element of falsehood, I undertake to implore you strenuously with demanding entreaties intermingled with love, that, when all these things are truly perceived, you hasten to resuscitate the gift of natural genius, which is within you, and do not extinguish the knowledge of humane literature and the spiritually burning fire of divine understanding with watery mud and moist dust of earthly greed, but being mindful of the psalm-writer pronouncing a judgment about the blessed man … and Moses in Deuteronomy … "and thou shalt meditate upon it day and night," moreover with all the obstacles of other unprofitable things abolished, you strive to pursue the study of sacred scripture with concentrated mind, and from it acquire the beauty of glorious and true pulchritude, that is divine wisdom, which is more splendid than gold, more lovely than silver, more fiery than carbuncle, brighter than crystal, more precious than topaz, and according to the sanction of the gifted haranguer [Solomon]: "every precious thing is not worthy of her (i.e. virtue)."]

I.B1. *Aldhelm, Ep. 3, p. 479.20–480.6 (to Wihtfrid)*

Porro tuum discipulatum ceu cernuus arcuatis poplitibus flexisque suffraginibus, feculenta fama compulsus, posco, ut nequaquam prostibula vel lupanarium nugas, in quis pompulentae prostitutae delitescunt, lenocinante luxu adeas, quae obrizo rutilante periscelidis armillaque lacertorum tereti utpote faleris falerati /curules comuntur, sed magis ***edito aulae fastigio*** spreto, quo patricii ac praetores potiuntur, gurgustii humilis receptaculo contenta tua fausta fraternitas feliciter fruatur necnon contra ***gelida brumarum flabra e climate olim septentrionali emergentia neglecto***, ut decet Christi discipulum, fucato ostro potius lacernae gracilis amictu ac mastrucae tegmine incompto utatur. (88 words)

Alliteration: ceu cernuus, feculenta fama, pompulentae prostitutae, lenocinante luxu. faleris falerati, curules comuntur, patricii ac praetore potiuntur (*run of 3*), fausta fraternitas feliciter fruatur (*run of 4*)
Internal alliteration: rutilante periscelidis armillaque lacertorum

Pleonasm: arcuatis poplitibus flexisque suffraginibus ("with arched knee and bent leg")
Chiasmus: none
Hyperbaton: edito ... fastigio
Triple hyperbaton: gelida ... flabra ... emergentia / climate ... septentrionali ... neglecto
Lexica abstrusa: pompulentae *for attested* pomposae
APrW, p. 155

[Moreover, I, compelled by this foul report, beg your Discipleship, genuflecting, as it were, with arched knee and bent leg, that you in no wise go near the whores or the trumpery of bawdy houses, where lurk pretentious prostitutes with luxury as their pander, who are adorned with the flashing burnish of leg-bands and with smooth arm bracelets, just as ornamented chariots are adorned with metal bosses; but rather, having spurned the exalted summit of the banquet hall, where patricians and praetors hold sway, let your fortunate Fraternity enjoy happily and contentedly the shelter of the lowly hovel, and rather than the dusky purple of a graceful mantle, let it employ a common cloak and the inelegant covering of the sheepskin – as befits a disciple of Christ – against the freezing blasts of winter that arise in the once-neglected region of the North.]

I.B2. *Aldhelm, Ep. 5 (to Heahfrith), p. 488.4–489.6*

Primitus pantorum procerum praetorumque pio potissimum ***paternoque praesertim privilegio*** panagericum poemataque passim prosatori sub polo promulg*antes* ***stridula vocum simphonia*** et melodiae cantilenaeque carmine modulaturi ymnnizemus, praecipue quia tandem ***almae editum puerperae sobolem*** ob inextricabile sons protopla<u>storum piaculum priscorumque cirografum oblitteraturum terris tantundem /destinare dignatus est, luridum qui ***linguis celydrum trisulcis*** rancida ***virulentaque vomentem*** **per aevum venena** torrentia tetrae tortionis in tartara trusit, et ubi pridem eiusdem nefandae natricis ermula cervulusque cruda ***fanis colebantur stoliditate in profanis***, versa vice discipulorum gurgustia, immo ***almae oraminum aedes*** architecti ingenio fabre conduntur. (90 words)

Alliteration: Primitus ... promulgantes (*run of 15!*), cantilenaeque carmine, protopla<u>storum piaculum priscorumque (*run of 3*), terris tantundem, destinare dignatus, *l*uridum ... *l*inguis ce*l*ydrum trisu*l*cis

… viru*l*entaque (internal alliteration), *virulentaque vomentem*, torrentia tetrae tortionis in tartara trusit (*run of 5*), cervulusque cruda … colebantur, versa vice

Chiasmus: none

Hyperbaton: paternoque … privilegio, stridula … simphonia, luridum … celydrum, linguis … trisulcis, rancida virulentaque … venena torrentia, ermula … cruda, fanis … profanis, almae … aedes

Double hyperbaton: almae editum puerperae sobolem

Lexica abstrusa: pantorum, prosatori, sons, cirografum, ermula (hermula)

Figura etymologica: fanis profanis

APrW, pp. 160–1 (slightly modified)

[Principally, with particularly pious and paternal privilege, publicly proferring beneath the pole panegyric and poems promiscuously to princes and praetors, let us raise a hymn in measured rhythms with a loud blending of voices and with song of melodious music, especially because He who thrust into Tartarus of terrible torture the ghastly three-tongued serpent, who vomits torrents of rank and virulent venom through the ages, deigned in like measure to send to earth the offspring begotten of holy parturition in order to obliterate from the earth the criminal offence of first matter and the record of the first men on account of their inextricable sin; and [because], where once the crude pillars of the same foul snake and the stag were worshipped with coarse stupidity in profane fanes, in their place dwellings for students, not to mention holy houses of prayer, are constructed skilfully by the talents of the architect.]

II. Letters to Abbesses and Nuns Resident in Britain

II.A1. *Boniface, Ep. 10, p. 30.10–15 (to Abbess Eadburg, a. 716)*

Modo siquidem gratias omnipotenti Deo refero, quia in hoc dilectionis tuae voluntatem eo plenius liquidiusque, Deo patrocinium praestante, implere valeo, quia ipse cum supradicto fratre redivivo, dum nuper de transmarinis partibus ad ***istas pervenit regiones***, locutus sum, et ille mihi stupendas visiones, quas extra corpus suum raptus in spiritu vidit, ***proprio exposuit sermone***. (51 words)

Alliteration: patrocinium praestante

Pleonasm: none

Chiasmus: none
Hyperbaton: istas ... regiones, proprio ... sermone
Lexica abstrusa: none
Rhyming cola: pervenit regiones ... stupendas visiones

[Now indeed I give thanks to almighty God, because I am able in this matter to satisfy your wish all the more fully and clearly, with God offering his guidance, because I myself spoke with the aforesaid brother who had been revived, when recently he arrived in these regions from parts overseas, and revealed to me in his own words the amazing visions, which he, taken outside his body, beheld in the spirit.]

II.A2. *Boniface, Ep. 5, p.114.14–18 (to Eadburg, a. 735), opening sentence*

Deum omnipotentem retributorem et remuneratorem omnium bonorum operum deprecor, ut tibi in celestibus mansionibus et in aeternis tabernaculis omnium beneficiorum tuorum, quae mihi prestitisti, aeternalem mercedem et in superna curia beatorum angelorum restituat, quia sepe sive **solamine librorum sive vestimentorum adiuvamine** pietas tua tristitiam meam consolata est ... (closing sentence): Fac ergo, soror carissima, de hac petitione nostra, sicut benignitas tua de cunctis precibus meis semper solebat, ut et hic opera tua ad gloriam caelestis patris aureis litteris fulgeant. (80 words)

Alliteration: retributorem et remuneratorem, sepe sive solamine (*run of 3*), semper solebat
Internal alliteration: sive vestimentorum adiuvamine (*run of 3*)
Pleonasm: none
Chiasmus: solamine librorum sive vestimentorum adiuvamine
Hyperbaton: none
Lexica abstrusa: none

[I beseech almighty God, who repays and rewards all good works, that he remunerate you in his heavenly dwellings and in the eternal tabernacles and in the supernal council of the blessed angels with an eternal reward for all your benefactions, which you have performed for me, in that often your Goodness soothed my sorrow with the consolation of books or a gift of vestments ... Therefore, dearest sister, attend to our petition, just as your kindness was always accustomed [to do] with regard to all my requests, so that here too your works [i.e., the requested copies of the Epistles of Peter] may shine with golden letters to the glory of the heavenly Father.]

II.B1. *Aldhelm, Prosa de virg., p. 229.7–12 (to Abbess Hildelith and her nuns)*

Iamdudum ad ***pontificale proficiscens* *conciliabulum* / *fraternis sodalium caterivs*** comitatus, almitatis vestrae **scripta meae mediocritati allata** satis libenter suscipiens, ***erectis ad aethera palmis***, **immensas Christo pro sospitate vestra gratulabundus impendere grates** curavi; quo stilo non solum **ecclesiastica promissorum votorum foedera,** quae fida pollicitatione spopondistis, ubertim claruerunt, verum etiam ***melliflua divinarum studia*** scripturarum sagacissima sermonum serie patuerunt. (55 words)

Alliteration: pontificiale proficiscens, catervis comitatus, meae mediocritati, studia scripturarum sagacissima sermonum serie (*note run of 5*)
Pleonasm: gratulabundus ... grates
Chiasmus: scripta meae mediocritati allata, ecclesiastica promissorum votorum foedera, immensas ... pro sospitate vestra ... grates
Hyperbaton: pontificale ... conciliabulum, fraternis ... catervis, erectis ... palmis,
Double hyperbaton: melliflua divinarum studia scripturarum
Lexica abstrusa: none
Rhyming cola: ubertim claruerunt ... serie patuerunt
APrW, p. 59

[Some time ago, while proceeding to an episcopal convention accompanied by brotherly throngs of associates, I received most pleasurably what had been written by your Grace to my humble self and, with hands extended to the heavens, I took care joyously to extend immense thanks to Christ on behalf of your welfare. In your writing, not only were the ecclesiastical compacts of [your] sworn vows – which you had pledged with a solemn promise – abundantly clear, but also the mellifluous studies of the Holy Scriptures were manifest in the extremely subtle sequence of your discourse.]

II.B2. *Aldhelm, Ep. 8, p. 497 (to the nun Sigegyth), entire letter*

Cognoscat vestra almitas de baptismo sororis me interrogasse pontificem, qui licentiam dedit baptizari illam sanctimonialem, sed tamen clam et latenter. Saluto te diligenter, o Sigegyth, ex ***intimo cordis cubiculo*** subnixis precibus obsecrans, ut ***assidua scripturarum meditatione*** mentem tuam occupare non desistas, quatenus psalmigrafi sententiam compleas dicentis: "In lege eius meditabitur die ac nocte" et idem psalmista hoc item testator dicens: "Quam dulcia faucibus meis eloquia tua" et reliqua. ***Orationum vero mearum*** ut memores sint, omnes sorores per Christum suppliciter obsecro, quia dicit apostolus: "Multum valet deprecatio iusti assidua." Vale dilectissima, immo centies et milies; te Deus valere faciat. (105 words not counting scriptural quotations)

Alliteration: cordis cubiculo, meditatione mentem, mearum ut memores
Pleonasm: none
Chiasmus: none
Hyperbaton: intimo cordis cubicula, assidua scriptuarum meditatione, orationum vero mearum (dubious because of normal position of *vero*)
Lexica obstrusa: none
AprW, pp. 166–7

[Let your kindness be aware that I petitioned the bishop regarding the baptism of the sister, and he gave leave for that religious person to be baptized, although in a private and confidential manner. I greet you earnestly, O Sigegyth, from the deepest chamber of my heart, and I treat you with hopeful prayers that you do not cease to occupy your mind with continual meditation on the Scriptures, that you may fulfil the words of the Psalmist, when he said: "And on his law he shall meditate day and night" [Ps. I.2], and the same Psalmist avers this again, saying: "How sweet are they words to my palate!" [Ps. CXVIII.103] I suppliantly beseech all the sisters in Christ that they be mindful of my prayers, because the Apostle says: "For the continual prayers of a just man availeth much." [Iac. V.16] Farewell, ten times, nay a hundred and a thousand times beloved, and may God cause you to fare well!]

III. *Letters to Bishops Resident in Britain*

III.A1. *Boniface, Ep. 33, p. 108.19–28 (to Nothelm, archbishop of Canterbury, a. 735 × 739)*

Almitatis vestrae clementiam ***intimis obsecro precibus***, ut mei in vestris sacrosanctis orationibus memores esse dignemini, et navem mentis meae **variis Germanicarum gentium tempestatum fluctibus** quassatam precibus vestris in portu firme petrae stabilire studeatis, et ut communioni fraternae non aliter quam ut **mihi venerandae memoriae antecessor vester Berhtwaldus archiepiscopus exeunti** a patria concessit, vobiscum adunatus sim nexu spiritali et glutino caritatis coniunctus, simul cum fraternis comitibus peregrinationis meae catholicae fidei unitate et spiritalis amoris dulcedine semper sociatus vobis esse merear. (79 words)

Alliteration: mentis meae, stabilire studeatis, caritatis coniunctus, semper sociatus
Pleonasm: none
Chiasmus: variis Germanicarum gentium tempestatum fluctibus, mihi ... exeunti (*note degree of separation*)
Hyperbaton: intimis ... precibus
Lexica abstrusa: none

[I beseech the clemency of your Grace with inmost entreaties, that you deign to be mindful of me in your holy prayers, and that in your petitions you strive to make stable in a port of stout rock the ship of my mind, shaken by varying fluctuations of the storms of Germanic peoples, so that I may be united by a spiritual bond and tie of love to [your] fraternal community in the same way as your predecessor Archbishop Berhtwald granted to me as I was departing from the fatherland, and together with the fraternal companions of my pilgrimage I may ever merit to be associated with you in the unity of the Catholic faith and the sweetness of spiritual love.]

III.B1. *Aldhelm, Ep. 1, p. 476.1–6 (to Bishop Leutherius)*

Fateor, o beatissime antistes, me dudum decrevisse, si rerum ratio ac temporum volitans vicissitudo pateretur, **vicinam obtati natalis Domini sollemnitatem** ibidem in consortio fratrum trepudians celebrare et postmodum, vita comite, vestrae caritatis affabili presentia frui. Sed quia ***diversis impedimentorum obstaculis*** retardati, quemadmodum lator praesentium /viva voce / plenius promulgabit, illud perficere nequivimus, idcirco difficultatis veniam, precor, impendite ... (penultimate sentence): Haec idcirco, carissime pater, cursim pedetemptim perstrinximus, non ***garrulo verbositatis strepitu*** illecti, sed ut scias, ***tanta rerum arcana*** examusim non posse intellegi, nisi frequens et prolixa meditatio fuerit adhibita. (87 words)

Alliteration: dudum decrevisse, rerum ratio, volitans vicissitudo, viva voce, praesentium ... plenius promulgabit, pedetemptim promulgabit
Chiasmus: vicinam obtati natalis Domini sollemnitatem

Hyperbaton: diversis ... obstaculis, garrulo ... strepitu, tanta ... arcana
Pleonasm (*redundant genitive*): impedimentorum obstaculis, garrulo verbositatis strepitu
Lexica abstrusa: examusim
APrW, p. 152

[I declare, O most blessed bishop, that I decided some time ago, if the course of events and the swift mutations of time permitted, to celebrate joyfully in the same place the approaching feast of our Lord's longed-for birth, in the company of the brethren, and afterwards, if life is our companion, to enjoy the affable presence of your Goodness. But because we were delayed by various obstacles [and] hindrances, as the bearer of the present [letters] will propound more fully in oral delivery, we could not achieve that aim; therefore, I beg you, grant me pardon on account of that hardship ... Therefore, dearest father, we have touched on these matters carefully and cautiously, not [because we are] enticed by the garrulous chatter of verbosity, but that you might know that so many hidden matters of subjects cannot be accurately understood without the application of frequent and extended concentration.]

IV. *Letters to Kings Resident in Britain*

IV.A1. *Boniface, Ep. 73, p. 214.1–7 (to Æthelbald, king of Mercia, a. 746–7)*

Confitemur coram Deo et sanctis angelis, quia quandocumque prosperitatem vestram et fidem in Deo et opera bona coram Deo et hominibus per nuntios fideles audivimus, quod inde gaudentes et pro vobis orantes, laeti gratias agimus Deo postulantes et obsecrantes salvatorem mundi, ut vos sospites et in fide stabiles et in operibus coram Deo rectos in principatu christiani populi longo tempore custodiat. (61 words)

Alliteration: Confitemur coram, quia quandocumque
Chiasmus: none
Hyperbaton: none
Rhyming cola: orantes ... postulantes ... obsecrantes
Lexica abstrusa: none

[We profess before God and the holy angels, that whenever we heard from reliable messengers of your prosperity and faith in God and good works in the presence of God and men, that rejoicing because of it and praying for you, we cheerfully give thanks to God, petitioning and beseeching the saviour of the world, that he keep you safe for a long time and stable in the faith and upright in works before God at the head of the Christian people.]

IV.B1. *Aldhelm, Ep. 4, p. 481.4–12 (to King Geraint and the bishops of Devon)*

Nuper cum essem in concilio episcoporum, ubi ex tota paene Britannia **innumerabilis Dei sacerdotum** caterva confluxit, ad hoc praesertim congregata, ut pro ecclesiarum sollicitudine et animarum salute ab omnibus **decreta canonum et patrum statuta** tractarentur, et in commune Christo patrocinium praestante conservarentur – his igitur rite peractis omne sacerdotale concilium meam parvitatem pari praecepto et simili sententia compulerunt, ut ad vestrae pietatis praesentiam ***epistulares litterarum apices*** diregerem, et eorum paternam petitionem /salubremque suggestionem per script<ur>ae stilum intimarem, hoc est de ecclesiae catholicae unitate et christianae religionis concordia, sine quibus fides otiosa torpescit et merces futura fatescit. (95 words)

Alliteration: caterva confluxit, patrocinium praestante, parvitatem pari praecepto, simili sententia, pietatis praesentiam, paternam petitionem, salubremque suggestionem per script<ur>ae stilum, futura fatescit.
Chiasmus: decreta canonum et patrum statuta, innumerabilis Dei sacerdotum caterva
Hyperbaton: epistulares … apices
Lexica abstrusa: none
Rhyming cola: statuta tractarentur … praestante conservarentur, otiosa torpescit … futura fatescit
APr W, p. 155

[Recently when I was present at an episcopal council, where, out of almost the entirety of Britain an innumerable company of the bishops of God came together, having assembled for this purpose expressly, that out of concern for the churches and the salvation of souls, the decrees of the canons and the statutes of the (Church) Fathers might be discussed by all and be maintained in common, with Christ offering his protection – when these matters were duly accomplished, the entire episcopal council compelled my insignificant self with like precept and similar sentiment to direct epistolary letters to the presence of your Loyalty, and through the style of writing, to intimate their fatherly request and wholesome suggestion, that is, respecting the unity of the Catholic Church and the harmony of the Christian religion, without which an indifferent faith grows sluggish and future gain is exhausted.]

Interpretatio Monastica: Biblical Commentary and the Forging of Monastic Identity in the Early Middle Ages

SCOTT DEGREGORIO

The ancient monastic collection known by the title *Apophthegmata Patrum* attributes to one Abba Alonius the following saying: "If I had not destroyed myself completely, I should not have been able to rebuild and shape myself again."[1] These words capture very well the peculiar ideal that animates the spirituality of monastic existence – the razing of one identity to make way for another, self-obliteration as the catalyst for rebirth, a new sense of who one is. The intention to live as a monk begins with the personal decision to embrace what is effectively a kind of death, towards oneself, one's relations, indeed everything worldly. Since ancient times, investing the candidate with the monastic habit has in this regard pulled double duty, being a constituent element of monastic formation in addition to a powerful symbol in its own right, namely of the monk's resolve to change his whole way of life – in short, to undergo conversion.

But this is to dwell on one half of Alonius's remark; he speaks just as potently of rebuilding the self anew. But how? In the *Vitae Patrum*, another ancient collect of monastic sayings, an answer of sorts is found in the words of St Anthony: "Whatever you do," he says, "follow the example of Holy Scripture."[2] The injunction is unremarkable until it is recalled what, for the monk, following Scripture entailed. Cassian, in a passage from his *Conferences* heavily indebted to Origen, puts it this way:

> ... hoc tibi est omnimodis enitendum, ut expulsa omni sollicitudine et cogitatione terrena adsiduum te ac potius iugem sacrae praebeas lectioni, donec

1 Ward, *Sayings of the Desert Fathers*, 35.
2 Ward, *Desert Fathers*, 1.

continua meditatio inbuat mentem tuam et quasi in similitudinem sui formet, arcam quodammodo ex ea faciens testamenti, habentem scilicet in se duas tabulas lapideas, id est duplicis instrumenti perpetuam firmitatem.[3]

[... once all worldly cares and preoccupations have been cast out, you must strive in every respect to give yourself assiduously and even constantly to sacred reading. Do this until continual meditation fills your mind and as it were forms it in its likeness, making of it a kind of ark of the covenant, containing in itself two stone tablets – that is, constant steadfastness under the aspect of twofold Testament.][4]

Cassian continues with the suggestion – incredible to us today – that *all* the books of Scripture should be "diligenter memoriae conmendanda est et incessabiliter recensenda" (diligently committed to memory and ceaselessly reviewed).[5] The recasting of the monk's identity on the rubble of the old self was, then, centrally a project of scriptural reformation. The goal was effectively to create a scriptural self, a new textual identity, the biblical text becoming so engrained within the monk that any part of it may, to use St Benedict's phrase, be recalled *ex corde*, "by heart."[6]

There were of course many levels to the scriptural saturation of the individual that monastic culture so programmatically sought to achieve: the common prayers of the liturgy, built as they were out of Scripture; private reading and study, to which the expression *lectio divina* was originally applied; teaching in the monastic schoolroom, with its focus primarily on the study of the Bible itself; finally the organizing of the whole of life through a *regula* or rule, which was always no more than an attempt to apply Scripture to the practical situation of living.[7] But I shall set these worthy topics aside so that I may focus on scriptural commentary. What I want to do is home in on this genre's capacity to catalyse a monk's identity, using the figures of Gregory the Great and Bede as models. The approach suggests

3 Cassian, *Conlationes* XIV.10, ed. Petschenig, Corpus scriptorum ecclesiasticorum latinorum, 13, p. 410, lines 12–18.

4 Trans. Ramsey, *Conferences*, 514.

5 Cassian, *Conlationes* XIV.10, ed. Petschenig, Corpus scriptorum ecclesiasticorum latinorum, 13, p. 411, lines 11–12; trans. Ramsey, 514.

6 Fry, ed. and trans, *Rule of St Benedict*, 204–5: "Post hos, lectio apostoli sequatur, ex corde recitanda" (This ended, there follows a reading from the Apostle recited by heart). For comment on the phrase, see Kardong, *Benedict's Rule*, 177.

7 On these practices, see Driver, *John Cassian*, and Robertson, *Lectio Divina*, esp. 72–103.

itself for two reasons. First, it is significant that so much of our surviving medieval exegesis derives from monastic quarters. I shall begin therefore by looking at how scholarship has identified and mapped that tradition and target a problem with its current configuration. Second, the way Gregory and Bede approached the understanding of sacred texts opens a wide window onto their self-conceptions as exegetes within the monastic tradition. My next task, then, will be to use the comparison to ask in what way their identities may be construed as effects of the exegetical styles and textual strategies they deploy. While much may be found here to unite them, what will ultimately emerge are some revealing discontinuities that can be used to historicize their identities. Contrary to those earlier strains in the scholarship that proverbially figure Bede's identity as subsumed by a desire to emulate his beloved patristic forebears, the evidence shows Bede did not always follow their footsteps, as his favourite Latin tag had it,[8] but instead evolved his own approach – and with that, his own identity.

Monastic Exegesis: The Identity of the Tradition

The scholarly category of a distinctly "monastic exegesis" arose in the middle of the last century from the pioneering work of Henri de Lubac and Jean Leclercq.[9] Both scholars approached the topic through contrast: they were pressed to distinguish a "university" brand of exegesis from another suited to the cloisters. Where the former sought a *lectio* structured towards *scientia* and systematized it into genres to achieve this (e.g., the *diuisio*, the *expositio*, the *quaestio*, the *glossa*), the latter had its soil in the *lectio diuina*, a more discursive mode of reading sacred texts geared to foster spiritual desire.[10] In the pages of Leclercq and de Lubac as well, the phenomenon is thus elucidated best in the high medieval period, particularly the twelfth century. To be sure, Gregory gets a nod – the second

8 The phrase "patrum uestigia sequens" (following in the footsteps of the Fathers) is a favourite of Bede's: e.g., *In primam partem Samuhelis*, ed. Hurst, CCSL 119, p. 10, lines 52–4; *In Cantica Canticorum*, ed. Hurst, CCSL 119B, p. 180, lines 501–4; *Expositio Actuum Apostolorum*, ed. Laistner, CCSL 121, p. 3, lines 9–10; *De temporum ratione*, ed. Jones, CCSL 123B, p. 287, line 86. For wide-ranging discussion of his calculated use of the phrase, see the essays in DeGregorio, ed., *Innovation and Tradition*, esp. 1–35 and 143–68.

9 de Lubac, *Medieval Exegesis*, esp. 2:143–53; and Leclercq, *Love of Learning*, esp. 71–88.

10 On this distinction see also the classic discussion of Smalley, *Study of the Bible*, 37–82.

chapter of Leclercq's *Love of Learning* is entitled "St. Gregory, Doctor of Desire" – but the real heroes come later. Leclercq, tellingly, begins his book by pitting Bernard of Clairvaux against Peter Damian.[11]

Unsurprisingly, neither scholar pays much attention to Bede. Yet there is no doubt that Bede's work is noteworthy in this context. His exegesis was monastic in every sense of that word – written by a monk in a monastery for other monks about teachings especially appropriate for monks.[12] Long before Bernard, Bede wrote a massive commentary on the Song of Songs, always a major source for monastic devotion.[13] In his brief autobiographical epilogue to the *Ecclesiastical History*, one of the precious few places Bede can be heard speaking directly about himself, he characterized his interaction with Scripture in purely monastic terms:

> cunctumque ex eo tempus uitae in eiusdem monasterii habitatione peragens, omnem meditandis scripturis operam dedi, atque inter obseruantiam disciplinae regularis, et cotidianam cantandi in ecclesia curam, semper aut discere aut docere aut scribere dulce habui.[14]
>
> [I have spent my whole life in this monastery, applying myself entirely to the study of Scripture; and, amid the observance of the discipline of the Rule and the daily task of singing in church, it has always been my delight to learn or to teach or to write.]

Then he added, crucially, that whatever exegetical work he undertook was done "meae meorumque necessitati" (for my own benefit and that of my brethren).[15] No wonder, then, that when Bede sought to imagine what it

11 Leclercq, *Love of Learning*, 3–4.

12 See DeGregorio, "Bede, the Monk, as Exegete" and "Bede and Benedict of Nursia."

13 This important work is now available in English translation: Holder, *Bede: Song of Songs*. For comment on some of its "affective" strains, see DeGregorio, "Affective Spirituality."

14 Originals and translations are from Bede, *HE* 5.24, p. 566.

15 Bede, *HE* 5.24, p. 566. The full quote runs, "Ex quo tempore accepti presbyteratus usque ad annum aetatis meae LVIII haec in Scripturam sanctam meae meorumque necessitati ex opusculis uenerabilium patrum breuiter adnotare, siue etiam ad formam sensus et interpretationis eorum superadicere curaui" (From the time I became a priest until the fifty-ninth year of my life I have made it my business, for my own benefit and that of my brothers, to make brief extracts from the works of the venerable fathers on the holy Scriptures, or to add notes of my own to clarify their sense and interpretation).

would be like for an illiterate cowherd to come face-to-face with Scripture, he could only imagine him in his own image, in the guise of a monk "rememorando secum et quasi mundum animal ruminando" (memorizing it and ruminating over it, like some clean animal chewing its cud),[16] and doing so moreover *sub regula* for the betterment of his *fratres*.

It is critical to recognize all this in Bede; it will not do to race over four centuries to get from Gregory to Bernard. The view of the monastic exegetical tradition as ultimately a late medieval development perhaps makes for an easier, maybe more appealing concept, but it needs to be resisted. The existence of a predominantly monastic mode already well established in Bede, nurtured as he was by a wholly monastic experience of Scripture, is perhaps the greatest sign of his Gregorianism.[17] Here it may be that what is more clearly identifiable in Gregory can help to elucidate what is less discernible in Bede. Take the question of working methods. We know that Gregory's commentaries on Job, the Song of Songs, and Ezekiel were composed for monastic audiences.[18] We know further that they began as *collatio*, spoken discourses delivered by Gregory as he reflected and ruminated on these portions of Scripture before small, probably quite elite

---

16 Bede, *HE* 4.24, p. 418. For further comment on both this passage and Bede's treatment of Cædmon generally, see DeGregorio, "Literary Contexts."

17 The trend has been to emphasize pastoral theology as Bede's greatest Gregorian inheritance. See, e.g., Thacker, "Bede's Ideal" and "Monks, Preaching and Pastoral Care."

18 The preface accompanying Gregory's first major exegetical enterprise, the *Moralia in Iob*, makes this context for his work very clear. See *Moralia in Iob*, *Epistula ad Leandrum* 1, ed. Adriaen, CCSL 143, 43–53: "Tunc eisdem fratibus etiam cogente te placuit, sicut ipse meministi, ut librum beati Iob exponere importuna me petitione compellerent et, prout ueritas uires infunderet, eis mysteria tantae profounditatis aperirem. Qui hoc quoque mihi in onere suae petitionis addiderunt, ut non solum uerba historiae per allegoriarum sensus excuterem, sed allegoriarum sensus protinus in exercitium moralitatis inclinarem, adhuc aliquid grauius adiungentes, ut intellecta quaeque testimoniis cingerem et prolata testimonia, si implicita fortasse uiderentur interpositione superadditae expositionis enodarem" (Then it pleased those brethren, as you will recall encouraging them, to force me by their repeated requests to comment on the book of blessed Job and, as far as truth should give me strength, to reveal to them such profound mysteries. To the burden of their petition they added as well that I should not only discuss the words of the story through their allegorical meanings, but should also direct the allegorical meanings towards moral edification; and that I should also (a still heavier burden) support my interpretations with other scriptural texts and should even add explanations of those passages if they seemed difficult enough to require more elucidation). For exhaustive comment on the monastic setting of Gregory's exegesis, see McClure, "Gregory the Great."

groups of monks. Only later did he produce the written versions, relying on the short-hand of notaries who recorded his original pronouncements.[19] Such insight into how Gregory worked does much to explain the characteristic features of his exegesis: the unrestrained flow of ideas, the absence of fixed structures, the multiple digressions, the recursiveness seen on nearly every page. Now these are features all found in Bede's commentaries as well, but usually to his detriment. The limpid style of his historical prose has been adduced recently by Richard Sharpe to reveal by contrast the muddledness of his exegetical Latin.[20] But might it be that Bede's commentaries, like Gregory's, began too as *collatio* in the presence of the Wearmouth-Jarrow monks before undergoing redaction on their way towards incarnation in writing? Such a view, while admittedly unprovable, is not at all implausible given his monastic environment, and may well explain, say, the piling up of interpretations, the syntactic looseness, the leisurely flow of thought, not to mention the distinctive themes that mark his commentaries.

Exegetical Identities in Context: Gregory and Bede

Neither Gregory nor Bede bothered to expound a theory of monastic exegesis, but examination of their actual habits and practices can indicate much that is essential to their approach. I shall delimit my comparison to just two works, Gregory's *Homilies on Ezekiel* and Bede's *On Ezra and Nehemiah*.[21] These two texts pair well together, and are especially illuminating for our purposes. Both are major works of Old Testament allegorical exegesis born from periods of crisis in their authors' lives. Deeply personal creations, they can tell us much about the habits of mind and spiritual outlook that produced them. Gregory's *Homilies on Ezekiel* is a seemingly integrated edition of two books, but in fact each section is rather distinct, representing a different stage of composition in the original homilies. Gregory first delivered the homilies *coram populo* around 593, then eight years later, probably in 601, worked them up into a written

19 Meyvaert, "Date of Gregory the Great's Commentaries."

20 Sharpe, "Varieties of Bede's Prose."

21 Gregory, *Homiliae in Hiezechihelem*, ed. Adriaen, CCSL 142, hereafter cited as *HEz*; and Bede, *In Ezram et Neemiam*, ed. Hurst, CCSL 119A, hereafter cited as *In Ezram*. All translations from the latter will be cited from DeGregorio, trans., *Bede: On Ezra and Nehemiah*.

edition with the help of records made by his notaries.[22] Book 1, containing twelve homilies, treats Ezekiel's opening vision and prophetic call, and so stops near the beginning of Ezk. chapter 4. Strangely, the ten homilies of book 2 then deal exclusively with Ezk. chapter 40, the prophet's vision of the new temple. The preface to book 2 explains why: the Lombard encroachment on Rome in 593 had greatly curtailed Gregory's time, forcing him to move directly to the temple vision which his audience had implored him to elucidate.[23]

By contrast with this, Bede's *On Ezra and Nehemiah* is more straightforward: in three books it proceeds verse by verse, offering detailed treatment of the Ezra-Nehemiah story, with its focus on the return from exile and the reconstruction of the temple under the priestly scribe Ezra. But the choice of biblical time-frame very much aligns with what we find in Gregory's Ezekiel, namely the events surrounding the Babylonian Captivity, and likewise reveals to us an author writing under duress: not because of besieging Lombards, but because of a decline in morals in Bede's present-day Northumbrian world.[24] Bede of course knew Gregory's *Homilies* well and cited them in *On Ezra and Nehemiah*, but we must look beyond that kind of contact if the goal is to characterize their monastic approach to Scripture and to see, in turn, how that approach as it were characterizes them. So instead I shall direct my focus to three wider areas of overlap that can, I think, reveal at once Bede's debt to this Gregorian work as well as his calculated departures from it. These are, first, their choice of biblical book; second, their treatment of one dominant image within it (viz. the temple); and third, their association with the titular characters Ezekiel the prophet and Ezra the priestly scribe.

---

22 *HEz* 1, praefatio, p. 3, lines 1–8: "Homilias, quae in beatum Hiezechihelem prophetam, ita ut coram populo loquebar, exceptae sunt, multis curis irruentibus in abolitione reliqueram. Sed post annos octo, petentibus fratribus, notariorum schedas requirere studui, easque fauente Domino transcurrens, in quantum ab angustiis tribulationum licuit, emendaui" (Because many troubles were besieging me I had abandoned the homilies on the blessed prophet Ezekiel which were taken down just as I delivered them before the people. But after eight years, at the request of the brothers, I was eager to acquire the clerk's notes and, glancing through them with the Lord's support, I have amended them, insofar as the difficult circumstances have allowed).

23 *HEz* 2, praefatio, p. 205, lines 10–12: "Aliud, quod iam Agilulphum Langobardorum regem ad obsidionem nostram summopere festinantem Padum transisse cognouimus" (The other is that we know that the Lombard king Agilulphus has crossed the Po and is proceeding with utmost haste to besiege us).

24 See DeGregorio, "Bede's *In Ezram et Neemiam*," and "Bede's Commentary."

I

One thing that firmly embeds Gregory and Bede within a monastic interpretive tradition is their shared love for obscure Old Testament narratives requiring extensive allegorization. Neither Ezekiel nor Ezra-Nehemiah were high on the to-do lists of the Fathers. Only Origen, Jerome, and Theodore of Cyr had offered full-scale treatments of Ezekiel before Gregory took it up.[25] Meanwhile, no one had touched Ezra-Nehemiah: Bede's is the first and only complete commentary on that book.[26] Given their high degree of literal obscurity and irrelevance to the Christian story, it is no mystery these were rather neglected texts. This is precisely why, however, Gregory took up Ezekiel, and its most difficult portions at that. A good part of Gregory's radically monastic approach to Scripture depends on the heuristic role of *arcana*. He commends the *obscuritas* of Holy Writ for being replete with *utilitas*, welcoming the free-play of signification thereby opened up for the interpreter.[27] In the *Homilies* Gregory offers a profusion of metaphors for this hermeneutic process: Scripture is a gate to be opened, a dark forest to be illumined, a wheel to be turned, and of course – a monastic favourite – food to be chewed up and consumed.[28] Here there is none of the older Augustine's trepidation about allegory, just pure delight in reading the text *multipliciter*.[29] Whatever attention Gregory pays to the literal level of the text is clearly of

25 Borret, ed., *Origène: Homélies*; Jerome, *Commentarii in Ezechielem*, ed. Glorie, CCSL 75; Theodore of Cyr, *Interpretatio in Ezechielem*, PG 81, cols 808–1256. See also Christman, *What Did Ezekiel See?*

26 See DeGregorio, "Footsteps of His Own."

27 *HEz* 1.6, p. 67, lines 8–14: "Magnae uero utilitatis est ipsa obscuritas eloquiorum Dei, quia exercet sensum ut fatigatione dilatetur, et exercitatus capiat quod capere non posset otiosus. Habet quoque adhuc maius aliud, quia Scripturae sacrae intellegentia, quae si in cunctis esset aperta uilesceret, in quibusdam locis obscurioribus tanto maiore dulcedine inuenta reficit, quanto maiore labore fatigat animum quaesita" (The very obscurity of divine speech is of great benefit, because it trains thought to enlarge itself through exhaustion, and when it is trained it seizes what it could not seize if idle. And it has something still greater because the understanding of holy Scripture, which would become cheap if it were opened up to all, when found in certain more obscure places refreshes with greater sweetness, the more the search for it exhausts the spirit).

28 As gate: *HEz* 2.3, p. 238, lines 43–7; as forest: *HEz* 1.5, p. 57, lines 1–5; as wheel: *HEz* 1.6, p. 67, lines 16–32; as food: *HEz* 1.10, p. 145, lines 17–35.

29 On the Augustine-Gregory contrast, see Markus, *Signs and Meaning*, 45–51.

ancillary importance. Its role may be compared to that of a springboard for contemplative flight to higher things.

Much of this is paralleled in Bede's treatment of Ezra-Nehemiah. In the prologue to the work, Bede calls the literal level of this Old Testament story a husk to be peeled away, so that the nourishing pith in the marrow may be ingested.[30] Repeatedly he tells us that the events, places, people, and objects in the text are there "certi mysterii gratia" (for the sake of a certain mystery).[31] He equates the Nathinnites dwelling in the fortified hill of Ophel, which in Hebrew means "a tower that rises into the clouds," with those who read meditatively and thereby seek to penetrate the "abdita scripturarum" (hidden things of the Scriptures).[32] And Neh. 8:15, "Go out into the mountain and bring back branches of olives and the most beautiful wood," he glosses with this injunction: "Et nos egrediamur de mansione quasi quadam generalium cogitationum in altitudinem sanctarum scripturarum crebrius meditandam" (Let us too go out from the dwelling, so to speak, of our general thoughts onto the height of meditating frequently on

30 *In Ezram*, p. 237, lines 13–17: "quia donet nobis propitius retecto cortice litterae altius aliud et sacratius in medulla sensus spiritalis inuenire quod uidelicet ipsum dominum ac templum et ciuitatem eius quae nos sumus propheticis quidem figuris sed manifesta ratione designet" (to give us [the ability] to find, when the bark of the text is peeled back, something deeper and more sacred in the marrow of the spiritual sense, since by prophetic figures but in a clear way it designates the Lord himself and his temple and city, which we are; trans. DeGregorio, *Bede: On Ezra and Nehemiah*, 1–2).

31 *In Ezram*, p. 237, lines 316–22: "Quem etiam certi nobis mysterii gratia Hebraice Graece et Latine conscripsit quia nimirum omnis diuina lex quam habebant Hebraei omnis sapientia mundana in qua gloriabantur Graeci omne regnum terrestre in quo tunc maxime praeminebant Romani Christum regem contestatur omnium sanctorum et confitentium Deum" (For the sake of a certain mystery for us, [Pilate] wrote this inscription in Hebrew, Greek, and Latin, doubtless because all the divine law which the Hebrews had, all the human wisdom about which the Greeks used to boast, and all the terrestrial kingdom in which the Romans at that time were especially preeminent, bear witness that Christ is the king of all the saints and of those who confess God; trans. DeGregorio, *Bede: On Ezra and Nehemiah*, 18–19).

32 *In Ezram*, p. 353, lines 568–72: "Item Nathinnei habitant in Ofel cum quique religionis habitu insignes abdita scripturarum de quibus dictum est, tenebrosa aqua in nubibus aeris, hoc est mystica scientia in prophetis illustrato corde penetrare atque in horum lectione die noctuque meditari didicerint" (Similarly, the Nathinnites dwell in Ophel when all those distinguished by the religious habit have learned to penetrate with illuminated heart the hidden things of the Scriptures, about which it was said, *the dark water in the clouds of the air* (that is, the mystical knowledge contained in the prophets), and to meditate day and night on the reading of these; trans. DeGregorio, *Bede: On Ezra and Nehemiah*, 175).

the Holy Scriptures).[33] The Gregorian ring of these passages is evident: the *raison d'être* of the monastic exegete is to expound Scripture's darkest mysteries through a process of meditative reflection akin to *lectio divina*. Indeed for both of these monastic interpreters, exegesis is not a technique so much as a contemplative *askesis* in its own right, a search for the invisible Creator through the physical medium of page and word. Such observations go quite far in explaining the complexion of both works: inspired as much by personal meditation as organized teaching, they are long and diffuse in character, full of digressions and driven by a free associative play of ideas. In this they exhibit deeply engrained monastic habits of reading, wringing the text for all its significations.

II

Next it is worth considering their treatment of the temple. Here we can continue to chart Bede's debt to Gregory while noting some key differences in their respective approaches. The temple is of course integral to both Ezekiel and Ezra-Nehemiah. Ezekiel concludes with the prophet's vision of a rebuilt temple (Ezk. 40–8), and Gregory, as noted, devotes the second book of his *Homilies* to explicating this vision. The whole Ezra-Nehemiah story, meanwhile, is predicated on the return of the Jews from captivity in Babylon to rebuild their sacred shrine in Jerusalem. Now Gregory and Bede adopt the same interpretative scheme for the idea of the return itself: it represents the return of souls from sin to righteousness through penance.[34]

---

33 *In Ezram*, p. 369, lines 1221–3; trans. DeGregorio, *Bede: On Ezra and Nehemiah*, 197.

34 *HEz* 1.10, p. 155, lines 380–7: "Saepe enim quis postquam in confusione uitiorum ceciderit, erubescens mala quae perpetrauit, ad paenitentiam redit, seque a suis lapsibus bene uiuendo erigit. Quid ergo iste nisi usque Babylonem uenit, et ibi liberatus est? Qui postquam, confusus mente, peruersa perpetrauit, haec ipsa erubescens mala quae fecit, se contra se erigit, et bene operando ad statum recititudinis redit. In Babylone itaque liberatus est, qui per diuinam gratiam ostenditur etiam de confusione saluatus" (For often someone, after he has fallen into the confusion of vices, ashamed of the evils which he has committed, returns to penitence and raises himself by a good life from his failings. What therefore did this man do if he did not come all the way to Babylon and was freed there? He who after he has committed perversities in confusion, blushing for the evils he had done, raises himself in spite of himself and by doing good returns to a state of uprightness. And so he was freed in Babylon who through God's grace is shown as saved even from his confusion). Cf. Bede's prologue, *In Ezram*, pp. 241–3, lines 1–88, where he elaborates at length precisely this allegorical scheme as the main interpretive framework for his commentary.

Here a crucial point of overlap between Gregory and Bede must be noted: for all the high-flying allegoresis, much of their non-literal, spiritual reading is rooted in an ascetic emphasis on proper conduct, on *how* to live the Christian life. Constantly the focus is on putting precept into action; the perfection of the monastic ideal in this way suffuses both texts.[35]

And yet, a compelling difference between Gregory and Bede here begins to emerge. Much more than Bede, Gregory is ready to jump from the literal to the spiritual level, or to forsake the letter entirely. Their respective treatment of the architecture of the temple and its precincts makes this all very clear. Gregory begins his discussion of Ezekiel's temple with this observation: "Cuius uidelicet ciuitatis aedificium accipi iuxta litteram nullatenus potest" (Indeed it is by no means possible to accept the building of this city according to the letter).[36] True, Ezekiel's is a visionary temple, but Gregory's concern to treat every dimension of Ezekiel 40ff with a broad allegorical brush should be noted, as should the mystical level to which his allegorizing aspires.[37] Consider, for example, his interpretation of the two doors in the outer court of the East Gate:

> In cognitione uero omnipotentis Dei primum ostium nostrum fides est, secundum uero species illius, ad quam per fidem ambulando peruenimus. In hac etenim uita hanc ingredimur, ut ad illam postmodum perducamur. Ostium ergo contra ostium est, quia per aditum fidei aperitur aditus uisionis Dei. Si quis uero utraque haec ostia in hac uita uelit accipere, neque hoc a salubri intellegentia abhorret. Nam saepe uolumus omnipotentis Dei naturam inuisibilem considerare, sed nequaquam ualemus, atque ipsis difficultatibus fatigata anima ad semetipsam recedit, sibique de seipsa gradus ascensionis facit, ut primum semetipsam, si ualet, consideret, et tunc illam naturam quae super ipsam est, in quantum potuerit, inuestiget. Sed mens nostra si in carnalibus imaginibus fuerit sparsa, nequaquam uel se uel animae naturam considerare sufficit, quia per quot cogitationes ducitur, quasi per tot obstacula caecatur.[38]

> [Truly in the knowledge of Almighty God our first door is faith, but the second is the likeness of him to which we come by walking in faith. For in this

35 For more on this, see DeGregorio, "The Venerable Bede and Gregory the Great," esp. 54–7.

36 *HEz* 2.1, p. 208, lines 51–2.

37 DeGregorio, "The Venerable Bede and Gregory the Great," 58–60.

38 *HEz* 2.5, p. 281, lines 213–28.

> life we enter the latter so that we may later be led to the former. Therefore one door is opposite the other because through the way of faith the way to the vision of God is revealed. But if anyone wishes to interpret these two doors in regard to this life, this too is not inconsistent with a profitable understanding. For often we wish to ponder the invisible nature of Almighty God but are by no means able to, and the soul, wearied by these difficulties, withdraws into itself and makes for itself and from itself the steps of its ascent, so that it may first consider itself, if it can, and then examine insofar as it can that nature which is above it. But if our mind has been dissipated in carnal images, it is by no means capable of considering either itself or the nature of the soul because it is as if blinded by as many obstacles as the thoughts it is led through.]

By contrast, in discussing the temple Bede keeps his eye firmly on the literal details, treating them often meticulously and at some length, before moving to a spiritual meaning. To cite one instance, he spends some time working out the historical details of exactly where the Sheep Gate stood, when it was built, and by whom, then uses that history to distil a moral framework for his audience. And so he concludes as follows:

> Portam ergo gregis in primordio aedificandae ciuitatis dei sacerdotes aedificant cum sancti praedicatores auditores suos ante omnia fide ueritatis quae per dilectionem operetur imbuunt per quam uictimas bonorum operum introducere et in altari sui cordis Deo offerre debeant, et huius portae aedificium per centum cubitos extensum usque ad turrem Anenehel, id est gratiae Dei, sanctificant cum ab initio fidei usque ad firmitatem bonae actionis quae non nisi Deo inspirante atque auxiliante perficitur sola aeternae retributionis intentione pertendunt.
>
> [Thus the priests build the Sheep Gate at the commencement of the building of God's city when, before all else, holy preachers imbue their listeners with true faith which works through love, the kind of gate through which they should bring the sacrificial victims of good works and offer these to God on the altar of their hearts; and they sanctify the building of this Gate which extended one hundred cubits through the Tower of Hananel when from the inception of faith they strive towards the firmness of good action with a singular determination for everlasting reward.][39]

39 *In Ezram*, p. 345, lines 241–51; trans. DeGregorio, *Bede: On Ezra and Nehemiah*, 163.

Here as elsewhere, it is as if Bede attends more carefully than Gregory does to his own dictum stated at the start of the *Moralia*, where he writes: "Nam primum quidem fundamenta historiae ponimus; deinde per significationem typicam in acrem fidei fabricam mentis erigimus; ad extremum quoque per moralitatis gratiam, quasi superducto aedificium colore uestimus" (First we lay the foundations of historical fact; then we lift up the mind to the citadel of faith through allegory; finally through the exposition of the moral sense we dress the edifice in its coloured raiment).[40]

III

This contrast between Gregory and Bede can be sharpened further by returning third and finally to their choice of biblical book or, even better, their choice of Old Testament prophet. For in many ways, the contrast between Ezekiel and Ezra can be used to sum up the contrast between the personal identities of Gregory and Bede. Of course, we know far more about Gregory the individual than we do Bede. Famously, Bede's slender biography at the conclusion of the *Ecclesiastical History* is remarkable for its exclusion of any real personal detail; rather Bede uses that space to construct an ideal image of a life dedicated to monastic observance and scholarship, and leaves it at that.[41] By comparison Gregory is an open book: from multiple sources we know something of his family origin with its posh patrician roots, his secular career as prefect of Rome, his monastic conversion deferred continually, his rise through the clergy, which would take him to Constantinople as papal ambassador before his final ascent to the papal office itself. And though Gregory rarely speaks in the first person, there is at times a self-referentiality to his writings that acts further to reveal him to our gaze: think, for instance, of those passages on his stomach illness, or on the burden of pastoral responsibilities, which, as he lamented in the preface to the *Dialogues*, were like a tumultuous storm devastating his longing for monastic *quies*.[42] All this of course Bede was quick to suppress, tellingly, when he constructed his little portrait of Gregory in book 2 of the *Ecclesiastical History*. There Bede crafts an ideal

40 *Moralia in Iob*, *Epistula ad Leandrum* 3, p. 4, lines 110–14.

41 Ray, "Who Did Bede Think He Was?"

42 Stomach illness: *Moralia in Iob*, *Epistula ad Leandrum* 5, p. 6, lines 189–90; longing for *quies*: de Vogüé, ed., *Grégoire le Grand: Dialogues*, pp. 12–14, lines 14–56.

Gregory as Bede himself might have wished to see him – humble monk, papal evangelist, saviour of the *gens Anglorum*.[43]

But if we place this Bedan Gregory to one side, as we surely must, and ask rather how Gregory perceived himself, there is striking evidence in the *Homilies on Ezekiel*, in Gregory's very personal reading of Ezk. 3:17, which reads "Son of man, I have given thee as the watchman to the House of Israel."[44] Ezekiel, a Zadokite priest, was a prophet obsessed by the nature of his prophetic vocation. In this verse, the task of the prophet is described in terms of the watchman; his prophetic role is to foresee what God is about to do and then stir up the people to respond. Thus if the prophet remains silent, ignoring God's directive, or otherwise fails to call the people to account for their sins, he, as their watchman, is held responsible. The historical context for Ezekiel is the Babylonian siege of Jerusalem resulting in the destruction of the Temple and the fall of Judah in 587 BC, and like other prophetic writings the biblical book justifies the tragedy as divine punishment for the people's sin and points to God's mercy in the new temple of the future restoration. All these details resonated powerfully with Gregory, whose own Greek name, Gregorius, let us recall with Gregory's biographer Paul the Deacon, corresponds to the Latin *vigilantius* "watchful." While Jerome, Ambrose, and other exegetes had equated the role of the watchman with the office of bishop, only in Gregory do we find a deep internalizing of the image and a strong sense of personal involvement with all it conveys. Thus in the *Homilies* Gregory devotes several paragraphs to his own struggles as watchman or *speculator*, made all the more uncanny given that Babylonians have now been replaced by Lombards, and the siege of Jerusalem by the siege of Gregory's own Rome. Gregory's identity, in effect, thereby becomes that of a modern-day Ezekiel, and other parallels between the two – for instance, the heavy symbolism and striking imagery of the Book of Ezekiel and Gregory's own mystico-allegorical exegetical style – can be educed to buttress that recognition. Gregory apparently felt a similar sense of identification when he commented on Job in the 580s, remarking in his prefatory letter to Leander that "fortasse hoc diuinae prouidentiae consilium fuit, ut percussum Iob percussus exponerem, et flagellati mentem melius per flagella sentirem" (perhaps this was the divine plan, that in my trials I should tell of the trials

43 Bede, *HE* 2.1, pp. 120–34.
44 *HEz* 1.11, pp. 170–2, lines 68–122.

of Job and that I would better understand the mind of one so scourged if I felt the scourge myself).[45]

In light of all this, it is striking indeed that Bede's reading of the Ezra-Nehemiah story is marked by a similar personal treatment of the characters themselves. It is as if they are models not in some general way but specifically for Anglo-Saxon clergy and even for Bede himself. Now the figure of Ezra is most resonant in this regard. In the biblical story his role pertains not to the material reconstruction of the temple but to the building up, as it were, of the Jews as a people – a *gens*, so Bede might say – under their God. In this connection Bede's repeated focus is Ezra 7:6, where Ezra is called "a swift scribe in the Law of Moses." For as Bede well saw, Ezra's primary activity was textual: he restored the books of Law which the Babylonians destroyed when they sacked Jerusalem, in order that the returnees might themselves be rebuilt through sound instruction.[46] This Jewish priest and scribe who reforms his people through texts and teaching may have been a mirror in which Bede could see his own reflection, giving point to the nature and meaning of his own hermeneutic vocation and, perhaps as well, a powerful set of images for imagining his own identity. Bede's perception that Ezra's mission in some senses reflected his own may reveal much about this otherwise odd yoking of biblical past and Anglo-Saxon present. Indeed, it may well account for his decision to take up this neglected biblical story, but also for the unique portrait of Ezra in the front matter of the Codex Amiatinus, perhaps the grandest extant statement of Bede's Ezra-like mission.[47]

But my larger point, to be sure, is not so much that Bede and Gregory have followed similar strategies – namely replacing personal with textual

45 *Moralia in Iob*, *Epistula ad Leandrum* 5, p. 6, lines 195–7.

46 *In Ezram*, p. 307, lines 791–6: "Scriba autem uelox in lege Moysi appellatur Ezras eo quod legem quae erat consumpta reficeret non solum legem sed etiam ut communis maiorum fama est omnem sacrae scripturae seriem quae pariter igni consumpta est prout sibi uidebatur legentibus sufficere rescripsit" (Now Ezra, who is called a swift scribe in the Law of Moses for having restored the Law that had been destroyed, rewrote not only the Law but also, as the common tradition of our forebears holds, the whole sequence of sacred Scripture that had likewise been destroyed by fire, in accordance with the way that seemed to him to meet the needs of readers; trans. DeGregorio, *Bede: On Ezra and Nehemiah*, 109). For additional comment on this passage, see DeGregorio, "Bede's *In Ezram et Neemiam*," 16–20.

47 DeGregorio, "Figure of Ezra."

identities – as that their imagined identities are so differentiated. If Gregory could see himself most readily in Ezekiel the prophet-visionary, Bede, ever hesitant about such heady experience, opts instead for Ezra the priestly reformer. These choices must be emphasized and their implications given due weight. I'll close with just two. First, support is added to our earlier observation that Bede's hermeneutics involve a more careful appreciation of the literal-historical sense. He evidently saw that the Book of Ezra-Nehemiah, in its literal storyline and array of historical personae, could readily be mapped onto and concretized within his own Northumbrian setting, with little need for allegorical pyrotechnics to further his moral agenda of ecclesiastical and spiritual reform.[48] Bede thus stands out among monastic exegetes with their penchant for arriving at tropology via allegory, and it is important for scholarship not to overlook his innovations within that tradition. Second, while textual selves are not, strictly speaking, real selves, the attempts of both our subjects to align their behaviour with established scriptural models are real attempts at a kind of self-fashioning, suggestive as much for its discontinuities as for whatever affinities underlie it as a practice. As much as Bede may have revered Gregory as an *auctor* par excellence deserving of rote emulation, the concrete circumstances not just of place and time but also of temperament and outlook seemingly necessitate that Bede depart from his hero's footsteps, by imagining himself in terms of constructs better suited to the frameworks of his own self-understanding and the vicissitudes of his particular historical-cultural situation.

48 Again, I have discussed this idea at length in several publications, but see esp. DeGregorio, "Bede's *In Ezram et Neemiam*."

Æthilwulf *poeta*

EMILY V. THORNBURY

It did not do to call oneself a poet too freely during most of the Anglo-Saxon period. From the distance of a millennium or more, it is difficult to understand the social or semantic reasons why it was almost unheard-of for Old English authors to call themselves *scopas*, and very rare for Anglo-Latin writers to describe themselves as *uates* or *poetae*. The tendency itself, however, is clear, as a survey of the referents of words for "poet" indicates (see table 4.1). Surprising as it may seem, Cynewulf, Bede, Frithegod, and Wulfstan Cantor – though all people to whom the art of verse seems to have been important – never refer to themselves as poets in any surviving writings.

Even Aldhelm of Malmesbury, self-proclaimed first English author of quantitative Latin verse, called himself a poet only obliquely.[1] At the end of the *Carmen de uirginitate*, for instance, as he asks the nuns of Barking to defend his poem against detractors, he adds that

> Cum tamen haud metuam scurrarum dicta legentum,
> Qui malunt uatum scedas lacerare canentum …
> Nec tamen emendant titubantis gramma poetae …[2]

---

1 In *De metris et enigmatibus et pedum regulis*, Aldhelm quotes Vergil's appropriation of the bucolic mode and applies it to his own poetic labors (Ehwald, ed., *Opera*, 202). On the accuracy of this claim, see Ruff, "Place of Metrics," 154n13, and for more general commentary, see Lapidge and Rosier, *Aldhelm: The Poetic Works*, 19 and 24, and Thornbury, "Aldhelm's Rejection," 71–2.

2 Ehwald, *Aldhelmi Opera*, 468, lines 2835–6, 2843. Aldhelm goes on to compare such nitpickers to a goat chewing up flowers in a vineyard. He uses this line again in the comic verse epilogue to his letter to Heahfrith (Ehwald, *Opera*, 494: on the letter and the verses, see Lapidge and Herren, *Aldhelm: The Prose Works*, 143–6).

Table 4.1. Referents of words for "poet" in Anglo-Latin

Referent	poeta	uates	uersificus	lyricus	comicus	satiricus
Self	16	12	0	0	0	0
Contemporary	0	4	0	0	0	0
Historical poet:	64	14	5	0	5	2
With quote	60	9	2		5	2
Without quote	4	5	3		0	0
Psalmist	0	5	0	0	0	0
Non-specific (a poet in general)	71	13	2	1	1	1
A non-poet	0	80	0	0	0	0
Total	151	128	7	1	6	3

Texts searched: All Anglo-Latin texts edited in the MGH and CCSL; Wulfstan Cantor, *Narratio metrica* ...; Frithegod, *Breuiloquium*; Lapidge, ed., "Three Latin Poems from Æthelwold's School at Winchester" and "A Tenth-Century Metrical Calendar of Winchcombe"; Campbell, ed., *Chronicle of Æthelweard*.

> [Though to be sure I'm hardly afraid of the words of caddish readers who prefer to shred the pages of poets as they sing ... yet still won't correct the faltering poet's letters.]

But though Aldhelm has included himself in the category of those who need protection from criticism, he has not precisely identified himself with the poet-victims – indeed, it seems unlikely he would consider himself guilty of the grammatical and metrical flaws pounced upon by *scurrae legentes*, and so he seems to be speaking on behalf of *poetae* more hapless than himself. Even when quoting his own works, Aldhelm evades the first-person voice. In his *De metris*, he attributes to a "poeta" a line contrived for the sake of example – though a reader without Aldhelm's range of reading would have no way of knowing the line was not the work of Prudentius, Sedulius, Arator, or another of the Christian-Latin poets whom he cites elsewhere as *poetae*.[3] Three times, too, he attributes to a *poeta* the line "Clauiger aethereus, portam qui pandit in aethra" (Heavenly key-bearer, who opens the door in the heavens), which derives from his

3 Ehwald, ed., *Opera*, 93; see further Thornbury, *Becoming a Poet*, chapter 1.

titulus for a church dedicated to Sts Peter and Paul.[4] If we knew more about the circulation of Aldhelm's *Carmina ecclesiastica*, it would be easier to ascertain just how obscure Aldhelm's self-reference was, for in order to understand that he called himself a poet, his readers would have to know the poem or have it to hand. Given that the line is a confection of two verses from Arator, it is even possible that this is a misremembered quotation rather than a self-reference.[5]

Among Anglo-Saxon poets, then, Aldhelm is both unusual in his use of masked self-citations and typical in his refusal to call himself a poet outright. In the face of this widespread reluctance to self-identify as a poet – which seems to have been as prevalent in the tenth century as the seventh – it is remarkable indeed to find two Anglo-Latin authors openly and repeatedly describing themselves as *poeta* or *uates*. Alcuin and Æthilwulf between them seem to open a window onto a different mode of poetic self-conception. In the case of Alcuin, we know a good deal about the literary climate that gave rise to his view of himself as a poet, for he was not the only *uates* at the court of Charlemagne. But the Northumbrian monk Æthilwulf, whose poem is all that remains of his small abbey, is a figure all the more striking in his solitude, for he seems to have been the only English poet to adopt a poetic persona in the early Carolingian tradition. In this essay, I will consider how and why Æthilwulf constructed himself as a *poeta*, and offer some thoughts as to why he remained unique.

History is both the subject and context of Æthilwulf's only surviving poem, now called *De abbatibus*.[6] Addressed to Ecgberht, bishop of Lindisfarne (*r.* 803–21), it narrates the foundation, successive abbots, and illustrious inhabitants of an unnamed cell in Northumbria.[7] In each of the three

4 Ehwald, *Opera*, 11, *Carmen ecclesiasticum* I, 6. It is also found (slightly modified) in an inscription for an altar in *Carmen ecclesiasticum* IV.i, 2 (Ehwald, *Opera*, 19). The three citations occur in the *Epistle to Geraint*, *Prosa de uirginitate*, and the treatise on the number 7 that opens his metrical textbook (Ehwald, *Opera*, 485, 314, and 68); each is in the course of a reference to St Peter's authority.

5 For the line and its source, see Lapidge and Rosier, *Poetic Works*, 233n3, and (on the circulation of the *Carmina ecclesiastica*) 38.

6 For the poem's editorial history, including its title's permutations, see Campbell, ed., *Æthelwulf: De abbatibus*, ix, xi–xv.

7 The identity of the cell is a matter of dispute. Thomas Arnold, who edited *De abbatibus* as an appendix to Simeon of Durham's *Historia* (as well as other Durham material), argued for Crayke, Yorkshire, mainly on the basis of its topographical similarities to the description in §vi of the poem (*Symeonis monachi opera*, 1: xxxiii–xxxix); more recently Lapidge has endorsed this view in light of Crayke's proximity to York, and the 1937

known manuscripts, *De abbatibus* is juxtaposed with authoritative prose histories of English church foundations: Bede's *Historia ecclesiastica* in two cases, and Simeon of Durham's *Historia Dunelmensis ecclesiae* together with the *Historia de Sancto Cuthberto* in the third.[8] For compilers of the eleventh and twelfth centuries, the poem seems to have been most valuable as a kind of appendix to more capacious histories of the northern Church. Considering the obscurity of Æthilwulf's cell, which may have been destroyed or dispersed sometime during the later ninth or early tenth century, it is somewhat surprising that the poem should have been preserved at all.[9] That it *was* preserved is most likely a testimony to its literary appeal. Like the books of Simeon and Bede as well as the *Historia de Sancto Cuthberto*, Æthilwulf's poem includes visions, marvels, and narratives of exemplary lives, all of which provide an interest that overcomes the loss of chronological and geographical specificity. Indeed, as we shall see later, part of Æthilwulf's motive in creating his persona as a poet may have been a desire to authorize and acknowledge these transcendent fictions.

De abbatibus displays a close and self-consciously literary relation to its Anglo-Latin predecessors. Campbell and, more recently, Lapidge and Orchard have indicated the scope of Æthilwulf's borrowings and the nature of his sources: in addition to the hexameter verse of standard classical and Christian-Latin authors, Æthilwulf was evidently very familiar with the poetry of Aldhelm, Bede, the *Miracula S. Nyniae*, and – most importantly

---

find there of a metalworker's hoard ("Aediluulf," 394–8: with discussion of Cwicwine, the smith in §x). The *Historia de S. Cuthberto*, however, identifies Crayke as a gift to St Cuthbert by King Ecgfrith, for which there is some supporting charter and physical evidence (see Blair, *Church*, 222). Howlett has proposed Bywell (on the Tyne, between Hexham and Newcastle) as an alternative ("Provenance, Date, and Structure"), an identification cautiously endorsed by Wood ("Monasteries," 17n59).

8 With the *Historia ecclesiastica*: Winchester, Cathedral Library 1 + London, British Library, Cotton Tiberius D.iv, vol. ii, fols. 158–66 (s. x/xi or xi^{in}: G 759); Oxford, Bodleian Library, Bodley 163 (s. xi^{in}: G 555). With a dossier on Durham's history, including the late Old English *Durham* as well as Simeon of Durham's *Historia*: Cambridge, University Library, Ff.1.27 (s. xii). The Winchester and Oxford manuscripts are closely related: see Campbell, ed. *De abbatibus*, ix–xi, xv–xxi.

9 Though St Cuthbert's community sojourned at Crayke in 882 or 883, the house was evidently in secular hands by the early 900s: see Adams, "Monastery and Village," esp. 49–50. Bywell St Peter belonged to the Benedictines in 1174 (when it was transferred from St Albans to Durham), but it is not clear when or how St Albans had come into possession (see Hodgson, *History*, 103).

for our purposes – Alcuin.[10] Charlemagne's Yorkshire clergyman seems to have been an inspiration to his younger contemporary in many respects. The generic innovation of Alcuin's poem on York clearly impressed Æthilwulf, and that work's blend of episodic history, biography, miracle narrative, and encomium gives *De abbatibus* its shape. Kamphausen has pointed out that the large-scale structure of Æthilwulf's poem mimics his predecessor's: both end with a vision of members of the community in paradise.[11] The form of *De abbatibus*, however, actually resembles Alcuin's verse *Vita S. Willibrordi* more closely than it does any other Anglo-Latin poem, since both texts are framed with elegiac prologues and epilogues, and are arranged in short episodes with significant (and almost certainly authorial) rubrics.[12] Moreover, Lapidge has demonstrated that Æthilwulf's diction is saturated with Alcuinian phraseology, and suggests that he may have learned this from a pupil of Alcuin's.[13] Æthilwulf, in short, modelled his verse on Alcuin's in every important regard: in subject matter, form, and style. It is not surprising, then, that he should have adopted significant aspects of Alcuin's voice.

Charlemagne's court was a place where a poet's voice could have real influence, though it might need to be raised to hyperbolic levels (or sweetened with venom) to be heard among a crowd of rivals.[14] Whether satirical or serious, poems intended for the court were invested with personal

10 Campbell, ed., *De abbatibus*, xliv–xlviii; Lapidge, "Aediluulf," 386–9; Orchard, *Poetic Art*, 263–8. Æthilwulf seems to have had some familiarity with Vergil, Statius, and Lucan, and to have known well Juvencus, Sedulius, Arator, and Cyprianus Gallus; he may also (Lapidge suggests, 389) have known Paulinus of Nola, Prosper of Aquitaine, and Venantius Fortunatus.

11 Kamphausen, *Traum und Vision*, 88–90.

12 Arator's *De actibus apostolorum* also contains prose rubrics for the *capitula*: though they are much longer than those of the *Vita Willibrordi* or *De abbatibus*, their structural function probably influenced the Anglo-Latin poems. The *capitula* of the *Vita Willibrordi* are listed together before the main text in the three extant manuscripts (see Dümmler, MGH PLAC 1, 163, 207–8); this is also the case in the Cambridge manuscript of *De abbatibus*. There is little evidence for the circulation of the *Vita S. Willibrordi* in England (though Wulfstan Cantor occasionally seems to echo it); Æthilwulf, however, appears to quote it: see Lapidge, "Aediluulf," 390.

13 Lapidge, "Aediluulf," esp. 390–3. Orchard (*Poetic Art*, 264) notes that some of the phrases *De abbatibus* shares with Alcuin originated with Aldhelm; given that Æthilwulf knew the works of both poets, the two were probably mutually reinforcing.

14 On the influence and rivalry of poets at the court, see Schaller, "Vortrags- und Zirkulardichtung"; Godman, *Poets and Emperors*, esp. 38–92; Garrison, "Emergence" and "English and Irish."

significance by their authors' self-assertion, and while the status of *other* poets might be questioned (as in some of Theodulf's bitterer verses), the *poetae* surrounding the king did not undermine their own personae. For instance, extravagant as Angilbert's encomium on "uatorum ... gloria Dauid" might seem, it was carefully considered: its praise of Charlemagne in the figure of the poet-king spilled over to his minor prophets, the *uates* who advise him in their songs.[15] Alcuin, too, emphatically figured himself as a *uates* when addressing his patrons. In carmen 40, for example, he remakes an apparent loss of favour at court as the death of all poetry:

Nix ruit e caelo, gelidus simul ingruit imber:
Non fuit Albino "Exspecta paulisper in urbe"
Qui iam dixisset, "donec pertranseat imber,
Et calido pectus Parnasi fonte refirma."
Tristis abit senior ieiuno ventre poeta,
Et pueri tristes planxerunt carmine Flaccum.
Frigida quapropter taceat sibi fistula carmen,
Has tantum paucas balbutiat ore camenas:
Carmina non curat David, nec Delia curat.
Dum redeunt iterum calidi bona tempora Phoebi,
Mox pristina redit virtus in carmine Flacco,
Tunc ruet in David Musarum laetior odis,
Tunc pax, vita, salus David, tunc praelia Musis.[16]

[Snow falls from the sky, and cold rain comes in with it: for Albinus there was no one who would have said, "Wait in town for a while until the rain passes, and fortify your heart from the warm spring of Parnassus." The old poet departs sadly with an empty belly, and sad boys mourned Flaccus in song. Therefore let his chilled pipe quiet its song, let him stammer over these few verses with his mouth: David cares not for songs, nor does Delia care. When the pleasant seasons of hot Phoebus return again, Flaccus's former skill in song returns to him at once: then he shall fall more joyfully upon David with the Muses' odes; then peace, life, and health shall befall David; then there will be contests for the Muses.]

15 MGH PLAC 1, 360. II, 6. "David, the glory of poets." On this poem, and the political implications of Angilbert's persona, see Godman, *Poets and Emperors*, 65–7.

16 MGH PLAC 1, 253.

The reed-pipe falls silent, the Muses fail, and the skies weep in concert with a boys' chorus. The whole effect is grandly self-dramatizing, but its point would be lost if Alcuin's persona as "Flaccus" were not really and inseparably part of his identity. When tiring of Alcuin means that "Carmina non curat David, nec Delia curat," he becomes not merely *a* poet, but *the* poet, and restoring him to court means restoring harmony to the world. Whatever else in the poem might lack seriousness, two things cannot be doubted: the author's status as a poet, and the plea for patronage. The latter is affirmed by the concluding praise of "David," and the former by the poem itself.

This is not to argue that "Flaccus" embodied Alcuin's *primary* identity or function in Charlemagne's entourage.[17] Yet he – in company with many of his associates – did create for himself a public face as a poet, and he used this mask often in his relations with his patrons. Alcuin's self-performance as a poet was at core a practical endeavour: it helped him further the king's political and cultural interests while maintaining his own status in a world which valorized poets – the *uates* surrounding their King David. That Alcuin had helped to *create* this world makes his role in it all the more significant.

To Æthilwulf, reading Alcuin's works in a small monastic cell in Northumbria, the world of these courtier-poets must have seemed very exotic indeed. It is difficult to imagine the peculiar blend of Christianized encomium and classical love-elegy we see in carmen 40 being produced anywhere in the Anglo-Saxon kingdoms of the eighth or ninth centuries.[18] Though northern monastic foundations were closely interlinked with royal authority, the ascetic cast of their religious culture – perhaps combined with a greater degree of actual financial independence – rendered almost unthinkable the degree of servility and of self-promotion seen in early Carolingian verse.[19] Neither was necessary. Though Bede, for instance, was heavily invested in the acceptance of his work's authority, he had no need to promote *himself* within his own community. His place at

17 On the subordinate role of poetry in the lives of Charlemagne's clerical courtiers, see Garrison, "English and Irish," 105.

18 On Alcuin's knowledge of Tibullus, and manipulation of the *exclusus amator* trope in carmen 40, see Garrison, "Alcuin and Tibullus."

19 On royal power and early Anglo-Saxon monasticism, see Blair, *Church*, 84–91, and Wood, "Monasteries."

Jarrow was secure, and unlike Alcuin, he had no cause to fear that the loss of any individual's favour would mean the loss of his livelihood.

Yet despite writing from what was most likely a similar position of security, Æthilwulf seems to have perceived the utility of Alcuin's persona in relating to a patron. Five of the seven instances in which Æthilwulf calls himself a *poeta* or *uates* occur in the prefatory sections or the epilogue, all of which are addressed to Bishop Ecgberht of Lindisfarne in the second person.[20] The opening *salutatio* even positions *De abbatibus* as a kind of encomium, since the history of the cell is a history of Ecgberht's illustrious kinsmen:

> cum te sancta manuṣ prestantem reddidit Anglis
> haec tibi conplacuit rustica dona dare ...
> nam tibi dum proceres propria de sanguine signant,
> iam domino placidus gaudia magna capis.[21]

> [When the holy hand rendered you excellent among the English, it seemed fitting to give you these rustic gifts ... for even as they point out to you distinguished men of your own blood, you now in your gentleness receive great joy from the Lord.]

The abbey was governed by two sets of brothers in succession. The latter pair are described in particularly effusive terms, as "pastor praeclaro nomine Sigbald" (the priest Sigbald of most renowned name) and his "germanus premitis ... Siguinus" (431; 473–4) (most mild brother Sigwine).[22] Sigbald's building of a Lady Chapel, his gifts to the church, and his devotion to Mary are described at length, while Sigwine is shown secretly distributing goods to the poor in the manner of a confessor-saint, even as God increases the monastery's agricultural wealth during his reign. These men, it seems most likely to me, were Ecgberht's "proceres propria de sanguine," and it may even be that the accounts of their generosity were

---

20 These are the rubrics to chapters I and XXIII; and lines 1, 27, and 814.

21 *De abbatibus*, lines 13–14, 17–18. Further line references to this work will be in the text. The "sancta manus" presumably refers to the element of apostolic succession in Ecgberht's consecration as bishop.

22 Æthilwulf devotes §xiv (42 lines) to Sigbald, and §xv (34 lines) to his brother. The reigns of their predecessors, the brothers Eorpwine and Aldwine, are combined into §xiii (28 lines).

intended as a hint. This, however, is inference, since Æthilwulf never directly identifies the bishop's relations.

Whatever his familial connection to the cell, Ecgberht is requested in the series of prefatory addresses to *De abbatibus* to grant favour as a patron. Curiously, though, the actual aid which Æthilwulf seeks is impossible for the bishop to immediately provide:

> Sume, pater, placidus modulantis uota poete,
> quatinus aeterno capias cum rege quietem,
> atque petas superas meritis splendentibus arces.
> nunc memorare libens semper, lectissime presul,
> sancta supernorum conscendens sceptra polorum
> mercedemque tuam, quam iussit reddere caluus. (1–6) [23]

> [Receive graciously, O father, the wishes of the poet as he sings, that you might receive repose with the eternal King and seek through your shining merits the citadels above. Gladly now remember [him] always, most outstanding bishop, as you attain the holy realms of the heavens above and your reward, which the Tonsured One promised to grant.]

Æthilwulf's temporal markers are often somewhat disorienting. Here, the speaker's desire for the bishop's welfare is pushed into the (postmortem) future by "aeterno capias cum rege quietem" (that you might receive repose with the eternal King). As a result, the combination of "nunc" and "semper" in line 4 effectively tips the participles in 4 and 5 from a transient immediate present to an eternal future: the poet, in other words, requests that Ecgberht will pray for him as the bishop dies and attains his heavenly reward. Doubtless a professed monk, as the bishop had been, would find such good wishes less disconcerting than would a layman; but however Æthilwulf's request was received, its form indicates that the immediate temporal effect he hoped his poem would produce was, effectively, nonexistent. Ecgberht's prayers in this life are also solicited in the poem's conclusion, but the contrast with Alcuin's courtly verse remains striking. For Æthilwulf, the patron-client relation is essentially unworldly.

23 The "Tonsured One" is Christ, whose crown of thorns prefigured the monastic tonsure: see Campbell, ed., *De abbatibus*, 2n1.

Besides prayer (either pre- or postmortem), the only other object of the poet's request is a negative one. He wishes the bishop to spare his poem harsh judgment:

si quid in his cartis te dignum reddere grates
  inuenias domino maxime nunc moneo;
sin alias, **uati** ueniam dignare canenti
  iam tribuere pius: quod potuit cecinit.
hanc tuo nam cupio requiem prestare labori,
  carmina que domino sanctificata sonant.
aduersum est quicquid moneo tolerare modeste,
  nec querula in quoque corda mouere tua.
mens requiem capiat semper sine fine benignam
  in domino Christo prosperitate pia. (§i, 25–34)

[Should you find anything worthy of you in these pages, I advise you to give thanks most greatly to the Lord; if not, in your kindness see fit to give pardon to the poet as he sings: he sang what he could. For I am trying to furnish some rest for your labour – poems which sound forth things consecrated to the Lord. I advise you to discreetly tolerate anything objectionable, and not incite your feelings of complaint in any respect. May your mind receive kindly repose forever and ever with holy prosperity in Christ the Lord.]

The request to withhold criticism is part of a long-lived rhetorical trope, the humility topos.[24] In Æthilwulf's case, however, it is also part of a complex set of negotiations with his patron's power, and must be read in conjunction with his final request for the bishop's prayers:

tu, pater, hec recitans nostros non sperne labores,
  quin magis hec cernens gaudia digna tene;
quod tua tam clari meruerunt sanguine patres
  esse, deo grates reddere te moneo.
me quoque nunc precibus domino mandare profusis
  iam dignare, precor, corpore, corde rogans,
quatinus hic trepido dimittat crimina **uati**
  omnipotens genitor, nec pietate uacat,

24 Curtius's formulation remains classic: see *European Literature*, 83–5 and 407–13.

cui decus, imperium, uirtus, sapientia perpes,
  laus et honor semper permaneat, uigeat.
te, pater, omnitenens seruet per secula mitis,
  inferni uinclis uerberibusque privans. (§xxiii, 808–19)

[As you read these things out, O father, do not despise our labours, but as you perceive them instead take fitting joys. I advise you to render thanks to God that fathers of your blood have been worthy to be so renowned. Now I pray you also, see fit to commend me to the Lord with prayers poured forth, beseeching with body and heart, that the almighty Father might here remit the frightened poet's sins, and that he might not be without kindness, with whom may glory, power, might, eternal wisdom, praise, and honour live and flourish forever. May the kindly All-ruler keep you safe forever, O father, and keep you from the chains and blows of Hell.]

In these passages, the serenely one-way conduit of postmortem obligation established in the poem's first lines is troubled by the implication that Ecgberht may need prayers himself. In the final lines, especially, the poet's plea for God's forgiveness of his own sins is paired with a request that the bishop be spared the pains of Hell. Without implying any doubt as to the feasibility of the opening prayer that Ecgberht be received into heaven, this juxtaposition does suggest that he may need to be remembered by others in order to reach such a blessed state.[25] By designating himself as a *poeta* in this context, Æthilwulf frames his own poem as a possible means to that end. Without directly suggesting that *De abbatibus* will act as a memorial for the bishop, the insistence that Ecgberht pray for the distinguished men of his own blood whom Æthilwulf praises in his verse generates a context in which the poem's potential usefulness to the soul of the *lectissimus presul* can be discreetly recognized.

The implication that Ecgberht too must undergo God's judgment casts a very particular light on Æthilwulf's plea for clemency towards his poem. Linking literary and divine judgment was very common in Anglo-Saxon literature, and I have argued elsewhere for the social implications of this pairing.[26] Here, it is clear that the message to the bishop is: As you judge,

25 On Anglo-Saxon ideas of postmortem judgment and purification, see Foot, "Anglo-Saxon 'Purgatory.'"
26 See Thornbury, *Becoming a Poet*, chapter 3.

so shall you be judged. This is most beautifully and concisely expressed in the near-anaphora of lines 808 and 818. In the first instance, Ecgberht is addressed in the vocative, as "tu pater," with the request that he not "spurn" the labours presented to him – and Æthilwulf's use of the plural possessive, "nostros ... labores," means that he is conflating his poem with the whole work and history of his cell. In the second, the pronoun is in the accusative ("te pater"), as the poet hopes that God will keep the bishop safe and free of Hell. The subtle contrast between subject and object encapsulates Æthilwulf's point.

An element of muted coercion, then, permeates the relations between patron and poet established in these passages. Alcuin's appeal to Charlemagne and "Delia"[27] in carmen 40 is founded on their love for poetry (and, by extension, their poet), and on their compassion for his unhappiness without them. He figures their former and prospective patronage as charity: freely given, unnecessary to themselves. Æthilwulf, however, creates a conjunction of divine and human judgment to suggest a direct relationship between poetry and efficacious prayer, and by doing so implies his addressee's *need* for his "rustica dona" (14) (homely gifts). As a poet capable of memorializing the worthy in verse and thus soliciting aid for their souls, Æthilwulf has the power to benefit the dead – among which, as the poem's first and last lines hint, Ecgberht surely will one day find himself. Judging *De abbatibus* kindly thus becomes less an act of charity than a wise investment.

The sense of power with which Æthilwulf invests his status as a poet in relation to his patron goes some way towards explaining the paradoxical confidence of his expressions of humility. Though he pleads for lenience, he never undermines either the essential value of his poem or his own status as a poet. Humility topoi were often accompanied by apologies for technical incompetence, such as ignorance of quantity or of grammatical categories; but as Aldhelm had before him, Æthilwulf avoids this form of self-abasement.[28] Instead, in his first *salutatio* quoted above, he proposes a standard of measure which flatters his addressee without denigrating himself, as he hopes the bishop will find "quid in his cartis te dignum" (§i, 25)

27 Probably Charlemagne's daughter Bertha (the name being derived from Tibullus's love-elegies): see Garrison, "Social World," 71–2, and "Alcuin and Tibullus."

28 See Curtius, *European Literature*, 83. Technical competence was an Anglo-Saxon poet's most prized attribute: see Thornbury, "Aldhelm's Rejection."

(something worthy of you in these pages). As he goes on to invoke the possibility of his failure in this regard, Æthilwulf points out that his subject matter, at least, is not open to criticism: "carmina ... domino sanctificata sonant" (§i, 30) (the songs sound forth things sacred to the Lord). The (somewhat passive-aggressive) juxtaposition in lines 31–4 of his hopes for the bishop's eternal peace with the advice not to let faults in the poem upset him completes the effect of a strikingly unapologetic *apologia* for the poem. Though Æthilwulf suggests he would be sorry if Bishop Ecgberht disliked his poem, he declines even to entertain the notion that this would make him any less a poet.

This protectiveness towards his status extends through his other humility topoi. When beginning a chapter on the lector Hyglac, Æthilwulf notes that he has already written of this man in an earlier poem:

tempore quo lector preclarus gaudia digna
accumulat patris Hyglacus nomine dictus,
de quo iam dudum perstrinxi pauca relatu,
Anglorum de gente pios dum carmine quosdam
iam cecini indoctus, uilisque per omnia scriptor.
que si quis cupiat cum gnaro noscere corde,
currat et haec sitiens se algosis mergat in undis,
littera quo docti non docte carmina patris
pompat, et aggreditur poterit quod dicere digne. (§xvi, 507–15)

[At that time, a renowned lector heaped up the father [abbot]'s fitting joys; he was called Hyglac, about whom I formerly briefly narrated a few things in a poem about certain holy men of the English race which I once sang, though I am unlearned and an altogether wretched writer. Should anyone happen to want to learn of these things with a knowing heart, let him hurry, and, thirsting for them, plunge himself in the seaweedy waves in which the letter unlearnedly adorns songs about the learned father, and ventures that which it will be able to fittingly tell.]

This work on the holy men of England (or the *Angli*?) has been lost: which is a pity, since Æthilwulf, at least, seems to think well of it. The self-deprecating aspects of this humility topos work on three levels, all of which tend to blunt the impact of their criticism of the poem. As far as this work itself is concerned, Æthilwulf speaks of it in a rather charming reworking of the literary-work-as-sea-voyage metaphor as "algosae ... undae" (seaweedy waves). Though seaweed certainly has its objectionable qualities, it does not taint or devalue the sea from which it comes.[29] As an image, the metaphor cannot effectively combine with Æthilwulf's self-criticism, which centres on his lack of learning (511, 514) and incapacity as a *scriptor*. Ignorance does not generate seaweed, and this dilutes the force of this passage's negative implications. Moreover, the juxtaposition of "docti ... patris" with "non docte ... / pompat" (514/15) makes it clear that at least some of Æthilwulf's protestations of his unlearnedness are meant to be relative: it is in comparison to the learned father Hyglac that he falls short. Even taking "indoctus" (511) at face value, it is interesting that it agrees in this line with "scriptor." Metrically, "uates" would have been considerably more elegant in the final foot.[30] By calling himself a "uilis ... scriptor," however, Æthilwulf avoids criticizing the essential elements of his works. A *scriptor*, in normal medieval usage, is a scribe. Though the Anglo-Saxons did not make Bonaventure's careful distinctions between "scriptor," "compilator," "commentator," and "auctor," nevertheless they did use the word "scriptor" to designate the person who physically formed the letters of a book, and who need not have had anything to do with creating its content.[31] Elsewhere, Æthilwulf describes a man famous for his beautiful books as a "scriptor" (§viii, 225), whose excellence is due to the surrender of his individual agency: "digitos sanctus iam spiritus auctor / rexit" (§viii, 214/15) (for the Author, the Holy Spirit, governed his fingers). Labelling himself a "scriptor," then, is at one level a gesture of humility – to use a modern phrase, he claims he is "typing, not writing" – but it also effectively distances his self-deprecation from his persona as a poet. The lost poem is insulated from criticism on a basic

29 On composition and sea-metaphors, see Curtius, *European Literature*, 128–30. Traube (*Karolingische Dichtungen*, 14–16) first interpreted the "waves" as Æthilwulf's poem, and suggested the emendation "algosis" from "ulgosis" (found in all three manuscripts); see Campbell, ed., *De abbatibus*, 40–1. Æthilwulf was not the only Anglo-Saxon to dislike seaweed; Aldhelm's *Enigma C* contains the phrase "spretis uilior algis" (line 26, "more worthless than despised seaweed").

30 The *a* in "omnia" must be short. Consonant clusters with *s* or a liquid can be counted as a single consonant (and thus need not make a preceding vowel long by position); however, a cluster of three consonants presses this rule, and would normally be avoided in such a position.

31 Bonaventure's enumeration of the kinds of makers of books is found in the proem to *In primum librum sententiarum* (and frequently quoted). On Æthilwulf's own use of "scriptor" with the technical meaning "scribe," see Nees, "Ultán the Scribe."

denotative level: a failed "scriptor" might produce a smeary or bungled text, but the words themselves need not be harmed in the process.

Æthilwulf, then, has enough invested in his status as *poeta* to make him reluctant to undermine it in any way, even through the traditionally patent insincerity of a humility topos. In his relations with his bishop, too, he seems unwilling to adopt a posture of abasement. This is consistent with his persona elsewhere in *De abbatibus*, where it seems that calling himself *uates* or *poeta* signals the assumption on Æthilwulf's part of a degree of personal authority – or, at least, the attachment of a certain credence to himself *qua* poet. The first such instance occurs in a chapter titled "De fratribus celle uel obitu pastoris" (On the brothers of the cell, or the death of the abbot):[32]

presbiteros, monachos, fratrum reliquamque cohortem,
quos me non dignum paruis concessit in annis
omnipotens genitor per cellae moenia sanctae
cernere, quos miris commirans actibus ipse
enituisse suo confirmo tempore certe,
quos si peccatis famulis imitare negarit
uatis adhuc modulans – tandem iam credo futurum
illorum precibus capiam quod dona salutis. (§xvii, 527–34)[33]

[The priests, monks, and the rest of the cohort of brothers whom the almighty Father granted me to know (though I am unworthy) in the years of my youth within the walls of the holy cell; whom I myself, admiring them, attest to have been in their time resplendent in remarkable deeds; whom, if the poet till now singing should have, with servile sins, refused to imitate – in the end indeed I believe that I shall receive the gifts of life through their prayers.]

The syntax of this passage is peculiar from beginning to end. The phrases describing the brothers of the cell in 527–31 are all in the accusative,

32 Campbell translates "uel" as "and" (*De abbatibus*, 42). Yet elsewhere in the rubrics (which are all in prose), Æthilwulf uses "et" (or in §xvi, "atque") for the copulative conjunction.

33 It is possible that the syntactic problems in the passage are due to textual corruption; if so, the problems must have occurred at or before the writing of the surviving manuscripts' lost archetype.

waiting for a main verb that never comes. Instead, the sentence breaks off in the middle of an ominous conditional clause, and resumes in the first person with Æthilwulf's reaffirmation of his faith in the efficacy of his brothers' prayers. The whole arrangement of these lines draws attention to the anacoluthon in 533, in which the apparent subject "uatis adhuc modulans" (the poet till now singing) is abandoned and replaced with the "I" of "credo." At this central moment, then, Æthilwulf designates himself a poet and dramatizes the limits of his art. His poetic facility "peccatis famulis imitare negarit" (with servile sins (or sinful services) declined to imitate), and those servile sins – whatever they may have been, and to whomever they may have belonged – are accordingly unrepresented. But through the structure of the sentence, the brothers of Æthilwulf's cell remain the objects of this verb which the sequence of accusatives in the first line of the chapter has primed readers to expect. Grammatically, artistically, and (it seems) morally, the representation of the *uatis* is set apart from that of the brothers whom he has "declined to imitate."

What this really means is unclear. Campbell points out a parallel couplet, which again refers to the monks of Æthilwulf's cell:

cum quibus hec cantans, cupiens sua miscere uota,
non cessat famulans, quandoque non uitiis. (§xxiii, 806–7)

[With these, may the one singing these lines, seeking to join in their devotions, not cease in his service, so long as it is not to sins.]

Campbell explains this as a reference to the Benedictine Rule.[34] It is, alternatively, possible that these allusions refer to some incident, perhaps known to Bishop Ecgberht, which might have cast doubt either on the value of the brothers' prayers or on Æthilwulf's own character. The attribution of "peccatis" here is crucial, yet painfully unclear. Campbell considers these sins to have been committed by the brothers; while Traube, emending "famulis" to "famulans," renders a meaning something like "whom, if the poet presently singing, being in service to sins, declined to imitate ...,"[35] a reading that could refer to an actual incident, or be read simply as a humility topos. Whatever happened (or ought to have happened and did not), its

34 Campbell, ed., *De abbatibus*, 62n1.

35 Ibid., 69, note to 532–3.

absence from the poem is emphatically circled by the anacoluthon in §xvii; the moral failure seems to have taken the sentence down with it. Yet the poet and his art have retained the subject position, enabling him simultaneously to elide the failure and to draw attention to it. In both actions, it is clear that the "uatis adhuc modulans" controls the representation of his community as well as of himself.

By the penultimate chapter, then, when Æthilwulf begins with the rubric "Somnium quod uidit poeta dominica nocte" (The dream which the poet saw on a Sunday night), the word "poeta" has been invested with multiple layers of significance. It is, first of all, his declaration of affiliation with a modern school of poetry, the Carolingian reinvention of the poet to which Alcuin's verse had introduced him. But the word "poeta" also forms the core of our understanding of the narrator, who – despite his protestations of being "indoctus" – has shown enough learning, and witnessed enough marvels, to make his personal testimony worthy of credence. Moreover, the episode of §xvii discussed above has established the discretion and control of his persona. He is not simply versifying the words of sources; he acknowledges that he has been shaping them – and here, with the concluding vision, he becomes the source of knowledge about his house. Interestingly, though, the word he chooses for his self-attribution is not "uates," but "poeta." On the face of it, "uates" would seem more appropriate: it means "prophet" as well as "poet," and was commonly used by Anglo-Saxon writers to describe saints, who were imbued with divine knowledge.[36] Perhaps the knowledge of this usage actually deterred Æthilwulf from employing it here: but whatever his reasons, he chose a word for himself which emphatically asserts the literary element of his historiographical enterprise.

In the vision of §xxii, Æthilwulf gestures openly towards his literary predecessors. The chapter's most obvious relation is to the conclusion of Alcuin's York poem, in which he narrates an incident "cui quoque praesentem testem me contigit esse" (1601) (to which I also happened to be present as a witness). Here, a devout young man praying alone at night sees an angelic messenger "uestibus albis" (1608) (in white garments) who reveals marvels to him in a book.[37] Later, the young man died, but returned to life with a report of paradise – in which "sanctae / illius ecclesiae laetos

36 Saints account for most of the "non-poet" referents of "uates" listed in table 4.1.

37 Cf. Campbell, ed., *De abbatibus* §xxii, 696, "uestibus album."

agnovit alumnos" (1624/5) (he recognized the joyful foster-sons of that holy church) – and the prediction of another monk's death. The visionary too died again within the year, and Alcuin says that "vigilans e fratribus unus, / vir probus et verax" (1642/3) (one of the brothers keeping watch, an honourable and truthful man) saw a shining being come to take the youth's soul to heaven.

In Æthilwulf's vision, though, *he* is the one who has been praying by night; and instead of falling terrified at the feet of the shining guide (as the youth at York had), he follows him to a marvellous field. The appearance of the field, and the behaviour of the guide – who disappears suddenly in line 727 – owe a great deal to the "Vision of Dryhthelm" from book 5 of Bede's *Historia ecclesiastica*, which Alcuin had also versified in lines 876–1007 of his York poem. In the early phases of his vision, then, Æthilwulf finds that the "callibus ignotis" (698) (unknown paths) on which he sets forth lead through regions mapped earlier by Alcuin and Bede. Yet once the guide has left him, he finds himself in a marvellous arcaded church unparalleled in earlier literature.[38] Here, the teachers of his youth, Wulfsig, Eadfrith, and Hyglac, preside over a perpetual feast, among shining vessels even more splendid than those in the temporal church where they once served; the house, Eadfrith tells him, was founded as a place of repose for blessed souls. And then "his dictis uigilans uisum iam scribere coepi" (§xxii, 795) (waking as I heard these words, I began to write down what I saw).

What Æthilwulf found in his vision was his own paradise: the living memory of his own house, transfigured almost beyond belief, but not beyond recognition.[39] What he derived from attributing this account of it to himself as *poeta* was, it seems to me, the ability to acknowledge control over the artifice of history. Throughout *De abbatibus*, Æthilwulf has been careful to avoid compromising his status as poet by associating it too closely with expressions of inadequacy. In §xxii, he exerts the power of this status to declare his artistic independence of his predecessors while acknowledging their perpetual presence. Bede and, above all, Alcuin have been his teachers just as much as Wulfsig, Eadfrith, and Hyglac; but when the Dryhthelmian guide derived from his Anglo-Latin models leaves him, Æthilwulf enters a landscape entirely of his creation. As historian, even as *uates*, he must have owed this vision to external forces; but as *poeta*, he can

38 See Taylor, "Architectural Interest."

39 On the complex layers of monastic memory present to Æthilwulf and other Anglo-Saxons, see Cubitt, "Monastic Memory and Identity."

intimate that it is his own. Though derived from Alcuin, then, Æthilwulf's persona as a poet becomes a force of liberation. It frees him from uncomfortable dependence on the judgment of his patron and diocesan, the bishop of Lindisfarne; from the rigid yoke of impersonal historiography; even from too close a connection to the literature which inspired his own.

This breed of authorial self-confidence was absolutely unique in Anglo-Saxon England: as *poeta*, Æthilwulf had no successor. Exactly why not is difficult to say. It seems perhaps most likely that the traditional explanation for literary discontinuity between the ninth century and the tenth – the Viking raids and conquest of much of the North – is the correct one. What is certainly the case is that when Anglo-Saxons began to write Latin poetry again in the tenth century, they looked further back for their models:[40] mainly to Aldhelm, who, as we have seen, was reluctant to openly call himself a poet. Æthilwulf's *De abbatibus* shows us that had Anglo-Latin literature been allowed to develop on its own course, in continued dialogue with the Continent, it might have looked very different: in some ways, perhaps, more like Carolingian poetry, but undoubtedly with its own unique modes. Certainly the circulation of Alcuin's verse in England had, on one poet at least, a revelatory effect. Yet instead of simply imitating the courtly persona of his predecessor, Æthilwulf adapted the role of the poet to his own circumstances and his own predilections. As *poeta*, he has given us a remarkable work, offering a tantalizing glimpse of a world that might have been.

40 Lapidge, "Hermeneutic Style."

The *Old English Martyrology* and Anglo-Saxon Glosses

CHRISTINE RAUER

The *Old English Martyrology* is an anonymous ninth-century prose text, in the simplest terms a compendium of saints' stories and feastdays: it provides information on the most important biographical details of a given saint, and on which day this saint should be venerated.[1] In general terms, the *Old English Martyrology* is characterized by relatively simple Old English prose which would also seem to suit its educational aim. Its syntax, for example, is often paratactic and almost formulaic in the recurrent phraseology with which the saints' martyrdoms are described.[2] Individual text sections (arranged by feastday and going through the liturgical year) are kept short and are usually restricted to describing narrative sequences, without much authorial comment or interpretation.

But one linguistic feature stands out as unexpectedly complex in this educational text: the vocabulary of the *Old English Martyrology* contains a surprising number of difficulties, including many terms which are relatively rarely attested in the transmitted corpus of Old English. This rare vocabulary could be grouped into four categories (allowing for some overlap between the groups): Anglian dialect vocabulary, which appears as rare in comparison with the late West Saxon material dominating the surviving Old English corpus;[3] technical vocabulary for concepts rarely referred to

1 The *Old English Martyrology* is edited in Kotzor, *Das altenglische Martyrologium*, and Rauer, *Old English Martyrology*. Both editions follow the same system of subdividing the text into numbered sections, which is also used here for citations (numbers in bold).

2 See Kotzor, *Das altenglische Martyrologium*, 1:409–21 for a survey of quasi-formulaic phrasing.

3 Ibid., 1:329–67.

in Anglo-Saxon literature;[4] authorial neologisms, including errors;[5] and vocabulary which appears to have parallels mainly in glosses. It is this last group on which the following discussion will concentrate.

One of the most obvious unusual aspect of the martyrologist's vocabulary is its Latin component: a surprising number of Latin terms appear interlarded into the vernacular prose of the *Old English Martyrology*, often with accompanying Old English translations and explanations, and apparently authorial. Günter Kotzor collected and categorized such phrases as follows:[6]

Latin Terms and Phrases in the *Old English Martyrology* (according to Kotzor)

a) explanations of personal names (selection):
- **22** *spiritus fornicationis*, þæt is dernes geligeres gast
- **23** æt *Sanctos Germinos*, æt þæm halgum getwinnum

b) geographical terms (selection):
- **98** *Silua Nigra*, se swearta wudu
- **72** *on Uicolonge*, þæt is on ðæm langan tune

c) terms for feasts and calendrical entries (selection):
- **111a** *Solstitia*, þæt ys on ure geþeode sungihte
- **69** *Laetania Maiora*, þæt is on þonne micelra bena dæg

d) terms for literary or liturgical texts (selection):
- **59** on *De Uirginitate*, ðæt is on fæmnena bocum
- **201** on Angolcynnes bocum, ðæt is on *Istoria Anglorum*.

e) miscellaneous:
- **5** *abritsum*, þæt is smætegold
- **8** *ursa*, þæt is on ure geðeode byren
- **30** nænig fulwa (L. *fullo*), þæt is nænig webwyrhta
- **38** *Ecce Dominus meus*; Hona la min Hlaford
- **42** He is ure *altor* and we syndan his *alumni*; ðæt is ðæt he is ure festerfæder on Criste ond we syndon his festerbearn on fullwihte
- **48** Fylleþflod bið nemned on Læden *malina*, ond se nepflod *ledo*

4 For example, *understregdan*, "to scatter underneath," **19**, or *writbred*, "writing tablet," **155**.

5 For some examples, see Rauer, "Old English *blanca*," "Pelagia's Cloak," and "Errors and Textual Problems."

6 Kotzor, *Das altenglische Martyrologium*, 1:245–8.

59 *larbo* [L. *larua*], þæt is egesgrima
60 *hic hic hic*, her, her, her
70 *furtum laudabile*, hergendlico stalo
71 on hire *palatium*, þæt is on hire healle
120 *podagre*, ðæt is on ure geþeode fotadl
133 hire *alabastrum*, þæt is hire glasfæt
146 *Deus miserere animabus*; God miltsa þu saulum
149 *meretrix*, ðæt is forlegoswif
163 *mima*, þæt is leasere
190 *theloniarius*, þæt is gafoles moniend ond wecgerefa
210 *mima* ..., þæt is scericge on urum geðeode
232 ealle weoruldwysdomas, þæt ys ærest *arythimetica*, þæt ys þonne rymcræft, and *astraloia*, þæt ys þonne tungolcræft, and *astronomia*, þæt ys tungla gang, and *geometrica*, þæt ys eorðgemet, and *musica*, þæt ys dreamcræft, and *m<ech>anica*, þæt y<s>weoruldweorccs cræft, and *medicina*, þæt ys læcedomes cræft

Günter Kotzor pointed out that a number of these bilingual word pairs, especially those of the last category e), have parallels in the two so-called Corpus glossaries, contained in Cambridge, Corpus Christi College 144, probably a southwestern English production of the first half of the ninth century:[7]

5 *abritsum*; smæte gold; cp. CorpGl 2, 13.24 (*obrizum*; smæte gold)
42 *altor*; festerfæder; cp. CorpGl 2, 1.493 (*altor*; fostorfæder)
42 *alumni*; festerbearn; cp. CorpGl 2, 1.450 (*alumnae*; fostorbearn)
48 *malina*; fylleþflood; cp. CorpGl 1, 216 (*malina*; fylled flod)
48 *ledo*; nepflod; cp. CorpGl 1, 196 (*ledo*; nepflod)
190 *theloniarius*; gafoles moniend ond wicgerefa; cp. CorpGl 2, 18.129 (*teloniaris*; uuicgeroebum)
111a *umbilicus terre*; eorðan nafola; cp. CorpGl 2, 19.243 (*umbilicus*; *nabula*)
190 gafoles moniend; cp. CorpGl 2, 5.518 (*exactio*; geabules monung)

7 Ibid., 1:250n.

Philip Rusche later contributed two further examples of this lexical overlap between the *Old English Martyrology* vocabulary and glosses, drawing particular attention to the Aldhelmian material contained in the Cleopatra glossaries (three glossaries contained in London, British Library, Cotton Cleopatra A.iii, a product of tenth-century Canterbury and thought to be related to the Corpus glossaries), and highlighting Canterbury as a possible place of composition for both the early Aldhelm glosses and the *Old English Martyrology*:[8]

59 *larua*; egesgrima, cp. CorpGl 2, 10.11 (*larbula*; egisgrima) and 11.358 (*musca*; egesgrima); ClGl 1, 3543 (*larbula*; egesegrima) and 3926 (*musca*; egesegrima); ClGl 3, 1974 (*larbam*; becolan, egesgrima)

198 *heahlæce*, "great physician"; cp. ClGl 1, 84 (*Archiatros*; heahlæcas oððe cræfgan) and 395 (*Archiatros*; heahlæcas); ClGl 3, 854 (*archiatros*; heahlæcas). The Old English term is very rare and seems to be restricted to the *Old English Martyrology* and Anglo-Saxon glosses.

As the last case of *heahlæce* shows, an important detail to emerge from Rusche's discussion is that conspicuous parallels with glosses emerge even from passages in the *Old English Martyrology* which present no Latin element. A similar picture arose from the numerous source studies undertaken by James Cross which unearthed further parallels between the *Old English Martyrology* and Anglo-Saxon glosses, not necessarily in parts of the Old English texts containing Latin phrases.[9] What is common, however, to most Old English words linked to gloss material by Kotzor, Rusche, and Cross is that the Old English terms in question are relatively rare, pointing to a very recherché component in the martyrologist's vocabulary.

In order to demonstrate further links between the *Old English Martyrology* and gloss contacts, it would therefore seem useful to identify vocabulary which only occurs in, or is overwhelmingly restricted to, the *Old English Martyrology* and glosses. Thanks to the recent developments

8 Rusche, "*Old English Martyrology* and the Canterbury Aldhelm Scholia"; for the sources and composition of the Cleopatra glossaries, see also Rusche, "Cleopatra Glossaries," 47–61, and "Isidore's *Etymologiae*."

9 Cross, "Apostles in the *Old English Martyrology*," 19–20 (on *besma*), and his "Influence of Irish Texts," 191–2 (on *fodder*).

in electronic tools, especially the searchable Dictionary of Old English Corpus, it is now comparatively easy to identify rare vocabulary in the *Old English Martyrology*, and then to ascertain whether that rare vocabulary presents any conspicuous overlap with glosses.[10] In the appendix below, I aim to present a more extensive, updated list of such vocabulary in the *Old English Martyrology* than previous commentators were able to compile, with a view to assessing possible reasons for the lexical overlap between the *Old English Martyrology* and Anglo-Saxon glosses.

At this stage of research, such a word list needs to be treated with caution. Although the *Old English Martyrology* seems to share rare vocabulary with a wide range of gloss genres, including various types of glossaries (*glossae collectae*, class glossaries, alphabetical glossaries), and a range of interlinear glosses (Aldhelm glosses, gospel glosses, psalter glosses, possibly also hymn glosses), it would be simplistic to misunderstand this vocabulary as evidence that the martyrologist used or was influenced by a wide range of gloss material in his composition of the *Old English Martyrology*.[11] It is not that such a scenario would seem implausible: the anonymous martyrologist's activity can be assigned to ninth-century southern England, his text presenting Anglian dialectal features with some West Saxon influence, and a possible Kentish component. Some glossing activity can indeed be traced to the same ninth-century southern background, including the production, collection, and usage of some early glosses.[12] But the transmission history of these various gloss genres is complex, and it is difficult to trace the origin of a particular word in the *Old English Martyrology* to prototypes of glosses which are now no longer in existence.[13] It is important to remember that the Old English translations of Latin terms used by the martyrologist may have entered Anglo-Saxon glosses

10 Healey et al., *Dictionary of Old English Web Corpus.*

11 On the distinction between various types of glosses, see Lendinara, "Anglo-Saxon Glosses and Glossaries," and "Glosse in volgare e in latino"; Gretsch, "Literacy and the Uses of the Vernacular," 277–81; Lendinara, "Glossaries"; Gretsch, "Glosses."

12 For ninth-century production and usage of glossaries, see Kuhn, "Dialect"; for early Aldhelm glossing, see Rusche, "Cleopatra Glossaries," 47–61, and "Dry-Point Glosses"; Gwara, *Aldhelmi Malmesbiriensis Prosa de Virginitate*, 274–308, and "Canterbury Affiliations." For the background on early psalter glosses, see Wilson, "Provenance of the Vespasian Psalter Gloss"; Gretsch, "Junius Psalter Gloss," 85–9, "Roman Psalter," and *Intellectual Foundations*, 18–21.

13 The early beginnings of Anglo-Saxon hymnal usage and hymn glossing are not at all clearly identifiable; see Gneuss, *Hymnar und Hymnen*, 122–56, and Milfull, *Hymns*, 3–6.

long after his period of composition, and could conceivably have been recoined independently of his earlier efforts. The disparate corpus of surviving Anglo-Saxon glosses, and the problems which its heterogeneity creates, particularly for lexicographers, make it difficult to assess why and when a term may first have been included in an Anglo-Saxon gloss, and in what way this gloss could have influenced an Anglo-Saxon author trained in using (or even producing) glosses.[14]

Nevertheless, several interesting points emerge from the word list here. The augmented list presented here certainly bears out the particular interest of Aldhelm glosses, particularly those surviving in the Cleopatra glossaries. For some specific passages in the *Old English Martyrology*, Aldhelm's *De uirginitate* has been identified as a source, and it is interesting to see that in some cases later Aldhelm manuscripts and *glossae collectae* linked to Aldhelm present the same collocations of Aldhelmian Latin terms with accompanying glosses as are presented in the corresponding passages in the *Old English Martyrology*; see, for example, the gloss parallels for *bytme*, *heahlæce*, *wyrmgaldere*, *geometrica* and *eorþgemet*, *larua* and *egesgrima*, and *obryzum* and *smæte gold*. In these cases, it is difficult to escape the conclusion that the martyrologist is likely to have used glossed Aldhelm manuscripts in the composition of his text, and that he integrated at least some vernacular glosses found in his source manuscripts into his own vernacular text. If the martyrologist was familiar with Aldhelm glosses, he could conceivably also have internalized standard vernacular translations of Aldhelmian vocabulary to such an extent that he applied them to the same or similar Latin words even when working from authors other than Aldhelm, which could explain other cases of overlap.[15] Philip Rusche has gone as far as to suspect some sort of "Canterbury vocabulary" behind some of the martyrologist's translations, and given the extent to which the martyrologist's vocabulary is paralleled in gloss material, Rusche's suggestion needs to be taken very seriously.[16]

---

14 See the remarks made by several contributors in Derolez, ed., *Anglo-Saxon Glossography*, esp. Derolez, "Anglo-Saxon Glossography"; Lapidge, "Old English Glossography"; McDougall, "Some Notes on Glosses," and Pulsiano, "Proposal for a Collective Edition."

15 Compare modern students of Old English and their traditional translation of *swiðe* as "exceedingly," derived from Mitchell and Robinson, *Guide to Old English*, 402, notwithstanding the obsoleteness of this unidiomatic word at least in British English, where its usage is now largely restricted to advertising Mr Kipling's Exceedingly Good Cakes.

16 Rusche, "*The Old English Martyrology* and the Canterbury Aldhelm Scholia."

How glosses could have been used by Anglo-Saxon readers and authors is another complex question.[17] In the case of the martyrologist, who may have recycled glosses in the composition of his own vernacular prose texts, two possibilities arise regarding the purpose of his inclusion of Latin vocabulary accompanied by what seem to be non-idiomatic translations: he may have been aiming to increase his readers' technical Latin vocabulary, to stop the most obscure gaps in their vocabulary, which would explain his inclusion of Latin terms in his Old English prose. Alternatively (or indeed additionally), the reason may be found in his aesthetic and linguistic ideals, which could have associated a high Latinate or learned component (however unidiomatic) in his vernacular prose with good translation practice. Given the peculiarity of some of his Old English vocabulary, it may even be the case that the Latin words included in his text came to function as some sort of gloss on the vernacular words. In that sense, his inclusion of bilingual word pairs in his text may not have been reader-oriented, but could have been more of an incidental result of his efforts to keep the new text as close to its Latin sources as possible. What appears to be some sort of "hermeneutic (or gloss-derived) vocabulary" in the martyrologist's language would in that case be less of a self-conscious affection, as could perhaps be said for the authors composing hermeneutic Latin, where there seems to be more "deliberate obfuscation" even for their contemporary readers.[18] The martyrologist's lexical idiosyncrasies seem to have caused problems above all for later readers, who were apparently less accustomed to guessing the meaning of rare vocabulary and translationese, as the many errors and garbled scribal interpretations of later manuscript copies of the text show.[19] The *Old English Martyrology* is one of several ninth-century vernacular prose texts which was revised at a later point during its transmission; unsurprisingly, lexical updating is the main characteristic of this revision, next to syntactic remodelling.

The extent to which the martyrologist's language follows his Latin sources also becomes apparent in the light of his other rare vocabulary, namely those terms in his vocabulary without parallels in Anglo-Saxon glosses. His translation technique is frequently literal to the point of matching Latin and Old English word for word, and sometimes even

17 On the production and usage of glosses, see Lapidge, "Study of Latin Texts," and Wieland, "Glossed Manuscript."

18 Lendinara, "Contextualised Lexicography"; Stephenson, "Deliberate Obfuscation."

19 Rauer, "Errors and Textual Problems."

morpheme by morpheme; several of his more unusual words look like neologisms, and in some cases may have been formed from Latin, for example the otherwise unattested *neahealand* ("neighbouring island," **89**, translating *uicina insula* in his source text). Given the problems of comprehension that rare vocabulary may have caused for the reader, the sheer number of *hapax legomena* in the text seems to run counter to what one would intuitively expect of a didactic text apparently compiled to cover the most basic hagiography.

If the *Old English Martyrology* really is so Latinate in style and vocabulary as to appear to be only one step up from representing a gloss itself, it is not the only ninth-century Old English prose text which leaves this impression. It has long been known that the Old English translation of Bede's *Historia ecclesiastica* also presents a conspicuous overlap with gloss vocabulary, and, in the light of the discussion here, it seems remarkable that it is again the Aldhelmian gloss vocabulary, particularly of the Cleopatra glossaries, which has been linked with the Old English Bede, notwithstanding the fact that Aldhelm can hardly be counted among the principal sources of that text, as is, however, the case with the *Old English Martyrology*. The distinctive strings of Old English doublets and synonyms in the Old English Bede have been seen to represent integrated glosses, as "a rhetorical accident growing out of the manner in which the translation was made," and Sherman Kuhn went as far as suggesting that the entire translation of the Old English Bede initially grew out of a set of glosses.[20] Christine Thijs has similarly highlighted the Latinate aspects of Wærferth's translation technique in his Old English version of Gregory's *Dialogi*, and Rebecca Stephenson has recently discussed Latinate syntactical features in the Old English translation of Orosius's *Historiae adversum paganos*, which seems to mimic the Latin tense system by employing periphrastic constructions, as if aiming to make a particularly Latinate impression, a technique which may have been influenced by translation techniques used in the production of psalter glosses.[21] One hopes that further comparative studies of the rare vocabulary in ninth-century prose texts will shed new light on the general status of vernacular composition in that century, and that the *Old English Martyrology* will then be included in such comparative work.

20 Waite, "Vocabulary of the Old English Version of Bede's *Historia ecclesiastica*," ch. 6; Kuhn, "Synonyms"; Rowley, *Old English Version*, 40–3.

21 Thijs, "Wærferth's Translation," and Stephenson, "Deliberate Obfuscation," esp. 69–108.

It would be tempting to see the absence of idiomatic language in some of the ninth-century Old English prose texts as indicative of a vernacular medium as yet unemancipated from an aesthetically dominant Latinity. But, as Malcolm Godden has cautioned, it is a fact that even a late Anglo-Saxon prose author and teacher like Ælfric chose to combine the usage of institutional translation vocabulary with his own experiments in more unusual lexis in his didactic prose.[22] His example and that of the martyrologist show that a didactic aim does not preclude the usage of difficult vocabulary. In the case of the martyrologist, much of the difficulty in his vocabulary seems to be bound up with his Latinity. It could furthermore be said that, at least according to modern educational principles, new content should ideally be mediated to its readership through a familiar medium; the combination of new subject matter and its communication via difficult language would perhaps be regarded as overambitious by modern pedagogues. But modern pedagogy is frequently concerned not to demotivate its learners by overambitious teaching. Keeping up a reader's motivation for learning may not have been among an Anglo-Saxon author's priorities, however. Moreover, early medieval biographies (as known to modern scholarship) sometimes seem to present an interesting combination of advanced levels of learning (and age) and a persistent effort to close fairly basic gaps in this learning, leading to what in modern times would be termed "life-long learning," and in that sense, glossing activities should therefore not be misunderstood as a beginner's pursuit.[23] The *Old English Martyrology*, with its simple vernacular syntax, difficult vernacular vocabulary (to some extent influenced by Latinate sources), basic hagiographical contents, and foolproof encyclopedic format is a good example of a text which mingles high learning and fairly basic information in just such a way.[24]

---

22 Godden, "Ælfric's Changing Vocabulary"; Gretsch, *Ælfric and the Cult of Saints*, 113–16; Hall, "Ælfric as Pedagogue"; Dekker, "Ælfric and His Relation to the Latin Tradition"; Sauer, "Language and Culture"; on standardization, see also Chapman, "Uterque Lingua."

23 See most recently Godden, "Glosses to the *Consolation*," which sums up earlier discussions of this topic.

24 An earlier version of this chapter was read at the International Medieval Congress at Leeds, 2011. I am grateful for several suggestions made by the audience on that occasion, and also for the many useful points made by the anonymous reader during the production of this volume.

Appendix

The vocabulary list below includes rarely attested vocabulary in the *Old English Martyrology* whose usage in other texts is completely or predominantly restricted to Anglo-Saxon glosses, or which presents other conspicuous overlap with gloss usage. It is important to note that the vocabulary listed here does not make a uniformly *learned* impression: several terms can be suspected to have belonged to an adult layperson's normal register, their absence from non-gloss texts being due perhaps to infrequent usage of such vocabulary in literary contexts. The more unusual terms in the vocabulary denoting family relationships ("mother-in-law," "paternal aunt") are good examples of such vocabulary which may have been unusual without being particularly learned. In general terms, the reader is again reminded of the caveat presented above, according to which rare vocabulary in the *Old English Martyrology* can be characterized by any combination of being dialectal, technical, neologistic, or learned, or none of these characteristics. Headwords appear in standardized spelling, not that used in the *Old English Martyrology*. Abbreviations used here are listed at the end of the article.

1. Old English Terms

adelseaþ, noun, m., "sewer," **164**, a section derived from part of the composite *Passio S. Laurentii*, the *Passio SS. Irenaei et Abundii* (*BHL* 4464), which presents *cloaca*. 12 occurrences of the Old English word survive in the Old English Corpus, "mainly in glosses to Aldhelm" (*DOE*); cp. AntGlB, 1315 (*cocleae*; adulseaþ); AldV 1, 4165 (*cloacae*; grypan adelseaþes), 4625 (*ad cloacam*; to grypan adelseaþe) and 4632 (*putido latibulo spurco*; mid fulum adelseaþe); AldV 13.1, 3319 (*cloacarum .i. lacuum*; adelseaþa).

asteorfan, verb, "to die," **70** "astorfen eten," "they ate that which had died (carrion)"; the relevant passage is probably derived from the *Passio S. Marci* (*BHL* 5276), which has *suffocata edentes*. There are 9 occurrences of the Old English word overall, with some gloss usage; AntGlB, 2950 (*sideratus ł ictuatus*; færunge astorfen); AldV 1, 3552 (*obeuntem, morientem*; astorfene. *obeuntem*; astorfenne).

aswengan, verb, "to fling," **79**, where objects "wæron aswengde"; the passage is based on Adomnán, *De locis sanctis*, which presents *excussis*. There are 6 occurrences of the Old English word (*DOE*), most of them in psalter glosses, e.g. PsGlA, 135.15 (*excussit pharaonem et exercitum eius in mari rubro*;

aswengde pharaon and weorud his in ðæm readan sae), but also in HlGl, E751 (*Excussit .i. deiecit*; fram aswengde ł todraf).

beflean, verb, "to flay," occurs in two passages, **87** and **162**, apparently translating *excoriari* in the *Passio S. Victoris* (*BHL* 8559), and *decoriari* in the *Passio S. Bartholomaei* (*BHL* 1002). There are 10 occurrences of the word in the Old English corpus, "mainly in glosses and glossaries" (*DOE*); cp. AldV 1, 3175 (*deglobere*; beheldan, beflean, *decoriare*); AldV 13.1, 3280 (*deglobere .i. decoriare*; behyldan, beflean).

besma, noun, m., "broom," **162**, "wings like a thorny broom"; the presumed source, the *Passio S. Bartholomaei* (*BHL* 1002), seems to present *hystrix*. There are 11 occurrences of the term (*DOE*); cp. CorpGl 2, 17.123 (*scopa*; besma), AntGlB, 29 (*scops*; bisme) and 765 (*uessiculum*; bysm ł scope).

bisceophired, noun, m., "episcopal household," **128**, without an identifiable Latin equivalent in the presumed source. There are only 3 occurrences of the word (*DOE*), the other two being ClGl 1, 1220 (*cleri*; biscophyrede); ClGl 3, 847 (*cleri*; biscophirede).

bloma, noun, m., "mass or lump of metal," **26**, tied around the saints' necks, translating *plumbo* in the presumed source, the *Passio S. Ananiae* (*BHL* 397). Only 6 occurrences of the word survive (*DOE*), most of them in glosses; AntGlB, 1282 (*massa*; dað ł bloma); ClGl 1, 4114 (*matallum*; bloma); see *DOE* for further gloss material.

brunbasu, adj., "purple," **130**, translating *purpurea* in the presumptive source. There are 29 occurences of the Old English term in the surviving corpus, "mainly in glosses and glossaries" (*DOE*). AldV 13.1, 1269 (*purpureo*; mid brunbasewum); ClGl 3, 1478 (*punicio*; ðy brunan oððe þy brunbasewan), AldV 1, 5007 (*coccineum*; brunbasne); see *DOE* for further gloss material.

brydrest, noun, f., "marriage bed," **38**, without a precise equivalent in the Latin source. There are only 3 occurrences of the Old English term word attested (*DOE*); ClGl 1, 2944 (*geneales*; brydræst) and OE *Dialogues*, 14.278.28 (brydræste).

burhgerefa, noun, m., "reeve," **30**, **112**, **161**; a relatively rare term with only 8 occurrences (*DOE*), of which two further ones are in glosses; AntGlB, 133 (*pretor uel prefectus uel prepositus uel questor*; burhgerefa) and 170 (*curiales ł decuriales*; burhgerefa).

byrst, f., "bristle, stiff hair," **27**, without a close equivalent in the Latin source. There are 12 occurrences of the term, which is "frequent in glossaries"; cp. ClGl 2, 507 (*seta*; byrst); see *DOE* for other gloss attestations.

bytme, noun, f., "keel," **125**; the passage is probably based on Aldhelm, *Carmen de uirginitate*, 2331–7. The saints' bodies float on the water like a ship's keel, an image perhaps taken from Aldhelm, *Carmen de uirginitate*, 2338, which presents *planca carinae.* There are 9 attestations of the word (*DOE*), of which 5 occur in a nautical context, translating *carina*; ClGl 1, 848 (*carina*; bytne); CorpGl 2, 3.134 (*carina*; bythne); BrGl 1, 288.3 (*Carina*; bytme); OE *Dialogues*, 59.347.23 (bytman).

cægbora, noun, m., "key-bearer," **164**; the source seems to have specified the saint as a *cloacarius* ("sewer-worker"), which may have been misinterpreted as *clauicularius* ("key-bearer"), and was then mistranslated as cægbora. The word occurs only 6 times, mainly in glosses (*DOE*); cp. ClGl 1, 1128 (*clauicularius*; cægbora); ClGl 2, 655 (*clauicularius*; cægbora).

domern, noun, n., "court chamber, law-court," **153**, without a close parallel in the Latin source. 27 occurrences of the word are attested (*DOE*), mainly with reference to the courts of Pilate, but also in a more general sense in glosses; AldV 1, 4376 (*praetorium*; domern); ClGl 3, 1198 (*precorum*; domhus, domærn); see *DOE* for further gloss material.

drædan, verb, "to dread," **211**. Some 30 occurrences of the term survive, "mainly in psalter glosses" (*DOE*); cp. PsGlC, 63.10.

drugung, noun, f., drought, **145**, perhaps translating *siccitas*. There are 13 occurrences of the Old English term, many of them in psalter glosses (cp. PsGlC, 105.14), but also in the OE *Dialogues*, 15.210.16.

duguþ, noun, f., "citizens, senate," **139, 139b, 235**; the martyrologist uses the word to refer to the Roman senate, a practice familiar from glosses; AldV 1, 3928 (*senatu*; dugheþe ł rædе); AntGlB, 165 (*senatus*; ealdormanna duguð) and 166 (*senatusconsultus*; gesiþa duguþ).

eacen, adj., "pregnant" **56**; refers to Mary's pregnancy with Christ; some 30 occurrences survive in the Old English corpus, mainly in poetic texts, but also in a number of glosses; MtGlRu, 24.19; AldV 1, 50 (*ex fecundo*; *fertili*, of ecnum); ClGl 1, 2618 (*foeta*; eacene); ClGl 3, 1871 (*feta*; eacene); HlGl, F281 (*foeta .i. fecunda plena grauida*; eacenu).

eastermonaþ, noun, m., "Easter-month," **58b, 73a**, used to translate *Aprilis*. The translation is traditional and can be found in Bede, *De temporum ratione*, 15, but the Old English term occurs 12 times elsewhere, esp. in notes and glosses (see *DOE*).

faþu, noun, f., "paternal aunt," **11**, where it translates *amita*; 11 occurrences are attested in the Old English corpus (*DOE*), with some gloss usage; ClGl 1, 335 (*amita*; faðe); AntGlB, 2395 (*amita mea*; min faþu).

festermodor, noun, f., "foster-mother," **122**, translating *nutrix*; the Old English term survives in only 4 occurrences, one of them in ClGl 1, 467 (*altrix*; festermodor).

fodder, noun, n., "case," "container," "bag," **153**, without an equivalent term in the Latin source. Some 11 occurrences survive, "mainly in glosses" (*DOE*); cp. CorpGl 2, 18.128 (*tehis*; tegum, fodrum); ClGl 3, 928 (*theca*; fodre); AntGlB 1503 (*theca*; fodder).

foregangan, verb, "to precede," **111**, translating *supergredior*; the word survives in some 18 occurrences, including gospel glosses; cp. MtGlLi, 21.31, and psalter translations (see *DOE*).

foretacnian, verb, "to prefigure," **75**, perhaps translating *portendere*; only 4 occurrences survive (*DOE*), one of them in MtHeadGlLi, 36.

gefylgan, verb, "to obtain," **67**, apparently translating *consequor*. Some 70 occurrences survive of the Old English term (*DOE*), with many attestations in Northumbrian glosses; cp. MtGlLi, 5.7 and DurRitGl, 34.16.

glitenian, verb, "to glitter," **226**, without a close parallel in the Latin source. Some 50 occurrences in the Old English corpus, "frequent in glosses" (*DOE*). AldV 1, 615 (*fulgescit*; glitenaþ), 1074 (*radians splendens*; gliteniende), 1716 (*coruscat rutilat*; glitenaþ), and 5119 (*fulgenti muricae*; glitniendre); see *DOE* for attestations in hymn glosses.

gnyþnes, noun, f., "scarcity," **73**, possibly translating *indigentia*; 4 occurrences survive of the Old English term (*DOE*), 3 of them in glosses; cp. ClGl 1, 4669 (*parsimonia*; gneðnes); see *DOE* for other examples.

godmodor, noun, f., "godmother," **210**, which here seems to translate *mater in baptismo.* Only 2 attestations exist, the other in ClGl 1, 4106 (*matrenas*; godmodra).

grymettung, noun, f., "roaring," **16**, without a close parallel in the Latin source. Some 21 occurrences survive, with some gloss usage; AldV 1, 4257 (*rugitus*; grunnunge gremetunge), and 2345 (*truculentos fremitus feroces sonos*; laþlice gremetunge).

heahlæce, noun, m., "great physician," **198**, the term (but possibly not the rest of the passage) is probably derived from Aldhelm's description of the two saints in question as *archiatros, De uirginitate* (prose), 275.9. Some 4 occurrences of the word survive, the others being ClGl 1, 84 (*Archiatros*; heahlæcas oððe cræfgan) and 395 (*Archiatros*; heahlæcas); ClGl 3, 854 (*archiatros*; heahlæcas).

healseta, noun, m., "hole for the head, neckline," **219**, translating *capitium*. The Old English term is very rare and only 2 further attestations seem to exist; ClGl 3, 1349 (*capitium*; healsed), and CollGl47.2 Merritt (*capitium*; halsetha).

læswian, verb, "to put out to grass," **122**, **136**, translating *pascere*; frequent articularly in psalter glosses; cp., for example, PSGlC, 22.2.

legerteam, noun, m., "sex," **190**, without a precise equivalent in the relevant Latin source passage. There seems to be only 1 further attestation; ClGl 1, 2740 (*flagitium*; legerteam ł tiht).

licþegnung, noun, f., "funeral," **94** (if the closest Latin text did serve as a source), perhaps translating *exequiae*. The term is rare, occurring also in the OE *Dialogues*, 10.84.3 (licþegnung), and SedGl, 391 (*exsequis*; licþeg, licþegnungum).

mynster, noun, n., the term is consistently used to translate *cymiterium* (more conventionally L. *coemeterium*), **10, 20, 28, 91, 143, 147, 202, 205**; closest is perhaps AldV 13.1, 4347 (*in cimiterio, s. in monasterio*; on licreste, lictune). Other glosses do not explicitly refer to a monastic context; ClGl 1, 1227 (*cymiterio*; byrgenstowe); CorpGl 2, 3.433 (*cimiterium pontiani*; licburg *a nomine põn p̃r qui construxit*) and 3.978 (*cymiterium locus ubi requiescunt corpora*); AntGlAlph, 345 (*cimiterium .i. poliandrum*; halig legen); Occ. Glosses (Gough) 5, "licrest."

nihtwæcce, noun, f., "vigil," **127**, apparently without a precise Latin equivalent term in the source text; a very rare term, occurring in AntGlB, 148 (*uigilie*; nihtwæccan), the Will of Æthelgifu (Ch 1497, l. 14), and in the gospel translation of Luke, 2.8 (LukeCCCC140).

sweger, noun, f., "mother-in-law," **156**, here applied to the Virgin Mary and translating *socrus* in the source text of the passge, Aldhelm, *De uirginitate* (prose), 292.6–8. The Old English term is relatively rare and is mainly restricted to glosses and gospel translation; cp. ClGl 3, 168 (*socrum*; sweger), and 248 (*socrus*; sweger); AntGlB, 2385 (*socrus*; sweger); LkGlRu, 12.53 (*socrus*; sweger).

sweorban, noun, n., "neck," **90**, translating *ceruix* in the Latin source. The Old English term is rare, occurring also in psalter glosses; cp., for example, PSGlC, 128.4 (*ceruices*; swirban).

teah, noun, f., "bag," **209**, translating *mantega* in the Latin source; cp. CorpGl 1, 215 (*mantega*; taeg); CorpGl 2, 11.118 (*mantega*; taeg); ClGl 1, 3936 (*mantega*; tig).

tindiht, adj., "spiked," **150**; very rare; translates *scorpio* (the torture instrument) in the source text. AntGlB, 352 (*scorpio*; ostig ł tindig); the Old English term translates *rostratum* or its cognates in other glosses; cp. CorpGl2, 16.208 (*rostratum*; tindecte); see *DOE* for other examples.[25]

getwin, noun, m., "twin," **23, 107, 196, 238**; gloss usage; AldV 1, 140 (*gemina*; getwinnum), 1482 (*gemina dupla*; to getwinre), 4048 (*geminis duobus*;

25 Cross, "*Passio S. Laurentii*," 206.

getwinnum) and 4970 (*typica*; getwinne twifealde); AldV 13.1, 1459 (*gemina*; .i. dupla getwinre), 2605 (*geminis*; getwinnum), and 4166 (*geminis, .i. duobus*; getwinnum); ClGl 1, 2229 (*e geminis*; of getwinnum), but also in a number of hymn glosses (see *DOEC*).

webwyrhta, noun, m., "fuller," **30**, **108**, translating *fullo* in the Latin source texts. The Old English term is very rare, and otherwise only seems to be attested in a gloss; HlGl, F968 (*fullo*; webwyrhta).

writbred, noun, n., "writing tablet," **155**, with no precise equivalent in the presumed Latin source. The Old English term is very rare and otherwise only attested in ClGl 3, 305 (*pugillarem*; writbret).

wyrmgaldere, noun, m., "snake-charmer," **124**, translates *Marsus* in the two Aldhelmian texts on which the passage is based, *De uirginitate* (prose), 310.3–4 and *Carmen de uirginitate*, 2433–8. The Old English is otherwise very rare, occurring mainly in glosses; ClGl 1, 3891 (*Marsum*; wyrmgalere), and 4037 (*Marsorum*; wyrmgalera); ClGl 3, 904 (*Marsorum*; wyrmgalera) and 2005 (*Marsum*; wyrmgalere); AldV 13.1, 3271 (*marsorum, .i. incantatorum*; þyrsa, wyrmgalera) and 4939 (*marsum wyrmgalere*; dre); AldV 1, 3166 (*marsorum*; þyrsa oþþe wyrmgalera. *Marsi .i. incantatores*; þyrsas wyrmgaleres) and 4822 (*marsum*; wyrmgalere gal dre); see also Gwara, 696.

2. Old English and Latin Word Pairs

alabaster; **glæsfæt**, noun, m., "box for perfumes," **133**; the relevant passage is likely to have been derived from Luke 7:37, which does present *alabaster*; cp. CorpGl 2, 1.442 (*alabastrum*; *uas de gemma propri nomen lapidis et uas nominat de illo lapide factum*); AntGlB, 573 (*alabastrum*; stæne elefæt); the Latin word also occurs in a number of gospel glosses, including the Lindisfarne gospels for Luke 7:37 (LkGlLi; *alabastrum*; oelefæt), although in all of them with a different Old English translation.

altor; **festerfæder**, noun, m., "foster-father," **42**; only 6 occurrences of "festerfæder" survive (*DOE*); cp. ClGl 2, 361 (*altor*; festerfæder) and OE *Dialogues*, 25.228.22–3 (festerfæder). See also glosses with the alternative Old English lemma fostorfæder; CorpGl 2, 1.493 (*altor*; fostorfæder); ClGl 1, 78 (*altor*; fosterfæder);ClGl 3, 803 (*altor*; fosterfæder) and 1701 (*altor*; fosterfæder); AldV 1, 2749 (*altor*; fosterfæder; *nutritor*); AldV 13.1, 2841 (*altor, .i. nutritor*; fosterfæder).

alumnus; **festerbearn**, noun, m., **42**; "festerbearn" is a *hapax legomenon*, but there are some 6 occurrences of "fostorbearn," predominantly paired up with Latin *alumnus* and its cognates; cp. CorpGl 2, 1.450 (*alumnae*; fostorbearn); ClGl 1, 273 (*alumne*; fosterbearn); ClGl 3, 1431 (*alumne*; fosterbearn).

ecce; **hona**, interj., "oh," **38**; an exclamation put in St Natalia's mouth. Together with the related forms "heonu," "ono," and "heona," the word frequently occurs in gospel glosses, for example MtGlLi, 1.23 (*ecce*; heonu).[26]

exomologesis; **hreowsunge dæg ond dædbote**, noun, f., "Rogation," **69**; cp. CorpGl 2, 5.463 (*exomologesin*; *confessio*) and CorpGl 2, 5.505 (*exomologesin*; *preces uel confesionem*).

geometrica; **eorþgemet**, noun, n., "geometry," **232**, a passage partially based on Aldhelm, *De uirginitate* (prose), 276.24–278.23 and 280.5–7 with the reference to *geometrica* at 277.4. Of the 15 attested occurrences of the Old English term, 14 are in glosses; cp. AldV 1, 3017 (*geometrica*; eorðcræft. *geometrica*; eorþgemet) and 5316 (*geometrica*; eorþgemet); ClGl 1, 2806 (*geometrica*; eorþgemet) and 3908 (*metricam*; eorþgemet); see also Gwara, 456.

larua; **egesgrima**, noun, m., "ghost," **59**, a section partly based on Aldhelm, *Carmen de uirginitate*, 2222–44, with the reference to *larua* at *Carmen de uirginitate*, 2224. The Old English term is attested 9 times, mainly in glosses: cp. CorpGl 2, 10.11 (*larbula*; egisgrima) and 11.358 (*musca*; egesgrima); ClGl 1, 3543 (*larbula*; egesegrima) and 3926 (*musca*; egesegrima); ClGl 3, 1974 (*larbam*; becolan, egesgrima); see *DOE* for further gloss material.

ledo; **nepflod**, noun, f., "neap-tide," **48**. The Old English term is very rare, occurring in CorpGl 1, 196 (*ledo*; nepflod); AntGlB, 2712 (*ledona*; nepflod ł ebba); BrGl 1, 289.4 (*ledo*; nepflod).

malina; **fylleþflood**, noun, f., "spring-tide," **48**. The precise collocation of these two terms only has a parallel in CorpGl 1, 216 (*malina*; fylled flod); cp. also AntGlB, 2713 (*malina*; heahflod).

obryzum; **smæte gold**, noun, n., "pure gold," **5**, a passage partially based on Aldhelm, *De uirginitate* (prose), 254.8–255.15, where *obrizum* occurs at 254.12. The collocation of the Latin and Old English term is frequent in glosses; cp. CorpGl 2, 13.24 (*obrizum*; smæte gold); AldV 1, 3421 (*obrizum aurum platum aurum optimi colouris*; smæte gold); AldV 13.1, 1808 (*in obrizum*; on smætum) and 3534 (*obrizum, .i. aurum optimi colouris*; smæte gold, platum); ClGl 1, 31 (*Auri obriza lammina*; ða smætegyldenan claðas), 4432 (*Obrizum*; þæt smæte), 4435 (*Obriza lammina*; þa smætegyldnan claðas); ClGl 2, 513 (*obrizum*; smæte gold); ClGl 3, 412 (*obrizum*; smæte) and 1477 (*obridzum*; smætegyldne); see also Gwara, 272.

26 On the dialectal relationship between the forms, see Kotzor, *Das altenglische Martyrologium*, 1:342–3 and 365.

palatium; **heall**, noun, f., "hall," **71**. The Old English is a common term; the word pair in conjunction is also attested in two glossaries; AldV 1, 4247 (*triclimium palatium*; healle); AldV 13.1, 4368 (*triclinium, .i. palatium*; healle).

solstitium; **sungihte**, noun, "solstice," **111a**. The Old English term seems to be a *hapax legomenon*; morphologically comparable is perhaps "gebedgiht"; AntGlB, 362 (*conticinium*; cwylttid gebedgiht); on "giht" see also F. Holthausen, *Altenglisches etymologisches Wörterbuch*, 3rd ed. (Heidelberg: Winter, 1974), 130–1. The Old English term "sunstede" is more widely attested as a translation of *solstitium*, despite the martyrologist's protestation that "sungihte" is the correct word "on ure geþeode."

telonarius; **gafoles moniend ond wicgerefa**; noun, m., "customs officer," **190**; the passage specifies the apostle Matthew as a tax collector, information which was circulating in a wider range of texts (cp. Matthew 9:9). The collocation of the Latin term and its Old English translation is only paralleled in CorpGl 2, 18.129 (*teloniaris*; uuicgeroebum), with "gafoles moniend" also appearing in CorpGl 2, 5.518 (*exactio*; geabules monung).

umbilicus terre; **eorðan nafola**, noun, m., "navel," **111a**; for the combination of the Latin and Old English terms, cp. CorpGl 2, 19.243 (*umbilicus*; *nabula*), and AntGlB, 1892 (*umbilicus*; nauela).

ursa; **byren**, noun, f., "female bear," **8**; 5 occurrences, of which 3 are in the *Old English Martyrology* (*DOE*); cp. AntGlB, 483 (*ursa*; byrene); see *DOE* for further gloss material.

Other Vocabulary

The following vocabulary also presents overlap between the *Old English Martyrology* and glosses, but further attestations in other texts are too numerous for inclusion in the list above.

ænlic, adj., "handsome," **38, 97**; **ætswigan**, verb, "to be silent," **66ap**; **æþellice, æþelice**, adv., "splendidly," **17, 180**; **ancorsetl**, noun, n., "hermitage," **63, 66**; **awefan**, verb, "to weave," **227**; **bær**, noun, f., "bed," **209**; **bedelfan**, verb, "to bury," **209, 211**; **beheonan**, prep., "on this side," **146**; **beobread**, noun, n., "honeycomb," **58**; **beorhtlice**, adv., "clearly," **79**; **bræcseoc**, adj., "epileptic," **124**; **brædan**, verb, "to cook," **40, 151**; **brymm**, noun, m., "sea," **94b**; **cleofa**, noun, m., "chamber," **124**; **deaw**, noun, m., "dew," **52**; **deofolseoc**, adj., "possessed by devils," **3**; **deofolseocnes**, noun, f., "possession," **102, 122, 124**; **gedwinan**, verb, "to dwindle," **197**; **ear**, noun, n., "ear (of grain)," **1**; **eardung**, noun, f., "dwelling," **97**; **ehtan, ehtian**, verb, "to persecute," **35, 234**; **facenfull**, adj., "deceitful," **152**; **feogan**, verb, "to hate," **173**; **forbregdan**, verb, "to drag someone," **30**, **233**; **gafol**, noun, n., "tribute," **190**; **godwebb**, noun, n., "expensive fabric," **38**; **hæren**, adj., "made of hair," **138**, **210**, **227**; **herigendlic**, adj., "praiseworthy," **70**; **hrace**, noun, f., "throat," **30**; **maniend**, noun, m., "collector," **190**; **soþlufu**, noun, f., "love, charity," **122**; **stanweall**, noun, m., "stone wall," **56a**; **wundswaþu**, noun, f., "scar," **110ap**.

References to Primary Texts

AldV 1 — Aldhelm Glosses, ed. L. Goossens, *The Old English Glosses of MS. Brussels, Royal Library 1650*, Brussels Verhandelingen van de Koninklijke Academie voor Wetenschappen, Letteren en Schone Kunsten van Belgie, Klasse der Letteren, 36 (Brussels: Paleis der Academiën, 1974) (cited from *DOEC* by line number)

AldV 13.1 — Aldhelm Glosses (prose *De virginitate*, 13.1, Napier), ed. A.S. Napier, *Old English Glosses*, Anecdota Oxoniensia, Medieval and Modern Series 11 (Oxford: Clarendon Press, 1900) (cited by gloss number)

AntGlAlph — Antwerp-London Alphabetical Glossary, ed. D.W. Porter, *The Antwerp-London Glossaries*, Publications of the Dictionary of Old English 8 (Toronto: Pontifical Institute of Mediaeval Studies, 2011), I, 8–44 (cited by line)

AntGlB — Antwerp-London Bilingual Class Glossary, ed. D.W. Porter, *The Antwerp-London Glossaries*, Publications of the Dictionary of Old English 8 (Toronto: Pontifical Institute of Mediaeval Studies, 2011), I, 45–131 (cited by line)

BHL — *Bibliotheca Hagiographica Latina*, ed. the Bollandists, 2 vols. (Brussels, 1899–1901) and H. Fros, *Novum Supplementum* (Brussels, 1986)

BrGl 1 — T. Wright and R.P. Wülcker, ed., *Anglo-Saxon and Old English Vocabularies*, 2nd ed. by R.P. Wülcker, 2 vols. (London: Trübner, 1884) (cited by page and line)

ClGl 1 — Cleopatra Glosses, ed. W.G. Stryker, "The Latin-Old English Glossary in MS. Cotton Cleopatra

A.III" (doctoral dissertation, Stanford University, 1951) (cited from *DOEC* by gloss number)

ClGl 2 — Cleopatra Glosses, ed. J.J. Quinn, "The Minor Latin–Old English Glossaries in MS. Cotton Cleopatra A.III" (doctoral dissertation, Stanford University, 1956), 15–69 (cited from *DOEC* by gloss number)

ClGl 3 — Cleopatra Glosses, ed. J.J. Quinn, "The Minor Latin-Old English Glossaries in MS. Cotton Cleopatra A.III" (doctoral dissertation, Stanford University, 1956), 69–219 (cited from *DOEC* by gloss number)

CollGl47.2 Merritt — Latin-Old English Glossaries, no. 34; H.D. Meritt, ed., *Old English Glosses: A Collection*, MLA General Series 16 (New York: Modern Language Association of America, 1945) (cited by gloss no. following edition)

CorpGl 1 — First Corpus Glossary, ed. J.H. Hessels, *An Eighth-Century Latin-Anglo-Saxon Glossary* (Cambridge: Cambridge University Press, 1890) (cited by line)

CorpGl 2 — Second Corpus Glossary, ed. J.H. Hessels, *An Eighth-Century Latin-Anglo-Saxon Glossary* (Cambridge: Cambridge University Press, 1890) (cited by section and line)

DOE — *Dictionary of Old English: A–G on CD-ROM*, ed. A. diPaolo Healey and others (Toronto: Pontifical Institute of Mediaeval Studies, 2008)

DOEC — *Dictionary of Old English Corpus*, ed. A. diPaolo Healey and others (Toronto: Pontifical Institute of Mediaeval Studies, 2005), tapor.library.utoronto.ca/doecorpus

DurRitGl — Durham Ritual Glosses, ed. A.H. Thompson and U. Lindelöf, *Rituale ecclesiae Dunelmensis*, Surtees Society 140 (Durham: Andrews, 1927), 1–125 (cited by page and line)

Gwara — S. Gwara, ed., *Aldhelmi Malmesberiensis Prosa de Virginitate*, Corpus Christianorum Series Latina 124A (Turnhout: Brepols, 2001)

HlGl — Harley Glossary, ed. R.T. Oliphant, *The Harley Latin–Old English Glossary*, Janua linguarum,

	series practica 20 (The Hague: Mouton, 1966), 21–208 (cited by letter and gloss number, following *DOEC*)
LkGlLi	The Lindisfarne Gospels (Luke): Skeat, 15–239 (cited by chapter and verse)
LkGlRu	The Rushworth Gospels (Luke), Skeat, 15–239 (cited by chapter and verse)
LukeCCCC140	Skeat, 14–238 (cited by chapter and verse)
MtGlLi	The Lindisfarne Gospels (Matthew), Skeat, 25–245 (cited by chapter and verse)
MtGlRu	The Rushworth Gospels (Matthew), Skeat, 25–245 (cited by chapter and verse)
MtHeadGlLi	Headings to Readings in the Lindisfarne Gospels (Matthew), Skeat, 16–22 (cited by heading number)
OccGl	Occasional Glosses, ed. J. Gough, "Some Old English Glosses," *Anglia* 92 (1974), 273–90 (cited by gloss number)
OE *Dialogues*	Old English Translation of Gregory's *Dialogi*, ed. H. Hecht, *Bischof Wærferths von Worcester Übersetzung der Dialoge Gregors des Grossen*, Bibliothek der angelsächsischen Prosa 5 (Leipzig: Wissenschaftliche Buchgesellschaft Darmstadt, 1900–7), 179–259 (cited by chapter, page, and line)
PsGlA	Vespasian Psalter Glosses, ed. S.M. Kuhn, *The Vespasian Psalter* (Ann Arbor: University of Michigan Press, 1965) (cited by psalm and verse)
PSGlC	The Cambridge Psalter Glosses, ed. K. Wildhagen, *Der Cambridger Psalter*, Bibliothek der angelsächsischen Prosa 7 (Hamburg: H. Grand, 1910), 1–370 (cited by psalm and verse)
Skeat	W.W. Skeat, ed., *The Holy Gospels in Anglo-Saxon, Northumbrian, and Old Mercian Versions* (Cambridge: Cambridge University Press, 1871–87)

Sequences and Intellectual Identity at Winchester

JONATHAN DAVIS-SECORD

The monastic community at Winchester in the late tenth and early eleventh centuries was impressively vibrant, with bold reforms spearheaded by Bishop Æthelwold, literary productions that rival those of Bede and Aldhelm, and musical vitality and innovation apparently unmatched by any other monastic centre at the time.[1] Although Æthelwold grounded his community's intellectual identity on uniquely Anglo-Saxon foundations, in several aspects the Winchester community owed debts to Continental sources.[2] Indeed, Continental scholars influenced Æthelwold himself during his formative time in King Æthelstan's court and while at Winchester.[3] Moreover, elements of the Winchester liturgy link to Corbie in West Francia, and the forms of musical notation in the Winchester Tropers

1 For accounts of Æthelwold's influence and his role in reforming Winchester in the mid-tenth century, see Yorke, ed., *Bishop Æthelwold*; Lapidge and Winterbottom, eds., *Wulfstan of Winchester*; and Gretsch, *Intellectual Foundations*. On Winchester's literary productivity, see again Lapidge and Winterbottom's *Wulfstan of Winchester*; various articles collected in Lapidge, *Anglo-Latin Literature, 900–1066*; and Lapidge, *Cult of St Swithun*. On Winchester's musical importance, see Holschneider, *Die Organa von Winchester*; Hiley, "Changes in the English Chant Repertories" and "Repertory of Sequences at Winchester"; and Rankin, ed., *Winchester Troper*.

2 Gretsch suggests that Æthelwold's affinity for Aldhelm and the inheritance of that affinity by Æthelwold's students seem in large part responsible for the widespread adoption of the distinctive hermeneutic style in tenth-century Anglo-Saxon England (*Intellectual Foundations*, passim and summarized on 427).

3 On Continental influences on Æthelwold, see Wormald, "Æthelwold and His Continental Counterparts"; Gretsch, *Intellectual Foundations*, passim; and Lapidge, *Cult of St Swithun*, 8–24 and 218–24.

strongly resemble Corbie notations.[4] Consequently, the intellectual identity of the Winchester monastic community is a remarkable mixture of Anglo-Saxon and Continental influences, making it difficult to identify easily or succinctly.

This chapter gauges the character of this identity by examining the Winchester compositions of one of the most distinctive and purely medieval literary genres, namely the sequence. The sequence is a chant element of the liturgy that was sung after the *Alleluia* just before the gospel reading. Barely a century old by Æthelwold's time, the sequence comprises a particularly fertile genre for this investigation, since it was viewed less rigidly than other liturgical elements due to its short history.[5] Association with Pope Gregory I seems to have inhibited the composition of new texts in more traditional Roman chant, while the creation of new texts for pre-existing melodies is one of the distinguishing features of sequences.[6] This sense of freedom with sequences presumably licensed greater ease and opportunity for incorporating and expressing a community's identity than would have been acceptable in other, firmly established genres. Moreover, chant in general was a powerful vehicle for performing and expressing Christian identity in the Middle Ages. As both performance and remembrance, chant unified the individual with tradition:

> The brilliance of Gregorian chant is that it is at once *both* a personalized experience and a collective rite. By becoming a *musical* space, a conceptual "place to be," chant allows the subjects to enter into that space, and thus enrich their own personalized memorial archive, while *at the same time* participating in the cultural memory demarcated by that space ... For the medieval

4 David Hiley writes that "the codification of chant at Winchester seems to have followed very closely patterns established elsewhere, specifically ... at Corbie," and he highlights the post-Pentecost *Alleluia* series shared between Winchester and Corbie in "Thurstan of Caen," 61–4. Susan Rankin notes the "close relation" between Winchester neumes and those of Corbie in "Neumatic Notations in Anglo-Saxon England," 131–2. In addition to these pieces of concrete evidence, Lapidge suggests that it is highly likely that Æthelwold's creation of the cult of St Swithun was inspired by Continental cults of local saints, about which he presumably learned from his advisors from Ghent and Fleury (*Cult of St Swithun*, 12).

5 For discussions of the origin of the sequence genre, see von den Steinen, "Die Anfänge der Sequenzendichtung," and Crocker, *Early Medieval Sequence*, 4–8.

6 Hiley, "Changes in the English Chant Repertories," 137, and Lapidge, *Cult of St Swithun*, 192–3.

> subject, to perform or listen to chant in this way is fundamentally to come to *know* something – one's own identity.[7]

Chant then was an individual performance within a corporate group that linked the participating individuals, both singers and listeners, to the large and long-held traditions of Christianity. The creation of new personal memory while also participating in the "corporate memory" of the Christian whole leads the singer to perform an identity that is simultaneously a recapitulation of a communal Christian identity and a creation of an individual addition to that community. Identity in the Anglo-Saxon Benedictine Reform, moreover, was fundamentally textual and "centred on the voicing of sacred texts in the round of monastic liturgies, and on the reading and hearing of scripture and religious writings."[8] Thus, the act of singing and the composition of new sequence texts allowed the Winchester community to participate in a traditional Christian identity as well as express and perform its own, idiosyncratic version of that identity.

That the maintenance and expansion of the musical repertory at Winchester formed a central element of the community's intellectual life is made clear by the Winchester Tropers: Cambridge, Corpus Christi College, 473 and Oxford, Bodleian Library, Bodley 775. These manuscripts contain a large corpus of sequence texts copied by many Winchester residents, a large number of which were composed at Winchester during the period between the Benedictine Reform and the Norman Conquest.[9] This corpus affords valuable information on the monastic community's sense of itself as a product of various influences. Specifically, the compositional techniques employed and the exemplars that the authors emulated subtly but effectively reveal the manner in which the monks constructed their communal intellectual identity from competing elements of both East Frankish and West Frankish literary and liturgical traditions. I show in this chapter that Winchester sequence texts present a hybrid identity that incorporates East Frankish style to a larger degree than previously recognized, belying the many connections to West Frankish traditions already known. The texts in fact blend the two styles while nonetheless retaining

7 Baker, "Sing to the Lord a New Song," 114–15, original emphasis. See also Coleman, *Ancient and Medieval Memories*; Carruthers, *Craft of Thought*; and Cubitt, "Monastic Memory and Identity."

8 O'Brien O'Keeffe, *Stealing Obedience*, 97.

9 Rankin, ed., *Winchester Troper*, 74.

a sense of autonomy that produces a uniquely Winchesterian identity beholden to no single intellectual strain.

The sequence genre initially gained renown through the *Liber hymnorum* of Notker Balbulus of St Gall, who produced a significant corpus of this newly developing genre in the late ninth century.[10] Notker composed the texts as mnemonic devices for melodies that originally grew out of the *Alleluia* – sung before the gospel reading in the mass – into what is known as the *jubilus*.[11] The texts follow the fundamental structural guideline that each musical note should generally be matched with a single verbal syllable.[12] Moreover, each melodic line was generally repeated with different text before moving on to the next melodic line, creating in response a textual structure of isosyllabic paired stanzas (or versicles) – that is, two lines of text of equal length, each yoked to one instance of a repeated melodic line.[13] In addition to these basic principles, I have elsewhere shown that, in Notker's sequences, portions of text that correspond to repeated melodic members are not only isosyllabic but also isotonic – that is, having identical patterns of natural stress.[14] In other words, every segment of text

10 A form of the following description of the sequence genre and discussion of Notker's compositional practices also appears in Davis-Secord, "Rhythm and Music." Notker's account of his introduction to the sequence genre appears in his preface to his *Liber hymnorum* (von den Steinen, *Notker*, 2:8–11). Lapidge posits that the sequence genre was introduced to Anglo-Saxon England during the Benedictine Reform (*Cult of St Swithun*, 94).

11 Notker viewed the sequences as tools to "hold together" ("colligare") the long melodies of the *jubili* (von den Steinen, *Notker*, 2:8).

12 The Latin reads "Singulae motus cantilenae singulas syllabas debent habere" (the movements of individual segments ought to have one syllable apiece), although there is some textual inconsistency, with some scholars preferring the variant "singuli" (von den Steinen, *Notker*, 2:8–10). For an in-depth exploration of this description, see Calvin Bower's forthcoming edition of Notker's sequences; I am very grateful to Professor Bower for giving me access to the introduction to his edition before its publication.

13 Aparallel sequences do not repeat melodic lines as parallel sequences do, thus lacking even this aspect of organization, and on the rare occasion one syllable will account for more than one note in either type of sequence.

14 It is clear that classical Latin scansion, involving the patterning of heavy and light syllables into various types of metrical feet, is not applicable to sequence texts; the stanzas simply cannot be divided into the feet of classical metre. I therefore follow the lead of scholars of rhythmical Latin verse and attend to the natural stress of each line instead. For a fuller treatment of these issues, see Norberg, *Introduction*, and the discussion in Davis-Secord, "Rhythm and Music," 121–2, which addresses in detail the behaviour and treatment of secondary stress, among other issues.

corresponding to an occurrence of a repeated segment of melody has the same stress pattern as all the other segments of text corresponding to the other occurrences of that segment of melody. As a result, text and melody always match rhythmically wherever the segment of music appears in any given sequence melody.

This aspect of Notker's compositional technique is not an interesting aside: it provides a fundamental litmus test for assessing the allegiance of Winchester's sequences to either the East Frankish or the West Frankish sequence tradition.[15] East Frankish sequence texts composed after Notker tend to follow his example by repeating rhythms in response to repeated melodic phrases. For example, the anonymous, tenth-century *Eia, recolamus* from St Gall almost perfectly employs Notker's style of repetition.[16] West Frankish texts, on the other hand, generally lack such repetition: parallel versicles are isotonic in some, but musical repetition is never systematically matched with rhythm repetition, to my knowledge. Thus, the presence or absence of a Notkerian style of rhythm repetition in Winchester sequence texts should suggest an affinity for one tradition or the other and therefore provide additional insight into the careful construction of the intellectual identity of the Winchester monastic community. While the following discussion involves close attention to minute technical details of stress and rhythm, those details comprise some of the very few extant vestiges of the community's sense of itself and its acts of self-definition. From the minutiae arises an understanding of Winchester.

Notker's *Congaudent angelorum* provides an excellent example of the phenomenon of rhythm repetition as a baseline for comparison. Figure 6.1 provides a reconstruction of the melody *Mater*, to which *Congaudent angelorum* is set, with labels for melodic members and indications of repeated or nearly repeated melodic members. The following lines are the segments of text from *Congaudent angelorum* that correspond to melodic member 5e and its repetitions, namely melodic members 6c, 7e, and 8c.[17] Because sequence stanzas, as far as I can tell, cannot be grouped into regular segments such as feet, there is no way to summarize stress patterns succinctly. I therefore follow the practice of some

15 The division of sequences into two distinct traditions applies only to texts from the early phase of the genre's development and not to later texts, which display an entirely different approach to the repetition of rhythm.

16 Davis-Secord, "Rhythm and Music," 138–9.

17 The full text of *Congaudent angelorum* can be found in von den Steinen, *Notker*, 2:66.

Figure 6.1 Reconstruction of *Mater*[18]

18 Calvin Bower provided this reconstruction of *Mater*. Note that, in spots important to my discussion, it differs somewhat from the reconstruction found in Crocker, *Early Medieval Sequence*, 162–3.

metrical studies and represent stress patterns visually in the examples below, with a stroke (/) representing a stressed syllable and an "x" representing an unstressed syllable.[19]

5e: súi sanctíssimi córporis
átque spiríttuum génuit
/ x x / x x / x x
6c: píis concélebrat méntibus
úna cum ángelis élevat
/ x x / x x / x x
7e: Chrístique[20] mártyres práedicant
ín castimónia[21] áemulans
/ x x / x x / x x
8c: téque carmínibus vénerans
/ x x / x x / x x

All four instances of the repeated melodic member are texted with the same rhythm, with all seven segments of text having stress on the first, fourth, and seventh syllables of each segment. Importantly, since the text corresponding to melodic member 8c is part of the final stanza, which has no parallel verse, its rhythm cannot be the result of simply matching the

19 One could, for example, summarize a line of dactylic hexameter with, say, SSSSDS, indicating a line consisting of four spondees followed by a dactyl and another spondee. Such shorthand is not available for representing the rhythm of a full line of rhythmic verse. Many scholars classify lines of rhythmic verse by the number of their syllables and the positions of the final main stress – paroxytone or proparoxytone, that is penultimate stress and antepenultimate stress (Norberg, *Introduction*, 81–2n2, and 84). Since the present argument evaluates the positions of all stresses throughout entire lines, even this shorthand remains unusable.

20 This non-classical stress pattern is relatively common in medieval verse, since medieval authors sometimes treated the enclitic *-que* as a separate word that did not alter the stress pattern of the preceding word (Norberg, *Introduction*, 21–2). This departure from standard classical stress rules happens frequently in Notker's sequences, but not universally.

21 Another notable difference between classical and medieval stress patterns is the possibility of monosyllabic words attaching proclitically to following polysyllabic words and taking the stress as though the two words together formed a larger, single word, leading to stress patterns such as *ín dies* instead of *in díes* (Norberg, *Introduction*, 14–21). This departure from standard classical stress rules happens frequently in Notker's sequences, but not universally.

rhythm of its (non-existent) twin.[22] Instead, the repetition of rhythm here must be a result of matching this segment of the text with the other six segments of text corresponding to the same melodic member. This same type of repetition of rhythm occurs in several other places as well, always matching a repetition of a melodic member. For example, melodic member 3b is a repetition of 2b, 5c of 5a, 8b of 7d, 8d of 8a, and 8h of 8f, and in each of these instances of melodic repetition each segment of text corresponding to a repeated melodic member employs the same rhythm as each other segment of text corresponding to that melodic member. This phenomenon is of course not restricted to *Congaudent angelorum* but occurs in the vast majority of Notker's sequence texts, suggesting that he saw it as a fundamental aspect of sequence composition.[23]

Turning to the Winchester texts themselves, I first consider *Ave pontifex Haedde*, set to the melody *Iustus ut palma minor*, which was copied in the first layer of CCCC 473 on fol. 118v–119r, placing it among the earliest sequence compositions at Winchester.[24]

1. Áve, póntifex Háedde, rútilans ín aula
   / x / x x / x / x x / x x
2a. Còntemplatíva qua ágmina iúbilant làetabúnda,
   / x x / x x / x x / x x / x / x

22 For a discussion of the irregularity of Notker's final stanza, see Crocker, *Early Medieval Sequence*, 160–88.

23 I calculate that, at a conservative estimate, approximately 83 per cent of Notker's parallel stanzas are isotonic; see Davis-Secord, "Rhythm and Music," 140n57, for a full explanation and discussion of this estimate.

24 *Ave pontifex Haedde* is edited in *Analecta Hymnica* (henceforth *AH*) 40:228 (i.e., volume 40, no. 228). Translation: (1) Hail, Bishop Haedde, shining in the palace (2a) where the contemplative, joyful throng rejoices, (2b) where with splendid tones the songs resound "Alleluia," (3ab) and in which angelic songs are sung day and night (4a) in the most intimate presence of the divine, (4b) which arranges all things according to its own might, (5a) balancing opposing elements, (5b) suffusing the heights, the middle, and the depths. (6a) Therefore, Haedde, hear now our harmonious praises, (6b) you who shine with the apostolic mitre above the heavens. (7a) Lift us up with your holy prayer, and release all our chains of sin, (7b) and help us in the terrible hour of cruel death, and lead us to the kingdom of heaven, (8a) where we may contemplate uninterrupted joys, (8b) singing delightful songs to our God. (9a) Let him supply lofty rewards who knows how to give the utmost; (9b) let the glory be his forever. (10) Let all things sacred say "Amen."

2b. Vóce praeclára qua órgana cóncrepant àllelúia
3a. Díe ac nócte et cántica
/ x x / x x / x x
3b. Ín qua cantántur angélica
4a. Córam praeséntia dèitátis íntima,
/ x x / x x / x / x / x x
x / x / x x / x / x / x x[25]
4b. Virtúte própria quáe dispónit ómnia,
5a. Contrária témperans èleménta,
(/)x / x x / x x / x / x[26]
5b. (Cél)sa média pénetrans ác profúnda.
6a. Érgo nunc cónsona, Háedde, praecónia áudi nóstra,
/ x x / x x / x x / x x / x / x
6b. Quí apostólica rútilas ínfula súper áethra.
7a. Préce túa sáncta nos súbleva, ét peccáti sólve nóstra ómnia víncla,
/ x / x / x x / x x / x / x / x / x / x x / x
7b. Átque ín treménda nos ádiuva dírae mórtis hóra, ét duc ád caeli régna;
8a. Úbi contínua còntemplémur gáudia,
/ x x / x x / x / x / x x
x / x / x x /x / x / x x
8b. Cantántes dúlcia Déo nóstro cármina.
9a. Práestet haec grándia, quí scit dáre máxima;
/ x x / x x / x / x / x x[27]
9b. Cúi sit glória pér aetérna sáecula.
10. Dícant cúncta Ámen sáncta.
/ x / x / x / x

Apart from two instances of seemingly aparallel stress, the versicle pairs have exact rhythm repetition, with each one employing the same stress

25 The first visual representation of rhythm corresponds to the line 4a, and the second to line 4b; this disjunction and the parallel one between versicles 8a and 8b are discussed below.

26 Versicle 5a has one fewer syllable than versicle 5b, which aligns with melodic line 5a having one fewer note than 5b; see figure 6.2. Possibly, although by no means necessarily, the first syllable of "contraria" could have been sung melismatically over two notes to maintain parallelism.

27 Parsing this line with this rhythm and number of syllables requires taking "cui" as disyllabic, which the diacritics added above the text in CCCC 473, fol. 119r corroborate.

pattern as its mate. Moreover, there are several instances of melodic repetition that the text reflects with rhythm repetition as well. Figure 6.2 presents *Iustus ut palma minor*, showing that melodic phrase 4 is repeated as phrase 8. The texts from *Ave pontifex Haedde* associated with those melodic phrases are versicles 4ab and 8ab, which just so happen to contain the text's two instances of seeming rhythmic aparallelism. While emendations could provide possible solutions, editorial intervention is unnecessary, since the aparallelism obtains only when the versicle pairs are taken independently. When all four lines are taken together, as the musical repetition encourages, it becomes clear that the first versicles of each pair are perfectly isotonic with each other, as are the second versicles with each other. That is, 4a and 8a are isotonic, and 4b and 8b are isotonic. Excepting the first two syllables of each line, the four lines of text all employ one exactly repeated rhythm: x x x / x x / x / x / x x, with stresses on syllables 4, 7, 9, and 11. The change in the rhythm in 4b is repeated in 8b, thus maintaining perfect isotonic repetition on the level of versicle pairs linked by musical repetition. Given the repetition of this change, it seems that the author writing this new text for the melody *Iustus ut palma minor* played with the melodic repetition in some way, producing textual rhythms that departed from systematic expectation but still in a regular and repeated manner.

In addition to this instance of musico-rhythmic repetition, melodic line 9b also repeats line 4, although its parallel line, 9a, only repeats the final seven notes of 4. This melodic repetition is again matched by rhythmic repetition in the text, with text line 9b employing the same rhythmic pattern as do 4a and 8a, i.e., stressing syllables 1, 4, 7, 9, and 11. Oddly, text line 9a also employs this same stress pattern, even though the melody as recorded in manuscripts of Notker's sequences is not a perfect repetition. Possibly, the version of the melody known in Winchester and texted with *Ave pontifex Haedde* did not accord perfectly in this instance with the version we know from Notker, instead making both 9a and 9b perfect repetitions of 4. The neumes for 9a and 9b in CCCC 473, fol. 119r, appear identical and therefore support this possibility, which would satisfactorily explain the perfect repetition of rhythm in text line 9a. Whatever the ultimate reason for the repetition of stress pattern, this practice of matching rhythm to melody clearly associates *Ave pontifex Haedde* with the East Frankish tradition. This text, written at Winchester and celebrating a local Anglo-Saxon saint, employs the style pioneered by Notker.

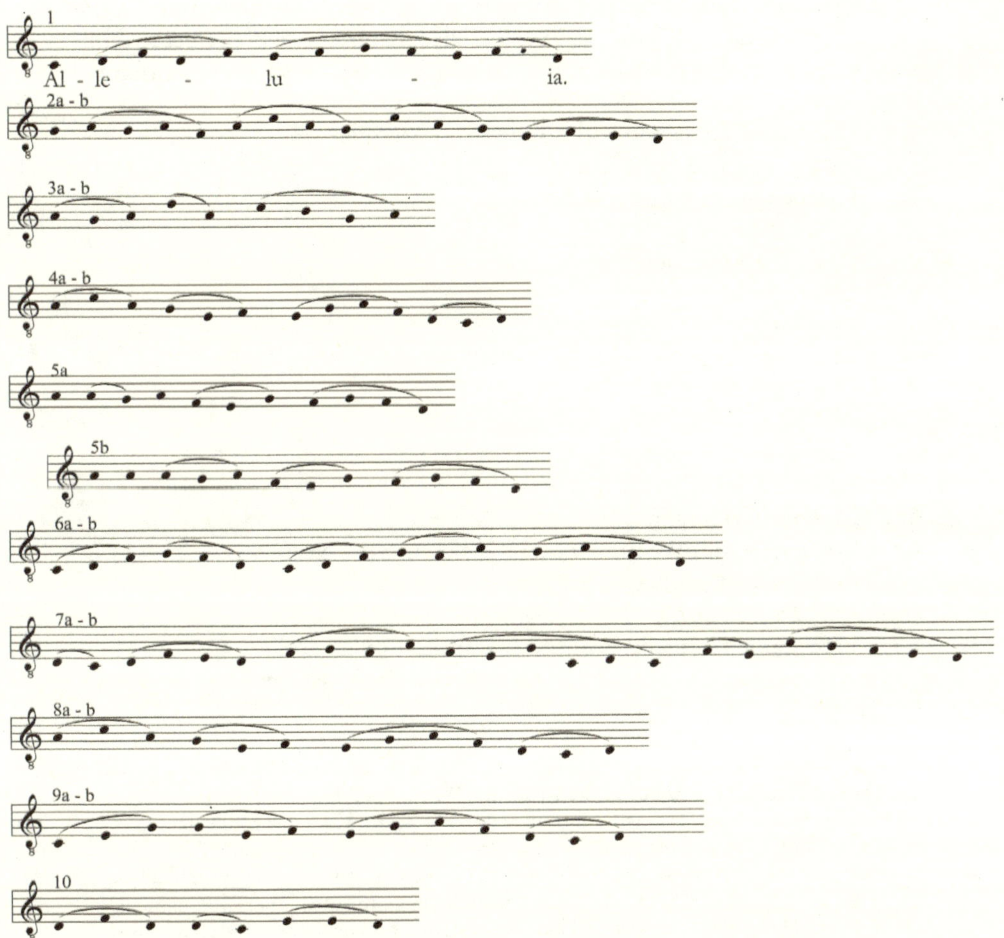

Figure 6.2 *Iustus ut palma minor*[28]

28 Calvin Bower provided this reconstruction of *Iustus ut palma minor*. Note that the version of the melody employed at Winchester agrees with Notker's version rather than a West Frankish one, probably due to Notker's version being the "mainstream" version (Hiley, "Repertory," 164). Hiley and, in personal correspondence, Bower point out, however, that the Winchester version creates better musical parallelism than other versions of the melody. Bower produced this reconstruction from the neumation in the Winchester Troper (CCCC).

Pange turma, another sequence composed at Winchester and copied in the first layer of CCCC 473 on fol. 98v–99v, also displays nearly perfect rhythm repetition in parallel versicles as well as in instances of melodic repetition.[29]

1. Pánge, túrma, córde, vúltu Chrísto praecónia,
   / x / x / x / x / x x / x x
2a. Concélebrans àdmiránda
   x / x x / x / x
2b. Paschália sàcraménta.
3a. Ó benefícia!
   / x x / x x
3b. Ó quam mirífica,
4. Ómni sáeclo pósita,
   / x / x / x x
5a. Álto pólo micántia,
   / x / x x / x x
5b. Mágna sólo fulgéntia!
6a. Quáe licet ámpla mirétur ecclésia sáncta cathólica,
   / x x / x x / x x / x x / x x / x x
   / x x / x x / x x / x x x / x / x x[30]
6b. Háec tamen álma praecéllunt instántia festíva gáudia

29 The text is edited in *AH* 40:22 and Misset and Weale, eds., *Analecta Liturgica*, 2:27–8, no. 436. Translation: (1) Sing, O throng, with your heart, with your countenance, praises for Christ, (2a) marking the miraculous (2b) Paschal celebrations. (3a) O, the blessings! (3b) O, how wonderful [they are], (4) ordained for every age, (5a) gleaming in the lofty heavens, (5b) greatly shining forth down to the earth! (6a) Although the holy universal church marvels at them in abundance, (6b) nevertheless, the redeeming joys of the present feast surpass them (7) through its miracles. (8a) So let the hymns resound loudly, (8b) and let the cosmos echo back. (9) Rejoice with melodious song, (10a) because, with night condemned and unceasing death crushed underfoot, (10b) Christ returns today to the lofty heavens in victory. (11a) The mysteries predicted before this age are fulfilled on this shining day; (11b) the holy, visionary words of the prophets are laid bare by this splendid light. (12a) Christ, the immaculate lamb of God, has risen today with immense glory after conquering death. (12b) O universal mother church, extended far and wide, rejoice, be glad, exult! (13a) With a joyous spirit, join song upon song. (13b) Merciful Christ on this glorious day, with death destroyed, has restored you to the high homeland. (14) Let everyone say "Alleluia."

30 The instance of stress mismatch in this pair of versicles would be resolved if "festiva" were parsed as proparoxytonic (/ x x), employing a germanicizing pronunciation, rather than paroxytonic (x / x) as classical stress rules suggest.

7. Súi pér insígnia.
/ x / x / x x
8a. Érgo clára cóncrepent órgana,
/ x / x / x x / x x
8b. Ét mundána réboet máchina.
9. Gáude, pràedulcísona,
/ x / x / x x
10a. Quía damnáta nócte et calcáta mórte perpétua
/ x x / x / x x x / x / x x / x x
10b. Chrístus ad áethra hódie praecélsa rédit victória.
11a. Ánte sáecla arcána pràenotáta compléntur hác die fúlgida;
/ x / x x / x / x / x x / x / x x / x x
11b. Pròphetárum praesága sácra vérba nudántur hác luce spléndida.
12a. Ágnus Déi síne mácula surréxit hódie mórte vícta, Chrístus, imménsa glória.
/ x / x / x / x x x / x / x x / x / x / x x / x / x x
/ x / x / x / x x x / x x / x / x / x / x x / x x / x x[31]
12b. Gáude, máter ó cathólica, laetáre, exsúlta, cìrcumfúsa lónge latéqu(e)_ecclésia.
13a. Méntis àlacritáte iúnge cánticis cántica.
/ x / x x / x / x / x x / x x
/ x / x x / x / x x / x / x x / x / x / x x / x x[32]
13b. Chrístus hác die clára mórte perémpta té clemens áltam rèstaurávit in pátriam.
14. Dícant ómnes *Àllelúia*.
/ x / x / x / x

31 This pair of lines presents a fairly complicated challenge. First, the rhythm as presented here depends on the presence of elision between "lateque" and "ecclesia"; certainly at least some monks at Winchester, for example Wulfstan Cantor, understood the concept of elision in metrical Latin poetry. Alternatively, *AH* 40:22 puts the "que" in parentheses, suggesting perhaps that the enclitic is superfluous and should be omitted. Second, the remaining rhythm aparallelism would be resolved if "exsulta" were parsed as proparoxytonic (σ́ σ σ), employing a germanicizing pronunciation, rather than paroxytonic (σ σ́ σ) as classical stress rules suggest.

32 The disjunction between versicles 13a and 13b is a product of the sequence's melody, *Pascha nostrum*, in which the melodic line for 13b is an elongated and embellished version of that for 13a.

The evidence of the rhythm repetition in parallel versicles is once again overwhelming, even with the two mismatched stresses that are unrelated to musical variation. As for melodic repetition, this version of the melody *Pascha nostrum* is idiosyncratic, generally matching the versions employed by Continental texts but with important, subtle differences.[33] Most importantly for the present discussion, several short melodic phrases repeat throughout all of the versions, but the placement of those phrases is unique in the version to which *Pange turma* is set.[34] The sequence scheme adopted in my presentation of the text above accords with this version of the melody as recorded in CCCC 473, fol. 82r–v, showing text lines 4, 7, and 9 to be stand-alone lines of text that all share a repeated melodic phrase. As with *Ave pontifex Haedde*, the repetition of music is matched by a repetition of rhythm, with all three lines stressing syllables 1, 3, and 5. Even though the melody is distinctive and likely confined to England and northern France,[35] the East Frankish compositional pattern is still present. Thus, this Winchester text also combines elements of both East and West Frankish traditions.

For a final example of this phenomenon of rhythm repetition reflecting melodic repetition, I present *Laude resonet*, again composed at Winchester and copied in the first layer of CCCC 473 on fol. 130r–v.[36]

---

33 See Crocker's discussion and various versions of the melody in *Early Medieval Sequence*, 241–61. This challenging variation likely led to the differing presentations of the text in *Analecta Hymnica* and *Analecta Liturgica*. The scheme adopted here is closer to that of the *Analecta Liturgica* version, but with the versicles renumbered to show the parallelism better.

34 For a reconstruction of this version of *Pascha nostrum*, see Bannister and Hughes, eds., *Anglo-French Sequelae*, 31.

35 Ibid.

36 The text is edited in *AH* 37:153 and Lapidge, *Cult of St Swithun*, 94–6. Translation (for comparison, see the translation in Lapidge, *Cult of St Swithun*, 94–5): (1) Let the humble throng devoutly resound with praise for you, Christ, (2a) you who raise the jewels of the church up from the dust of the earth to the stars, (2b) through which the vision of peace – mother Jerusalem – shines in adornment. (3a) [She] sent father Birinus from the Romulean citadel (3b) and Swithun, born in the English homeland, (4a) who, as golden candelabras of Christ, distribute heavenly grace, (4b) the first of whom bestows the baptismal font, the second rains down miracles triumphantly. (5a) This one heals hearts, that one cures bodies, (5b) this one also thunders as a leader, that one also shines like a light. (6a) One plants, one waters, one doubles talents, one consecrates the coin. (6b) One provides baptism, one blesses the chrism, one teaches, one prays, one fortifies. (7a) One is the helmsman of faith, one is the anchor, (7b) both bishops, who unite the English with the angels. (8) Through them, Christ, make us visible among the stars. Alleluia.

1. Láude résonet té, Christe, deuóte súpplex túrma,
/ x / x x / x x x / x / x / x
2a. ecclésiae quí gemmas dé mundi púluere tóllis ad sídera,
x / x x / x x / x x / x x / x x / x x
x / x x / x x / x x / x x x / x / x x[37]
2b. per quás pacis uísio, máter Ierúsalem, ornáta rútilat.
3a. Pátrem áb arce Bírinum míssum Romúlea,
/ x / x x / x x / x x / x x[38]
3b. mísit Suuíthunum pátria nátum et Ánglica,
4a. Quí candelábra Chrísti áurea spárgunt càrismáta supérna,
/ x x / x / x / x x / x / x / x x / x
4b. quórum lauácri príor dát fontem, séquens plúit sígna triúmphans.
5a. Sánat híc corda, cúrat hic córpora,
/ x / x x / x x / x x
5b. dúx et híc tonat, lúx et hic fúlgurat.
6a. Hic plántat, híc rigat, híc talénta dúpplicat, híc fidus cónsecrat nummísma.
x / x / x x / x / x / x x / x x / x x x / x[39]
6b. Baptísma híc prebet, crísma híc sanctíficat, híc docet, híc orat, hic fírmat.
7a. Híc proréta est fídei, híc est et ánchora,
/ x / x x / x x / x x / x x
7b. ámbo présules, ángelis Ánglos qui sóciant.
8. Nos prómere pér quos tú fac, Chríste, in ástris. *Àllelúia*
x / x x / x / x / x x / x / x / x

37 Parsing "ornata" as proparoxytonic (σ́ σ σ), i.e., with a germanicizing pronunciation, rather than paroxytonic (σ σ́ σ), i.e., with a classical pronunciation, would resolve the rhythm aparallelism.

38 This parsing assumes word-initial stress for "Birinum." Even if it would have been pronounced *Birínus*, there is precedent for the malleability of names at least in metrical Latin poetry, as Lapidge discusses concerning Wulfstan Cantor (*Cult of St Swithun*, 352).

39 While monosyllables can proclitically attach to following words and take stress, that pattern is optional (Norberg, *Introduction*, 14–21). In this stanza pair, while the anaphoric repetitions of "hic" sensibly act proclitically and take stresses in several places, the first and last instances can just as sensibly be interpreted as not taking stress. For the first instance of "hic," the pattern is not yet apparent, and thus I see no pressure for it to take the stress. For the last instance of "hic," the pattern is ending, which naturally calls for a change in the rhythm by having "hic" again not take the stress. Those two instances thus bookend the list, and that interpretation moreover allows for perfect rhythmic repetition between the parallel versicles.

Rhythm repetition is once again prevalent in this text, with only one stanza pair (2ab) having one stress mismatch out of nineteen syllables. Most importantly for the present discussion, the melody for this sequence, *Ecce quam bonum*, contains melodic repetition.[40] Lines 3ab share a melodic movement with lines 7ab; and, as the parsed rhythms above show, all four segments of text employ the same rhythm, stressing syllables 1, 3, 6, 9, and 12. Thus, this Winchester text also employs the Notkerian style of matching melodic repetition with rhythm repetition, marking it as yet another descendant of the East Frankish tradition.

These three examples – *Ave pontifex Haedde*, *Pange turma*, and *Laude resonet* – are not isolated accidents but are in fact representative of a significant portion of the Winchester sequence corpus. Of the thirty-one sequences contained in the two Winchester Tropers and probably composed at Winchester, approximately one-third displays excellent rhythm repetition with another third doing so imperfectly and with a fair number of mismatched stresses; the final third fails to employ rhythm repetition almost entirely.[41] In sum, then, many – but by no means all – Winchester texts employ rhythm repetition. Consequently, these representative texts also demonstrate that a significant portion of Winchester texts align with the East Frankish – as opposed to the West Frankish – style when it comes to this aspect of composing sequence texts. Although the Winchester liturgy and intellectual culture were replete with West Frankish influences in many other ways, this aspect of the sequence texts is decidedly East Frankish.

The dearth of East Frankish texts in the Winchester Tropers, however, presents a considerable obstacle to making this connection. Only two texts by Notker appear in the Tropers – *Scalam ad celos* and *Omnes sancti* – with West Frankish texts forming the vast majority of the corpus of foreign compositions in the manuscripts.[42] One might object that a tradition

40 For a reconstruction of *Ecce quam bonum*, see Bannister and Hughes, eds., *Anglo-French Sequelae*, 37–8.

41 These divisions must unfortunately remain preliminary, since the identification of rhythm repetition requires correlating text with music, even for parallel versicles, and doing so for all the Winchester sequences goes beyond the space of the present investigation. It is possible that such correlation might reveal rhythm repetition in some texts that seem to lack it currently. Unfortunately, four melodies cannot be reconstructed at this point because they are so rare, leaving at least four texts unresolvable (Hiley, "Repertory," 157; the four melodies are *Laudent te pie*, *Ploratum*, *Tractus iocularis*, and *Bucca*, with the first three being found nowhere other than in CCCC 473 and Bodley 775).

42 Hiley, "Repertory," 157. Moreover, the texts for *Scalam ad celos* and *Omnes sancti* appear only in Bodley 775, not in CCCC 473, which contains only the melodies.

of composition could scarcely have been transmitted through so small a number of texts. *Scalam ad celos*, however, employs excellent rhythm repetition in response to melodic repetition in its melody, *Puella turbata*, and thus would have been an outstanding example of the East Frankish style of sequence composition for the Winchester community to follow.[43] Specifically, the second half of melodic phrase 2 is repeated at the end of phrase 3, and the final six notes of phrase 2 are repeated at the ends of phrases 4 and 8; the texts set to those melodic members are as follows:

2a: cáutus invígilat íugiter
/ x x / x x / x x
2b: póssit insáucius scándere
3a: vétat exítium mínitans
/ x x / x x / x x
3b: rámum auréolum rétinet
4a: gládio tránsito
/ x x / x x
4b: láuream súmere
8a: íngemis íntegram[44]
(x) / x x / x x
8b: (per)suáseras vírgini

What might be termed a "dactylic" rhythm – that is, a stressed syllable followed by two unstressed syllables – repeats in each of the eight segments of text set to the repeated melodic member. The monks at Winchester, then, encountered in *Scalam ad celos* a text that provides an excellent example of Notker's penchant for rhythm repetition.

Omnes sancti, set to the melody *Vox exultationis*, presents a more complicated situation than *Scalam ad celos* and requires a nuanced evaluation

43 The text of *Scalam ad celos* is edited in von den Steinen, *Notker*, 2:90; a reconstruction of the melody, *Puella turbata*, along with the text can be found in Crocker, *Early Medieval Sequence*, 220–1.

44 Lewis and Short indicates that the medial *e* in oblique forms of *integer* can be long or short; moreover, vowels followed by consonant clusters consisting of a stop followed by a liquid, such as *gr*, can be treated as either heavy or light by position. Thus, parsing "integram" at the end of line 8a as proparoxytonic (/ x x) is acceptable, especially given the stress patterns of the other matching texts.

of the melody and text together.[45] On one level, one particular melodic segment occurs several times in *Vox exultationis*, and three of the six textual passages corresponding to instances of the melodic segment share a single rhythmic pattern, as follows:

3a: Quos ín Dei láudibus firmávit cáritas
3b: Nos frágiles hómines firmáte précibus
6b.2: placéntium pópulus suprémo Dómino
x / x x / x x x / x / x x

The first two of these three portions of text occur as parallel versicles, but the third comprises the second half of the b-versicle in stanza pair 6. While these three portions of text follow a single rhythmic pattern, the other three texts set to the same melodic segment do not:

5a: Vos quós Dei grátia víncere térrea
x / x x / x x / x x / x x
5b: Et ángelis sócios fécit ésse pólo
x / x x / x x / x / x / x
6a.2: cònfessóres, mártyres, mónachi, vírgines
/ x / x / x x / x x / x x

Each of these three portions of text has a slightly different rhythmic pattern: 5a and 6a.2 end with three "dactylic" words, but 5b does not; the rhythms of 5a and 5b align for the first four syllables, but 6a.2 does not match them. These seeming failures, however, are in fact the results of an understanding of the melody more nuanced than simply identifying the succession and pitches of individual notes. All six instances of the melodic segment indeed contain the same notes in the same order, but the notes are grouped into "gestures" differently.[46] Calvin Bower argues that these differences in stress patterns come not from a failure to recognize and respond

45 The following discussion of the rhythmic and melodic repetitions in *Omnes sancti* and *Vox exultationis* is heavily indebted to Calvin Bower's introduction to his forthcoming edition. Currently, the text of *Omnes sancti* is edited in von den Steinen, *Notker*, 2:78; a reconstruction of the melody, *Vox Exultationis*, along with the text can be found in Crocker, *Early Medieval Sequence*, 368.

46 For the use of the term "gesture" and the recognition of the different gestures in these six particular segments of texts, see the introduction to Bower's forthcoming edition of Notker.

to melodic repetition but rather from a deep recognition of that repetition that allowed Notker to "play with [the] expectation" that it creates.[47] For example, Bower argues that the stress pattern employed in 3a and 3b highlights the word-play between "firmavit" and "firmate"; the change in pattern from 5a to 5b reflects the move from the act of conquering terrestrial things (5a) to its transcendent result (5b), thus illustrating Notker's common practice of "expressing transcendence with exceptional accentual patterns"; and the need to include "confessores" in the list of types of saints necessitates the change in pattern in 6a.2.[48] Employing this nuanced understanding of the relationship between text and melody, one finds not just isotonic repetition in *Omnes sancti* but an underlying assumption that stress patterns interact with melodic patterns in both simple and complex ways. Thus *Omnes sancti*, illustrating this approach subtly but powerfully, demonstrates that a text newly composed for a pre-exisiting melody can not only follow that melody's patterns but can also respond to and play off of those patterns.

Thus, there is evidence of at least two examples of this East Frankish approach to texting pre-exisiting melodies present in the Winchester Tropers. Other manuscripts of Notker's texts could have circulated at Winchester with examples of his style, but direct evidence of definite sources remains *Scalam ad celos* and *Omnes sancti* only, although they illustrate the technique perfectly and in a deeply nuanced manner. That small set of certain evidence is problematic: without any other examples, it would have taken a very talented Latinist with excellent musical skills to recognize Notker's style from only those two sequences. Winchester, of course, had such an individual in the person of Wulfstan Cantor, whose metrical Latin ranks among the best that Anglo-Saxon England had to offer and whose musical abilities must have been prodigious to earn the cognomen "Cantor."[49] Indeed, Wulfstan's authorship of a portion of the Winchester sequence corpus is often suggested.[50] At the very least, Wulfstan would likely have

47 See the introduction to Bower's forthcoming edition of Notker, sections VII and VIII.

48 Again see the introduction to Bower's forthcoming edition.

49 Lapidge, *Cult of St Swithun*, 343–64; specifically, Lapidge comments that Wulfstan was "a Latin poet of outstanding calibre whose verse bears comparison with that of any early medieval Latin poet or even, in some small ways, with the poets of classical antiquity" (364).

50 See in particular Lapidge and Winterbottom, eds., *Wulfstan of Winchester: The Life of St Æthelwold*, xxxiv–xxxvi; Lapidge, *Cult of St Swithun*, 340–1; and Rankin, "Making the Liturgy," 51–2.

been able to recognize the subtle repetition of rhythm in *Scalam ad celos* and the subtle interaction of content, form, and melody in *Omnes sancti*, perhaps even reacting to the sequence genre much as Notker did decades earlier. His ability is unquestionable, although definite proof of such a reaction is unfortunately still lacking.

The composition of sequences at Winchester, moreover, seems to have continued after Wulfstan's death, with a second layer of texts having been added to CCCC 473 during the end of the eleventh century and beginning of the twelfth along with later additions to Bodley 775.[51] As with the early compositions, not every late addition employs repetition of rhythm, but several do.[52] The repetition employed by these later texts is not perfect, but the pattern is clearly present, with there still being relatively few mismatched stresses.[53] So, while Wulfstan certainly could have been the origin of the employment of the East Frankish, Notkerian tradition in Winchester sequences, he seems not to have been the end. This expansion of the musical repertory was a communal activity and not the work of one or even just two monks: at least seventeen separate scribes contributed to copying the sequences composed at Winchester into CCCC 473.[54] Even if only a handful of scribes were responsible for the actual composition of the texts, a significant portion of the community participated at least in updating the record of the repertory. This sustained interest in music, and sequences in particular, shows that such activity formed a central element of the identity of the monastic community at Winchester.[55]

Importantly, this discussion assumes intent on the part of the author or authors of the Winchester sequences. Indeed, accidence cannot account

51 Rankin, ed., *Winchester Troper*, 36 and 38–46, and Hiley, "Changes in English Chant Repertories," 154.

52 Of the five texts both composed at Winchester and recorded late (four in the second layer of CCCC 473 and one added late to Bodley 775), two have very poor rhythm repetition and three have decent repetition.

53 The best of the group, *Alme deus* (*AH* 40:43), has nine stanza pairs, some of which are fairly long (twenty-nine syllables, for example), with only twelve mismatched stresses in the entire text. Certainly, this proportion is higher than that of the best early Winchester sequence texts, but it is nonetheless much lower than that of texts that clearly fail to employ Notker's style.

54 See the descriptions in Rankin, ed., *Winchester Troper*, 36 and 38–46. Rankin also points out that "the *organa* were notated by as many as five scribes sometime in the half century following the time of Wulfstan's activity at the Old Minster" (*Winchester Troper*, 74).

55 Ibid., 74.

for the regularity of rhythm repetition in the sequences, considering the mobility of Latin stress and the complexity of Latin stress rules.[56] Lack of attention to stress placement would instead produce only occasional parallelism with many mismatched stresses and nothing like what occurs in the Winchester or Notkerian sequences. West Frankish sequences and pre-Notker East Frankish sequences, such as *Nostra tuba*, show what is most likely the result of such a lack of attention: little repetition of rhythm in parallel stanzas, with, at best, half the stresses aligning in any given stanza pair in *Nostra tuba*.[57] Later sequences also diverge from the patterns in the Winchester and Notkerian sequences, joining the trend of other musical genres that became strictly regular by repeating in every line a single rhythmic pattern dictated by an external verse form.[58] Indeed, later sequences, such as *Aurea personet lira*, are barely recognizable as sequences, with the repetition of melodic lines being the only link to early examples of the genre.[59] In comparison, then, the sequences by Notker and those composed at Winchester stand out with their distinctive pattern of rhythm repetition: the extent of the repetition is too great to be the product of accidence, but it is not as regular and slavishly repetitive as the later sequences. While claims of authorial intent must and should always be controversial, such a middle ground suggests nothing less than intention. Eliminating both an abstract verse form and accidence as explanations leaves, it seems, choice as the only alternative.

This conclusion should not be surprising, since such active incorporation of outside influences and attention to the rhythm of natural stress fit well with the rest of what we know about Winchester's literary milieu. Æthelwold himself set the initial example by incorporating many different influences and absorbing many different traditions, even displaying, for example, some knowledge of Greek in his use of *karessi* in an attestation in a charter.[60] Although the form is not a correct Greek form, its use reveals an openness to and thirst for outside traditions and knowledge. The use of East Frankish style in the Winchester sequences reveals again that same

56 A version of this discussion of authorial intent also appears in Davis-Secord, "Rhythm and Music," 124–6.

57 Norberg discusses *Nostra tuba* on pages 164–5 of *Introduction*; the original text is found in von den Steinen, *Notker*, 2:107.

58 Norberg, *Introduction*, 168.

59 Ibid., 168–9.

60 Lapidge, "Æthelwold as Teacher and Scholar," 184–9.

openness and thirst and shows that Æthelwold's example permeated the intellectual identity at Winchester for decades. Moreover, the attention to rhythm specifically fits well with Winchester's literary productions. Anglo-Saxons anywhere would have been sensitive to matters of rhythm, given the nature of the stress-based metre of Old English poetry, and Wulfstan Cantor, as already mentioned, mastered Latin metrical verse. In addition, Lantfred, a scholar from Fleury who spent time in Winchester and composed the *Translatio et miracula S. Swithuni*, was also very sensitive to the rhythm of natural language.[61] In particular, he cultivated a style employing particular patterns of *cursus*, that is, the pattern of stressed and unstressed syllables ending a clause or sentence.[62]

Of course, the most famous example from Winchester of an author carefully attending to rhythm must be Ælfric, who spent approximately two decades at Winchester being educated in "Æthelwold's school" and who wrote in a unique or at least idiosyncratic rhythmical Old English style. The significance of Ælfric's rhythmical style increases within the larger context of Winchester's other literary productions, since the extensive interface between Latin and English at Winchester certainly could have opened up a migration of stylistics from one language to another.[63] Lantfred's *cursus*, the East Frankish style of the Winchester sequences, Ælfric's rhythmical works – all fit together, linked by attention to rhythm as a stylistic feature in prose. Especially germane to this point is Ælfric's English-language grammar of Latin, which he based on the belief that both English and Latin could be understood through a single, shared set of grammatical categories expressed in the vernacular.[64] Indeed, Latin, with its well-defined inflectional and orthographic systems, seems to have been the model for Ælfric's and Æthelwold's efforts at standardizing English.[65]

61 For an edition and translation of Lantfred's *Translatio*, see Lapidge, *Cult of St Swithun*, 215–333.

62 Lapidge (ibid., 224–32) analyses Lantfred's prose style in detail.

63 On the possibility of Ælfric importing Latin style into Old English, see Gerould, "Abbot Ælfric's Rhythmic Prose"; Bethurum, "Form of Ælfric's *Lives of Saints*"; Pope, ed., *Homilies of Ælfric*, 1:108–12; and Nichols, "Ælfric and the Brief Style," 10–12.

64 For arguments that Ælfric indeed intended his treatise to apply to English, see Sisam, "The Order of Ælfric's Early Books," 301; Menzer, "Ælfric's *Grammar*" and "Ælfric's English *Grammar*." On the other hand, Law, "Anglo-Saxon England," argues that the treatise focuses solely on Latin.

65 Gretsch, "Ælfric, Language, and Winchester," 128.

A contemporary of Wulfstan Cantor, Ælfric was certainly familiar with Wulfstan's work, since he reworked Wulfstan's *Life of St Æthelwold*. Ælfric would have been familiar with the Winchester sequence corpus as well, whether or not any were composed by Wulfstan. Given Ælfric's interest in Latin and knowledge of the specific material in question, his homilies and saints' lives make a good deal of sense as products of a Winchester that attended to rhythm as an important, cross-linguistic feature of style.

This attention to form and style is not surprising for Winchester compositions, considering the prevalence and evident importance of the so-called hermeneutic style in Winchester's Latin works. The defining elements of this style, as it is currently understood, are a focus on form and the employment of elevated or poetic registers even in prose.[66] Moreover, in his *Enchiridion*, Byrhtferth presents knowledge of Latin and mastery of this challenging style as defining features of Benedictine monastics in Anglo-Saxon England.[67] The most common – or at least the most noticed – feature of the style is its difficult and rare vocabulary, once thought to have been culled from Greek-Latin glossaries known as "hermeneumata."[68] Ælfric's Latin works conspicuously avoid the showy vocabulary characteristic of the hermeneutic style, seemingly setting him apart as an exception to this Winchester practice.[69] The hermeneutic style, however, makes the most sense when understood less as an exercise in deploying difficult vocabulary and more as an evocation of poetic resonance in multiple ways, including but not limited to vocabulary, syntax, and rhyme.[70] As another widespread element of the Winchester style, attention to rhythm can also be seen as an evocation of poetic discourse, especially when considered in the light of Old English poetry. Indeed, Ælfric's rhythmical compositions adhere to the rules of late Old English metre and are thus considered

66 See primarily Winterbottom, "Style of Æthelweard"; Lapidge, "Hermeneutic Style" and "Poeticism"; Stephenson, "Ælfric of Eynsham," 117–24 and "Scapegoating the Secular Clergy," 107–12.

67 See Stephenson, "Scapegoating the Secular Clergy."

68 Lapidge, "Hermeneutic Style," 105n2, and Stephenson, "Scapegoating the Secular Clergy," 108.

69 Lapidge, "Hermeneutic Style," 139; Jones, "*Meatim sed et rustica*"; and Stephenson, "Ælfric of Eynsham."

70 Lapidge, "Poeticism"; Stephenson, "Ælfric of Eynsham," 117–24, and "Scapegoating the Secular Clergy," 107–12.

poetry by some.[71] Moreover, Ælfric himself identifies metre as the defining feature differentiating prose from poetry.[72] In this sense, then, he employs a device of poetry in what many still consider prose, a move very much in line with the fundamental strategy of the hermeneutic style, if not its most obvious specific tactics.

Ælfric's avoidance of the highest discourse register in his vocabulary but employment of some poetic elements elsewhere again links him with the sequence genre specifically. Although some Winchester sequences employ the difficult vocabulary characteristic of the hermeneutic style, most do not.[73] Moreover, both corpora have suffered the same fate in that they have sometimes been described as "artsy prose"; indeed sequences have literally been termed "art-prose" (*Kunstprosa*) by many scholars.[74] The ill-defined nature of these texts has sometimes made it difficult to determine exactly how to approach them, but perhaps this hybrid register resonated with Ælfric. Sequences were mass pieces, and most were likely intended for more general consumption than hermeneutic compositions, which often impeded access by all but the most learned with their unusual vocabulary. Ælfric's interests in pedagogy and accessibility precluded the highest register, but, given his application of the patterns of Old English metre, he clearly was uninterested in the lowest. What he achieves with his rhythmical style is what the sequences also achieve: a middle way involving elevated aspects but also avoidance of extremity. Hermeneutic Latin may have been the flagship mode of expression for Winchester compositions, but the sequences and Ælfric's rhythmical works are not as far removed as scholars once thought. Looking at Winchester style cross-linguistically in this way returns Ælfric to the fold, as it were, and demonstrates that the features of the sequences discussed here fit well into the larger picture of Winchester's intellectual identity.

71 See Skeat, *Ælfric's Lives of Saints*, 1:vi–vii; Bredehoft, *Early English Metre*, 70–98; and Beechy, *Poetics of Old English*. However, see Clemoes, "Ælfric"; Pope, *Homilies of Ælfric*, 1:105; and Mitchell, "Relation."

72 Zupitza, ed., *Ælfrics Grammatik*, 295–6.

73 See, for example, *Gaudens Christi* (edited in *AH* 40:337, and Lapidge, *Cult of St Swithun*, 97–8), which employs several lexical features characteristic of Winchester's hermeneutic style (Lapidge, *Cult of St Swithun*, 98).

74 See, for example, the discussion of the genre in Mantello and Rigg, eds., *Medieval Latin*, 601.

The sequences need not have *directly* influenced Ælfric; these approaches to style emerge so ubiquitously that they seem to have suffused the Winchester milieu. What becomes clear from this discussion, then, is that meticulous attention to language – not just one language or another, but language in general along with its stylistic and performative aspects – was a central, even defining, element of the intellectual identity at Winchester. The standardization of English, the Winchester vocabulary, the hermeneutic style, Ælfric's rhythms, the careful rhythms of the sequences – they all coalesce around general interest in language, both Latin and English. Perhaps this generalized linguistic interest was inspired by the supreme Anglo-Saxon scholarly exemplars of Aldhelm and Bede; perhaps by the works of Isidore; perhaps by the biblical centrality of the word. Regardless of its source, this interest is clearly present in a good portion of the sequences composed at Winchester, and ultimately it is quite fitting that the creation and maintenance of a distinctively "Winchesterian" intellectual identity within the bounds of Continental traditions should manifest itself through the sequence genre, since the sequence is itself a blend of the traditional (melody) and the novel (text).[75] So too with Winchester in general: building ultimately from the unique character of Aldhelm's work and nurtured by the international intellectual milieu at Æthelstan's court, Æthelwold founded an intellectual community that blended the Continental with the uniquely Anglo-Saxon.[76] This distinctive intellectual activity continued in the production of new sequence texts at Winchester, where the monastic community seized upon what may have been no more than a wisp of East Frankish tradition and blended it into the community's generally West Frankish liturgical identity and Anglo-Saxon intellectual roots. Study of the Winchester sequences thus ultimately reveals a community carving out and maintaining metaphorical space for its own intellectual identity, constructing a hybrid with two Continental traditions grafted onto its own native stem.[77]

75 Hiley, "Changes in English Chant Repertories," 137.

76 Gretsch, *Intellectual Foundations*, passim and summarized on 427.

77 This chapter benefited from, and I am indebted to, the advice of Calvin Bower, Sarah Davis-Secord, Michael Lapidge, Julia Schneider, and this volume's editors. All errors remain my own.

Saint Who? Building Monastic Identity through Computistical Inquiry in Byrhtferth's *Vita S. Ecgwini*

REBECCA STEPHENSON

While some saints, like the Venerable Bede, leave rich historical evidence of their presence, other saints, like St Ecgwine recorded by Byrhtferth of Ramsey, leave far fewer documents for the medieval hagiographer.[1] Michael Lapidge writes of St Ecgwine, "he was a very obscure saint indeed. Bede knows nothing of him. He is nowhere mentioned in the *Anglo-Saxon Chronicle*. There are very few early charters, in which Ecgwine is mentioned or appears as a witness, that are undoubtedly genuine."[2] In the absence of information about deeds, life history, or other distinguishing material, the hagiographer is free – and indeed required – to flesh out the saint's life as best as he or she can, incorporating common motifs, tropes, bits from other saints' lives, and stylistic tricks in order to develop a cult and an argument for sainthood. Unconstrained by facts or actual events, these otherwise unknown saints provide the perfect *tabula rasa* onto which the hagiographer can project issues surrounding both his own and the saint's respective identities. These saintly blank slates, therefore, provide an important context in which modern scholars can view the processes by which hagiographers form individual and corporate identities.

The process of identity formation is particularly on display in the life of St Ecgwine because, unlike the contemporary narratives of the equally unknown Swithun, which generally avoid his life and focus instead on his

1 All references to the *Vita S. Ecgwini* (abbreviated as *VSE*) will come from the standard edition: Lapidge, ed., *Byrhtferth of Ramsey: The Lives of St Oswald and St Ecgwine*, 205–303. This text supersedes the edition by J.A. Giles, "Vita Sancti Ecgwini," 349–96.

2 Lapidge, ed., *VSE*, 294.

translation and ensuing miracles,[3] Byrhtferth invents a life for Ecgwine in an endeavour of hagiographical fiction. In order to concoct this life, Byrhtferth claims to have cobbled together information from various sources including an old charter, which Michael Lapidge has shown to be spurious.[4] Rather than the sources that Byrhtferth claims to have used, it seems that he has in fact woven together a variety of literary texts common from the Anglo-Saxon monastic schoolroom with a toponymic miracle explaining the naming of Evesham.[5] Since the life itself is relatively free from facts or events, the style, literary allusions, and computistical digressions that would normally be in the periphery of a vita are pushed from the background into the foreground and become a major argument for Ecgwine's sainthood. Elsewhere I have argued that the style of this piece, the so-called hermeneutic style, encodes a certain kind of monastic identity, since the difficulty of reading and composing in this style offers proof of steady and sustained study, practices encouraged by the Rule of St Benedict.[6] Here, I will argue that the study of computus in the late tenth and early eleventh century is part and parcel of the same kind of identity formation. Byrhtferth's deployment of arithmetical and computistical information in a hagiographical work establishes sanctity for an otherwise unknown saint by situating Ecgwine in the intellectual context and language of a monastic schoolroom. In fact, these combined linguistic and esoteric concerns of computus and the hermeneutic style come to drive the plot and narrative of this tale, when actual events were otherwise lacking. Computus is a fertile field for this type of identity formation, since its mathematical and scientific foundations allow it to create relationships that appear to be natural and stable, but are in fact just as contrived as any other part of this narrative.

There is nothing new in my suggestion that the study of computus comprised an important aspect of monastic study during the Benedictine Reform. The prevalence of computistical inquiry in the late Anglo-Saxon

3 The four Anglo-Saxon lives of St Swithun can be found in Lapidge, *Cult of St Swithun*. The manuscript context of Lantfred of Winchester's *Translatio et miracula S. Swithuni* is relevant, since this work immediately follows Byrhtferth's *Vita S. Ecgwini* in Cotton Nero E.i, pt. 1 (a manuscript otherwise known as part 1 of the Cotton-Corpus Legendary).

4 Lapidge, "Byrhtferth and *Vita S. Ecgwini*," 305–6.

5 The sources and structure of Ecgwine's life are discussed in Lapidge, ed., *VSE*, lxxxiii–lxxxv.

6 Stephenson, "Scapegoating the Secular Clergy."

period is well documented by scholarship.[7] Byrhtferth presumably learned his computus from the great Benedictine and computist Abbo of Fleury, who was exiled at Ramsey from 985 to 987.[8] At the same time that Abbo was encouraging computistical exploration at Byrhtferth's home in Ramsey, the important reformed centre, Winchester, developed a standard computus.[9] Before the *Enchiridion*, Byrhtferth composed a computus in Latin, and Ælfric of Eynsham wrote *De temporibus anni*, which introduces the scientific aspects related to computus in an English-language format.[10] Byrhtferth's own comments in the *Enchiridion* further suggest a close monastic connection to computus, since he narrates the Legend of St Pachomius, the story of a monastic saint who received the Paschal verses from divine inspiration.

What is new, however, is to suggest that the practice of computus was constitutive of monastic identity in a manner similar to how the hermeneutic style suggests monastic affiliations for its users. When Dunstan's biographer petitioned to return to England, he composed in the hermeneutic style as a bid for favour from his English Benedictine superiors. Equally, nearly every named author connected to the Benedictine Reform – with the obvious exception of Ælfric – composed something in this style, including Æthelwold, Lantfred of Winchester, Wulfstan of Winchester, Frithegod of Canterbury, and Byrhtferth of Ramsey, to name a few.[11] Equally, a surprising number of manuscripts that contain documents constitutive of monastic identity, such as the *Regularis concordia* and the Rule of St Benedict, share space in their quires with computistical tables and treatises.[12] In addition,

7 For an introduction to the functional role of computus in Anglo-Saxon society, see Liuzza, "In Measure." For a more basic introduction to computistical terms, see Beate Günzel's introduction to *Ælfwine's Prayerbook*. For the history of computus, see Wallis, *Bede: The Reckoning of Time*, xviii–lxiii.

8 Baker and Lapidge, eds., *Byrhtferth's Enchiridion*, xx–xxiii.

9 The Winchester computus is reflected in Cotton Titus D.xxvi and xxvii (the *Prayerbook of Ælfwine*), Cambridge, Trinity College R. 15. 32, pp. 15–36, British Library, Cotton Vitellius E.xviii, British Library, Arundel 60, and Cotton Tiberius C.vi fols. 2r–7r. For a discussion and its relationship to Byrhtferth's computus, see Wallis, "Background Essay."

10 Ælfric's *De temporibus* has been released in a new edition by Martin Blake.

11 For a full history of the literary background of the Benedictine Reform, see the introduction to my *Politics of Language*. Ælfric's refusal to compose in the hermeneutic style is widely noted, particularly by Jones, "*Meatim sed et rustica*"; my "Ælfric of Eynsham"; and chap. 5 of my *Politics of Language*.

12 Cotton Tiberius A.iii offers a good example of monastic texts in close proximity to computistical texts, but one could also point to Ælfwine's Prayerbook, which combined computistical material with devotional material and was created for a Benedictine monk.

manuscripts that combine Anglo-Saxon curriculum authors prized by reformers, such as book 3 of Abbo's *Bella Parisiacae urbis*, with computistical works show how the discipline of writing in the hermeneutic style closely relates to the study of the more recherché realms of computus.[13] Both tend to be somewhat esoteric. While the hermeneutic style revels in rare vocabulary, Roy Liuzza argues that the monks structured their time by the liturgical year, a practice which would have been subtly distinct from that of the average Anglo-Saxon, who was likely more focused on agrarian concerns like the seasons and harvest.[14] Furthermore, since Benedictines were usually given as oblates,[15] it is possible that knowledge of computus might replace subtle nuances of the agrarian seasons that would be more common to their counterparts among the laity or the secular clergy. Equally, neither computus nor the hermeneutic style is intuitive, and they require skills to master, skills that come only from books. Although computus would seem to be accomplished by observing the heavens, the many collections of Easter tables and computistical material in fact encourage the study of written texts that replace the natural world. In the same way, the hermeneutic style is a highly literate phenomenon that is based on the strategic deployment of poetic language in order to reach an elevated style. Just as I have argued elsewhere that the practice of writing in the hermeneutic style shows the discipline of the monastic author and his distance from the affairs of the non-monastic clergy,[16] in the same way, serious knowledge of computistical esoterica shows a monk's discipline in his mastery of intricate details and his attention to liturgical affairs, rather than secular ones.

Discovering Computus in the *VSE*

One of the first problems when discussing how computus influences a hagiographical text is that the range of texts and fields considered by a medieval author to be computistical differs substantially from our own narrow

13 One example of this combination is Harley 3271.

14 Liuzza, "Anglo-Saxon Prognostics in Context," 211. These themes are more fully investigated in the introduction to his later edition *Anglo-Saxon Prognostics*.

15 For Byrhtferth's references to oblation in his community, see my *Politics of Language*, chap. 2. For a more general discussion of child oblation in early Anglo-Saxon England, see Foot, *Monastic Life*, 140–5. For a thorough discussion of child oblation centred on Carolingian Europe, see de Jong, *In Samuel's Image*. See also Nelson, "Parents, Children and the Church," with discussion of rituals concerning oblation at 107–12.

16 Stephenson, "Scapegoating the Secular Clergy."

definition, particularly as modern scholars divide computistical (computations of moveable feasts) from prognostical (computations about more superstitious concerns, e.g., good days for blood-letting) texts. Karen Jolly emphasizes the connections between computistical knowledge and prognostical healing calculations, since the Anglo-Saxons believed that the microcosm and the macrocosm were closely connected. Although Byrhtferth never discusses prognostical healing texts per se, Jolly argues, "Knowledge of astronomy, calendars, and computations constituted the skills of the literate few, who endeavored to create an accurate calendar, primarily for such religious purposes as the dating of Easter, but also for the healer."[17] László Sándor Chardonnens in his work on Anglo-Saxon prognostics further argues against an easy distinction between prognostical and computistical material during the Anglo-Saxon period, saying, "A corpus of prognostics does not exist as such: it is a group of writings which exist as a coherent unit in our minds only."[18] In the same way, the generic designation of computistical texts, as those treatises that calculate the date of Easter or the chronology of the world, probably is a designation with greater relevance to modern rather than medieval readers. Many manuscripts commonly include prognostical texts among what we might more carefully define as computistical texts.[19] Even manuscripts strongly connected to reformed centres show a similar conflation between orthodox computistical material and superstitious prognostical formulae, including Ælfwine's Prayerbook, said to be the personal prayerbook of the abbot of New Minster at Winchester,[20] or Cotton Tiberius A.iii, one of main texts of the *Regularis concordia*.[21] Although Ælfric certainly made statements in his sermons that have been construed as a rejection of prognostical texts, Liuzza argues that these remarks were directly from his source and did not address contemporary prognostical texts.[22] Furthermore, the combination of prognostical material in Anglo-Saxon manuscripts suggests that easy distinctions did not hold for many medieval authors, even those of the Benedictine Reform.

17 Jolly, *Popular Religion*, 113.

18 Chardonnens, ed., *Anglo-Saxon Prognostics*, 8–9.

19 For a full handlist of prognostical texts, see Liuzza, *Anglo-Saxon Prognostics*, 3–23.

20 For an edition, see Günzel, *Ælfwine's Prayerbook*.

21 For an edition, see Liuzza, *Anglo-Saxon Prognostics*.

22 Liuzza, "Anglo-Saxon Prognostics in Context," 193. Ælfric's comments are found in *Catholic Homilies* I.7 lines 116–23.

While Byrhtferth's writings do not require a consideration of the full range of prognostical texts, they do require a more complete understanding of how the calculation of liturgical feasts might bear on the human subject. Byrhtferth's famous diagram from Oxford, St John's College 17, a manuscript commonly regarded as Byrhtferth's computus,[23] vividly shows how computistical inquiry incorporates the interrelationships between the heavens, the human body, and astronomy. The outside arc represents the heavens and contains the names of the zodiac, while the centre of the diagram represents the earth with the four cardinal points. In between these two realms lies a diamond with roundels with the ages of man inscribed. Faith Wallis describes this middle circuit: "hanging between heaven and earth, these roundels are a graphic statement of man's amphibious nature, linked to the heavens through the stages of life as microcosm of celestial time, and to the earth through the name of Adam, formed from the initial letters of the Greek names of the cardinal directions."[24] In addition to this metaphysical consideration of man's place in the universe, the daily practice of computus was written onto the physical routines of the medieval monk in a far more practical way, since, as Roy Liuzza explains, "Monastic discipline is first and foremost a temporal discipline of punctuality and accurate timekeeping. The spiritual life was shaped by the cycles of the calendar – fasts and feasts, psalms and prayers, repentance and celebration were all performed according to calendrical calculations, and their observance was an outward sign of the universal unity of the Church. The *Regularis concordia*, whatever else it may be, is an elaborate timetable."[25] While the *Regularis concordia* is more commonly classified as a monastic customary, not a computistical text, Liuzza's assertion that timekeeping lies at the heart of monastic practice shows the broad range of texts that are inextricably interwoven with the monastic practice of computus. Equally, the writings of Bede show the wide range of genres in which computus can have a powerful influence, since he places the Synod of Whitby's Easter controversy at the centre of his *Historia ecclesiastica*.[26] In addition, Wallis

23 Baker, "Byrhtferth's *Enchiridion*." Faith Wallis has made this manuscript available online at *The Calendar and the Cloister*.

24 Wallis, *Calendar and Cloister*, Commentary on 7v (accessed 27 July 2012).

25 Liuzza, "Anglo-Saxon Prognostics in Context," 207.

26 "Bede's narrative of history and identity is framed by measurement and nature – in this case, by the problem of how divinely instituted natural time and the injunctions of the Bible could be faithfully mirrored in the timekeeping practices of the Christian people." Wallis, "Bede and Science," 113.

has argued that Bede's story of Cædmon has profound computistical implications.[27] It seems that for serious practictioners of computus, this discipline comes to pervade diverse works and genres that include monastic customaries, histories (especially regarding chronology),[28] and saints' lives. This range of textual material shows the central role of computistical inquiry in considering man's place in the universe, and, thus, computistical concerns become the glue that holds together the *VSE*.

An emphasis on numbers drives the discussion in certain sections of this saint's life. Notice the interweaving of arithmetical information in the following passage that occurs immediately after the description of the death of Ecgwine:

> Dominus Iesus octaua Kalendis Ianuarii erat natus in terris; Ecguuinus sanctus presul tertia Kalendis eiusdem mensis perducitur celis. Senarius numerus perfectus est, quia eodem die formauit protoplastum, in quo et istum transmisit ad celi gaudium. Si diuiseris hunc calculum (quem quidam "rithmum," nonnulli "laterculum" dicunt), inuenies fructum opimum et "opipare," quod nos "splendide" dicere possumus, <decoratum>. Si unum detraxeris, significat unitatem que est in Deo (quia unus est Deus), duo que secuntur, dilectionem Dei et proximi; tres quoque fidem, spem et caritatem congruenter demonstrant. Dominus quidem Iesus ante sex dies natus est in aruis; iste post sex dies perductus est ad astrigena regna glorie celestis – prestante gratia saluatoris nostri, qui cum patre sempiterno et almo flamine unus Deus in trinitate et trinus in unitate regnat et gloriatur per omnia secla seclorum. AMEN.[29]
>
> [The Lord Jesus was born on earth on the eighth kalends of January [i.e., December 25]; the bishop, St Ecgwine, was led into heaven on the third kalends of this same month [i.e., December 30]. The number six is perfect, because on that day he formed the first man [i.e., Adam], and even on that same day, he sent this same man [i.e., Ecgwine] to the joy of heaven. If you divide this sum (which some call "rithmus" and others "laterculus"), you will find reward that is rich and opiparously – which we may render "splendidly" – adorned.

27 Wallis, "Cædmon's Created World."

28 Calvin B. Kendall and Faith Wallis argue that Bede's computistical work was essential for his historical work, in which he created a new chronology that separated "the six World-Ages from a Septuagint *annus mundi* chronology" (*On the Nature of Things*, 30).

29 Lapidge, *VSE*, 278–80. All translations are mine, unless otherwise indicated.

> If you subtract one, it signifies the unity which is in God (because God is one), and the two that follow, the love of God and neighbour; the remaining three fitly represent faith, hope, and charity. Indeed the Lord Jesus was born on the earth six days before; this man was led to the starry realms of heavenly glory six days afterward – through the provision of the grace of our saviour, who with the eternal Father and the nurturing breath [i.e., Holy Spirit] as one God in trinity and threefold in unity reigns and rejoices and is glorified throughout all ages. Amen.]

Some might argue that this is not computus by any strict definition, but is rather an arithmetical discussion or perhaps numerology. But Byrhtferth would certainly have called this information computus, since most of the passage has roots in the numerological discussion that comprises the *Enchiridion*'s book 4.1, a text commonly described as a bilingual commentary on computus. As an extra piece of evidence that this would have been understood as a computistical passage, Byrhtferth uses the word "calculus," which in the *Enchiridion* he claims is the Macedonian word for "computus." The very similar passage at the beginning of the *Enchiridion* reads, "Compotus, Grece ciclus aut rithmus, secundum Egiptios latercus, iuxta Macedones dicitur calculus."[30]

Byrhtferth's use of the word "calculus" shows the close interaction of computistical information with the hermeneutic style, since this word, while not quite hermeneutic, show some idiosyncracies characteristic of the style. I translate it as "sum" since the Latin word "calculus" is a stone used in Roman calculations, and this stone can stand in metonymically for the process of calculating as a whole. Lapidge, however, translated it simply as "number," which as a translation makes better sense in English, since Byrhtferth seems to be using it as an identical synonym employed in free variation with that much simpler word. What makes this passage characteristic of the hermeneutic style is what follows: Byrhtferth has indulged in one of his favourite pastimes, glossing a relatively common, though strange, word with complex and unusual words. He explains "hunc calculum (quem quidam 'rithmum,' nonnulli 'laterculum' dicunt)" (This calculation (which some call "rithmus" and others "laterculus")).[31] Given the previous passage

30 "Computus is cycle or rhythm in Greek, among the Egyptians is 'latercus,' and according to the Macedonians is called 'calculus.'" Baker and Lapidge, eds., *Byrhtferth's Enchiridion*, 2.

31 Ibid., 2.

from the *Enchiridion*, it is immediately apparent that these synonyms are inspired by the discussion of computus that opens the other work. They do not, however, clarify the meaning of "calculus," but are instead added for their ornamental value. The end result is that any slight nuance of meaning between these words is lost as the explanatory synonyms become increasingly esoteric and rare. In the end, "numerus" carries the same meaning as "calculus," "rithmus," or "laterculus."

Interestingly enough, the words that would be identified as characteristic of the hermeneutic style are also related to Byrhtferth's computistical text, the *Enchiridion*. For instance, the word "opipare" is an archaism used in the *Enchiridion* in a very similar context to that recorded here, "videat sinceritas studiorum qualiter fructuosus duodenarius numerus fit opipare (id est splendide) decoratus" (Let the sincerity of our study see how the fruitful number twelve is richly (that is splendidly) decorated).[32] The words "fructum," "opipare," "splendide," and presumably "decoratum" are borrowed almost exactly from this earlier work. In addition, another feature of the hermeneutic style common to Byrhtferth is the use of partitive adjectives in place of cardinal numbers, as we saw in the "duodenarius numerus" of the previous passage from the *Enchiridion*. In the life of St Ecgwine, Byrhtferth has chosen the partitive form "senarius numerus" in place of the cardinal number "sex." While "senarius" is the customary form in conjunction with "numerus," the preference for this ADJ+NOUN formula rather than the simpler "sex" seems to be based in an ornamental affectation, rather than a nuance in the kind of number under discussion.

As a final example of the conflation between computistical features and those that mark this text as typical of the hermeneutic style, I offer the line "Dominus quidem Iesus ante sex dies natus est in aruis; iste post sex dies perductus est ad astrigena regna glorie celestis" (The Lord Jesus was born on earth on the eighth kalends of January [i.e., December 25]; the bishop, St Ecgwine, was led into heaven on the third kalends of this same month [i.e., December 30]).[33] Lapidge suggests that "in arvis ... ad astrigena" is a variation of the common Byrhtferthian formula of "in arvis ... in astris" (on the earth as in heaven).[34] Since this formulation seems to have its roots in poetry, it should be considered as characteristic of the hermeneutic

32 Lapidge, ed., *VSE*, 220.

33 Ibid., 278.

34 The full list of Byrhtferthian usage is in the notes for the *Vita S. Oswaldi* in ibid., 42n43.

style, which tends to use poetic conventions in prose.[35] While this idea is not explicitly related to computus, it does reflect the essential thesis of computistical inquiry, namely that the movements of the heavens accord in important ways with events on earth.

Beyond vocabulary and style, an arithmetical calculation plays an important role in the argument for Ecgwine's sanctity. He died on December 30, not in itself a significant date, except for the fact that it is six days (counting inclusively) from the nativity of Christ. Byrhtferth outlines the importance of the number 6 as the sum of 1, 2, and 3. The static nature of the figures and the authority of the interpretations, which in this case comes from Augustine (through Bede),[36] makes the positive associations with six appear to be relatively stable. The suggestion that six's exceptional nature comes from its constituent parts undermines this façade of stability, however, since the act of interpretation is thereby dependent on one's ability to manipulate numbers. A computist could always add or subtract in order to reach more felicitous numbers. Furthermore, while the number six receives a relatively thorough treatment in the *Enchridion* and is recognized as a "perfect" number since it is both the sum of 1+2+3 and the product of 1×2×3, a thorough reading of book 4 would assure a reader that Byrhtferth could have assigned equal importance to a date four, five, or ten days after Christ's birth, since all of these days are considered by Byrhtferth to be perfect.

And yet it is unclear what makes a number "perfect" for Byrhtferth. He certainly does not intend this word to mean what it does for mathematicians, since in addition to six, he considers two, four, five, nine, and ten to be "perfectus" as well. According to mathematics, a perfect number is one that is equivalent to the sum of its divisors. The smallest perfect number is six (1+2+3), followed by twenty-eight (1+2+4+7+14).[37] Yet Byrhtferth claims, "Quaternarius perfectus est numerus et quattuor uirtutibus exornatus: iustitia uidelicet, temperantia, fortitudine, prudentia" (Four is the perfect number and is adorned by the four virtues, namely justice, temperance, fortitude, and prudence).[38] Byrhtferth glosses this in English as "þæt

35 Lapidge, "Poeticism in Pre-Conquest Anglo-Latin Prose."

36 Byrhtferth bases his discussion on chapter 39 of Bede's *De temporum ratione*, which is based on a similar discussion in Augustine's *De trinitate*. Full discussion of both passages is found in Lapidge, ed., *VSE*, 278n44.

37 I would like to thank my colleague Brent Strunk for helping me understand the proper mathematical definition of perfect numbers.

38 Baker and Lapidge, eds., *Byrhtferth's Enchiridion*, 198.

feowerfealde fulfremed ys getæl and mid feower mægnum homo byð gewurðod" (That fourfold number is perfect and homo [man] is adorned with four virtues) and then goes on to list English translations of the virtues.[39] Byrhtferth's terminology is confusing, since *perfectus* is often used in a technical sense (either in the grammatical sense of a perfect tense or in the mathematical sense of a perfect number) and a form of *fulfremed* is the preferred translation for these Latin concepts. However, sometimes *fulfremed* renders *perfectus* in a more general sense to mean *completed*, as in Genesis 1:31, in which "ða wæron *fulfremode* heofonas & eorðe & eall heora frætewung" (The heavens and earth were completed and all their adornments).[40] Therefore, what Byrhtferth means by the number four being perfect is far from crystal clear. But yet, four's perfection probably lies not in mathematical theory but in the important correspondences between the heavens and the earth, as are outlined in his diagram in *Enchiridion* 4.1.

While Byrhtferth makes the value of a number like six appear to be natural, in effect, such numbers are composed of essentially separate numbers, which Byrhtferth can add and subtract at will in order to reach more advantageous numbers, many of which can later be declared "perfect," whether in a technical sense or not. The ease with which Byrhtferth declares a number to be perfect, and the ability to manipulate those very numbers through mathematical equations, suggest that through the knowledge of arithmetical trivia a Benedictine monk can create truths that appear to be static, and even natural, despite their essential malleability. Therefore, in this passage's sophisticated combination of the hermeneutic style and computus, Byrhtferth creates sanctity for Ecgwine by equating him to Christ through the flexible instrument of addition, while simultaneously bolstering his own credentials as a hagiographer by showing his knowledge of the hermeneutic style and computus, both of which were essential studies for a Benedictine monk.

The Narrative of Computus

This interest in numbers and computistical concerns drives the *VSE* from the very beginning, as it opens with a scholarly preface in the hermeneutic style that sets Ecgwine's life into the schema of salvation history and

---

39 Ibid.

40 These results were retrieved from the *Dictionary of Old English Web Corpus*, accessed 26 February 2013.

computistical inquiry. In this passage, Byrhtferth establishes the structural plan of the work, which is meant to follow a strictly numerological format. Byrhtferth explains the fourfold division in the preface as "Constat istius uita breuiter edita et in bis binis partibus diuisa; que quattuor partes demonstrant quid in pueritia uel adolescentia siue in iuuentute atque in senectute gessit" (The life of this man appears briefly published and divided into two times two parts; these four parts demonstrate what he did in childhood, adolescence, as a young man, and an old man).[41] This arrangement implies that part 1 narrates childhood, part 2 adolescence, part 3 the events of adulthood, and part 4 the affairs of his old age. Such a structure would be appealing to Byrhtferth's inner computist, who focused a fair bit of his scholarly work on the cosmic alignment of fours, as can be seen by his famous diagram, which positions the four ages of man in accordance with the seasons, the elements, the four directions, the zodiac, the four letters of Adam's name, and so on. Yet, this numerological structure is not conventional in saints' lives, which ordinarily narrate only a few select events from childhood and adolescence, so that the text can be focused on the adult actions of a saint along with a judicious helping of posthumous miracles. Despite Byrhtferth's elaborate numerical plan laid out in the preface, the text of Ecgwine's life proceeds in the customary way, quickly ticking off the events of his childhood, adolescence, and even much of his adulthood in part 1.

Beyond the failed plan of the preface, computistical concerns continue to drive the narrative from the very beginning of part 1, which concerns itself more with positioning the saint in the midst of salvation history than with physical details of his life. This section opens with neither Ecgwine nor his birth, but with Adam, moving quickly through a religious genealogy to the link with Christ, and followed by the martyrs and the confessors, thereby establishing Ecgwine's place in salvation history as a confessor. Just as the roundels of Byrhtferth's diagram hang between heaven and earth, so Ecgwine is situated above the plane of normal humans, but below Christ and the apostles, clearly positioned as a saint within the larger global community of saints. After this contextualization among the communion of saints, the events from childhood and adolescence are relatively stock for Anglo-Saxon saints: he was born of noble lineage and the

41 Lapidge, ed., *VSE*, 210.

early parts of his education are outlined, an important detail for the education-obsessed Benedictines. Then Byrhtferth moves on to Ecgwine's path on his sacerdotal career, quickly progressing to his appointment as bishop and his trip to Rome to receive the pallium. Taken from a large view, the structure of the earliest part of Ecgwine's life can be seen to be driven, not by details of plot, but rather by membership in communities, specifically his identity as a confessor and a monk.

The computistical material of the text is heavily involved in his membership in the monastic community, since the study of computus is often connected to monasticism, not just in monastic classrooms and monastic texts, but in the mythos that surrounds the study of computus, as can be seen in the Legend of St Pachomius recorded in Byrhtferth's *Enchiridion*. This text provides an originary narrative for the preservation and regulation of the study of computus. St Pachomius is a fourth-century Egyptian saint who is sometimes called the founder of monasticism, or at least the kind of organized, communal monasticism headed by an abbot and practised by Benedictine reformers.[42] I have printed the Old English prose legend as it appears in Byrhtferth's *Enchiridion*. Below that, I have printed the text in Latin, as it appears in Oxford, St John's College 17, the manuscript that holds Byrhtferth's diagram. The Latin text is quite common and similar to that in the Leofric Missal, the Missal of Robert of Jumièges, and several other computistical manuscripts (including Berlin 138).[43]

> We witon geare þæt þær næs æt ne gediht ne Virgilius gesetnyss, ne þæs wurðfullan Platonis fandung oððe Socratis his lareowes smeagung, ac we prutlice gecyðað uplendiscum preostum þæt we be þissum circule gerædd habbað: "An abbod wæs on Egipta lande fullfremed on Godes gesihðe, Pac<o>mius genemed on naman gefege. He abæd æt þam mihtigan Drihtne mid eallum his munucheape þæt he him mildelice gecydde hwær hyt rihtlicost wære þæt man þa Easterlican tide mid Godes rihte, þæne Pascan, healdan sceolde. Him sona of heofena mihte com unasecgendlic myrhð, engla sum mid blisse, se þas word geypte and þæne abbod gegladode and þas uers him mid gyldenum stafum awritene on þam handum betæhte, þe þus wæron on his spræce gedihte:

42 For the development of the legend of Pachomius, see Jones, "A Legend of St. Pachomius."
43 Baker and Lapidge, eds., *Byrhtferth's Enchiridion*, 420.

None Aprilis norunt quinos
eall to þam ende.[44]

[We know readily that there has been no literary work nor composition of Vergil, nor investigation by the worthy Plato, nor inquiry by his teacher Socrates concerning this cycle, but we proudly make known to the rustic clerics what we have read: "There was an abbot in Egypt who was perfect in God's sight, called Pachomius by name. He prayed to the mighty Lord with all of his company of monks that he mercifully make known to him when it was most correct to celebrate the Eastertide, or Paschal feast, according to God's ordinance. Immediately, by the power of heaven came unspeakable joy, an angel with grace, who made known these words and made the abbot glad and delivered these verses written with golden letters into his hands, which were thus composed in his language:

'The nones of April know five …
all the way to the end."]

Legimus in epistolis Grecorum quod post passionem apostolorum sanctus Pachomius abbas in Aegipto cum monachis suis in oratione a Domino rogauerit ut ostenderit eis quomodo Pascha deberent celebrare, et misit Dominus angelum suum et scripsit ad prephatum Pachomium cyclum nonodecimalem in uno philacterio hoc modo.[45]

[We have read in the letters of Greeks that after the passion of the apostles, St Pachomius, who was an abbot in Egypt, in prayer with his monks beseeched from the Lord that he show to them how they should celebrate Easter, and the Lord sent his angel and wrote to the aforementioned Pachomius the nineteen-year cycle on a phylactery in this manner.]

The verse "None Aprilis" that Pachomius allegedly receives from the angel is an easily memorized way to perform Easter calculations, without complicated formulae. This verse is often transmitted in computistical manuscripts and is much more common and much earlier than the prose legend that accompanies it. Notably, the verses themselves make no reference to St Pachomius and are only later ascribed to him. In both of these

44 Ibid., 138.
45 Ibid., 420 (Oxford, St John's College 17, 28r).

texts, the monastic connections are emphasized. Pachomius prays not alone, but with his "munucheape," and in the illustrations that accompany Pachomius's prose legend, his retinue of monks are always clearly displayed as an integral part of the image.[46] In Byrhtferth's introduction to this episode, literate monks are contrasted with "rustic clerics," who are here called "uplendiscum preostum" and are often depicted as lacking the same level of education in topics like computus that monks receive as young men.[47] Notably, the divine inspiration of the Pachomius legend is often promulgated by those emphasizing their monastic (as opposed to clerical) identity, since there is a competing story claiming that divine inspiration was given to the Council of Nicaea, founded before religious orders and led by members of the secular clergy.[48] (Incidentally, one story joins these two claims and asserts that the divine inspiration was given to Pachomius, who in turn gave it to the council of Nicaea, again awarding primacy to the monastic connections of computus.)[49]

While the monastic regulation of computus is central to many formulations of the Pachomius narrative, Byrhtferth adds an extra layer of complexity in his Old English text by strongly connecting this incident to the monastic schoolroom. Not only is the doggerel "None Aprilis" alleged to surpass the writings of Vergil (a dubious claim at best), but this section also appears immediately after a very famous passage in which Byrhtferth rejects the Muses, replacing their pagan writings with his Christian interpretation of computus. The dismissal of the Muses is effectively an English translation of a section from the *Carmen de virginitate* written by the Anglo-Saxon curriculum author Aldhelm.[50] By adapting an author as central to the Benedictine educational program as Aldhelm, Byrhtferth redefines both what it is to be an English-language author and the high status that should be accorded to computistical inquiry. Furthermore, in this close joining of Aldhelm and Pachomius, we see the important connections

46 Two Anglo-Saxon manuscripts have images of St Pachomius and his monks, Cotton Caligula A.xv and Arundel 155 (Eadwig Psalter).

47 When Byrhtferth uses the OE word "preost," he is referring exclusively to members of the secular clergy, as opposed to the monastic clergy of which Byrhtferth is a member. For a discussion of this word, see my "Scapegoating the Secular Clergy," 113–14.

48 Jones, "A Legend of St. Pachomius," 208–9.

49 Ibid.

50 Ehwald, *Aldhelmi opera*, 353 lines 23–30 and 356 lines 74–83. For a discussion of this section in the developing literary tradition of the Muses, see Thornbury, "Aldhelm's Rejection," 91.

among computus, monastic identity, and the Anglo-Saxon schoolroom – all of which are very relevant connections to the *VSE*, since Byrhtferth carefully crafted it to appear like many other central texts of the Anglo-Saxon classroom.

The *VSE* in a Monastic Classroom

The moulding of young monks in a monastic classroom provides an important intellectual background to the identity formation occurring in the *VSE*. We do not have evidence that this work was ever used in a classroom, but rather there are several deliberate ways in which Byrhtferth modelled this text after other works common to the Anglo-Saxon curriculum. The preface to the work establishes clear literary connections familiar to a monastic schoolroom. First of all, Byrhtferth explains the work by "tempus," "locus," and "persona," which are categories common to the *accessus ad auctores*, especially those associated with Remigius of Auxerre,[51] who wrote a commentary on Sedulius's *Carmen paschale*. This poetic reworking of the Gospels was a school text of the Anglo-Saxon monastic classroom, and Michael Lapidge argues that Remigius's commentary was also known in late Anglo-Saxon England.[52] While medieval grammarians commonly identify tempus, locus, and persona, as Byrhtferth did, Michael Lapidge explains that "in applying it to a saint rather than a literary work ... [Byrhtferth] imports an individual twist."[53] By explicitly naming these categories in the preface, Byrhtferth writes a kind of critical commentary of the kind that would be found in a schoolroom, at the same time that he writes a text with language and glosses resembling other school texts favoured by reformers, such as Aldhelm's *De virginitate* or Prudentius's *Psychomachia*. Notably, the commentaries on these common school texts were not written by their authors, but by later writers, like Remigius. Thus, the commentaries on these school texts occur as a result of an organic

51 For a discussion of the development of *accessus ad auctores*, see Copeland, *Rhetoric, Hermeneutics, and Translation*, 66–76. For evidence that Byrhtferth used manuscripts that included Remigius's commentary as marginal and interlinear glosses, see Lapidge, "Byrhtferth at Work," 27–34.

52 Lapidge, "The Study of Latin Texts," 481. Byrhtferth cites Remigius in both the *Enchiridion* and the *Vita S. Oswaldi*; for a list of citations, see Lapidge, *The Anglo-Saxon Library*, 273.

53 Lapidge, ed., *VSE*, 210.

process by which medieval texts gather paratexts in the form of lexical and explanatory glosses.[54] By writing the commentary himself, instead of allowing it to accumulate over many years, Byrhtferth automatically elevates his text to one worthy of having such a commentary, and at the same time clearly situates it in a monastic classroom.

In addition to the commentary integrated into the text, the *VSE* seems to have once had an elaborate structure of glosses, which were written by Byrhtferth himself.[55] Although authorship of glosses can be difficult to pin down, Lapidge argued that the glosses to the *VSE* were often written in the first person, employed typically eccentric Byrhtferthian vocabulary, and often quoted nearly directly from the *Enchiridion*, another work by Byrhtferth.[56] In both Cotton Nero E.i and Ashmole 328, the major manuscripts of Byrhtferth's saints' lives and the *Enchiridion*, respectively, the glossing is sporadic, tending to begin thickly in the opening sections, then tapering off or suddenly ceasing, only to reappear later.[57] The fact that the glossing begins and ends as eccentrically as it does suggests that these glosses came from a much more extensively glossed exemplar, but that the scribe became bored by copying the tedious and not entirely helpful commentary, which Lapidge describes as "expansions of the narrative rather than mere explanations of it."[58] Alternatively, if Byrhtferth himself tired of glossing his own text, it would still appear visually similar to many glossed copies of Aldhelm's *De virginitate* that circulated in tenth-century monastic centres and were read in monastic classrooms, many of which were also erratically glossed.[59]

Byrhtferth's reverence for such manuscripts can be seen in his own use of glossed copies of Aldhelm's *De virginitate* and in the heavy stylistic debt that he owes to Aldhelm. Byrhtferth occasionally interpolates Old English glosses into his running prose in the *Enchiridion*, and in some instances the Old English glosses that appear in the *VSE* are copied directly

54 Zetzel, *Marginal Scholarship*, 144–8.

55 Lapidge, ed., *VSE*, 305. Peter Baker discusses Byrhtferth's authorship of the glosses in the *Enchiridion* in "Old English Canon," 28–30.

56 Lapidge, "Byrhtferth and *Vita S. Ecgwini*," 313–15.

57 Lapidge, ed., *VSE*, 305. The glosses and eccentric formatting of the *Enchiridion* are disussed in chapter 1 of my *Politics of Language*.

58 Lapidge, "Byrhtferth and *Vita S. Ecgwini*," 313.

59 The glosses are edited in Gwara, *Aldhelmi Malmesbiriensis*. Mechthild Gretsch discusses the use of these Aldhelm glosses in the Anglo-Saxon classroom in *Intellectual Foundations*, 332–83.

from glossed Aldhelm manuscripts.[60] Incorporating not just Aldhelmian phrases but also their accompanying glosses into his own text suggests something of the audience and the reading situation that Byrhtferth imagined, since this manuscript would be visually similar to the most revered manuscripts in a Benedictine schoolroom. Martin Irvine underlines the central role of glossed manuscripts in medieval education, saying, "the transmission of glosses and commentary on the same page as the main text is a sign that a text had received institutional validation and had become an object of interpretation and knowledge."[61] By assigning a gloss to this saint's life, Byrhtferth marks his new text as one that has already received "institutional validation," as Irvine calls it, and connects his work to the grammatical culture of the monastic classroom, since Irvine goes on to say, "the appearance of glosses and commentary in a manuscript is a primary sign that a text was a part of grammatical culture, either as a part of the canon of *auctores* or as a text which is first constituted as such by grammatical methodology."[62] In short, the glosses of the *VSE* mark Byrhtferth as an important *auctor* and the text as worthy of grammatical study, even though the glosses were written by Byrhtferth himself, not acquired over years of reception and scholarly inquiry.

The visual consequences for the Anglo-Saxon reading experience should not be overlooked. Glosses such as those in Aldhelm's manuscripts were not written by the same author as the text, and such paratextual material accreted gradually over hundreds of years of use, not at the same time the text was written. In texts copied for schoolrooms, however, glosses were often copied by the same scribe as the main text, a fact that can create a certain kind of homogeneity between the gloss and text, suggesting that they are inextricably linked to each other. Thus, Byrhtferth's manuscript with its gloss and text both composed at the same time (and by the same author) has the same homogeneous appearance as other manuscripts, despite the fact that school texts have earned the institutional validation of glosses through years of continual study and use. Byrhtferth, on the other hand, adds this institutional mark himself and suggests an authority that the manuscript has not yet earned. Beyond institutional validation, this act makes an interesting claim. Particularly, it suggests that a saint's life is eligible for this kind of schoolroom reading. While Aldhelm's *De virginitate*

60 Lapidge, "Byrhtferth at Work," 35.
61 Irvine, *Making of Textual Culture*, 372.
62 Ibid.

is often read by those who study hagiography, it is much more than the life of a single saint, and was likely read more as a gold mine of vocabulary than as a model of sanctity. By presenting the manuscript in the same way as a revered school text, Byrhtferth argues that such contemporary saints' lives are worthy of studying and reading in monastic schoolrooms where the identities of young monks are formed.

Situating this text in the intellectual context of the monastic schoolroom might further illuminate the purpose of these saints' lives written in the hermeneutic style. Saints' lives generally support the creation of a cult and potentially enhance a given locale's reputation. But if the sole desire of the hagiographer is to propagate and disseminate information, the saint would be better served by a simpler, clearer English life, like those produced by Ælfric of Eynsham. Yet, there must have been an important social function for these saints' lives in the hermeneutic style, particularly for saints associated with monasticism, such as Swithun, Oswald, Dunstan, and Æthelwold. While the ostensible purpose of such lives may have been to celebrate the saint with a lofty tone appropriate to their important content, the social effects cannot be ignored, since their difficult style must inherently limit the audience to a monastic elite.[63] When computistical inquiry becomes the driving force behind the narrative, the difficulties are exacerbated, since computistical knowledge is even more esoteric, primarily focused in ecclesiastical centres, and mainly in monastic houses. Given the explicit references to computus and other texts commonly read in the monastic classroom, the computistical information within the text proved the sanctity of Ecgwine at the same time that it worked to build coherent identity among young Benedictine monks as Latinate and computistically skilled.

Conclusion

Unlike the English saints' lives of Ælfric, lives written in such an elevated style cannot easily encourage veneration of a saint or spread important stories of his or her history. Rather, the narrative of the *VSE* is less about the sanctity of an individual saint or even establishing his cult (though all hagiographies must ultimately fulfil this purpose to a certain degree). Instead, it establishes a strong connection between Evesham and a Benedictine

---

63 For a fuller explanation of how the hermeneutic style limits readership to a monastic audience, see my "Scapegoating the Secular Clergy."

identity that had a certain level of social cachet, and as the monks read the text together, that identity is enforced and reinscribed. By performing the valiant act of wading through the difficulties of the text, a monk proves his worthiness to be considered a Benedictine. Thus, this hagiographical work with its strong connection to computus becomes proof of Ecgwine's relevance to Benedictine monks, and at the same time the document itself becomes a test for the admission of others.

Therefore, when Byrhtferth weaves computus into the rather empty narrative of the *VSE*, he is in fact adding important markers of a certain kind of both literate and Benedictine identity, one that arises from a monastic schoolroom. We see a similar force at work in the extended allegory based on Prudentius's *Psychomachia* that sits where the powerful deeds of a saint might be, if this were the life of St Martin instead. These references to computus and monastic school texts perform three different acts constitutive of a monastic identity. First, they establish Byrhtferth's identity both as learned and as Benedictine, and thus a person with the authority to write this hagiography. Then, they connect Ecgwine to this world of monastic learning, even though the eighth-century saint probably would not have been considered a Benedictine by the strict standards of the reformers, nor do we have any evidence that he was a scholar. Finally, Byrhtferth creates a kind of textual community by connecting both himself and Ecgwine to the community of Benedictine monks at Evesham, who likely would have studied the same curriculum texts favoured by reformers alongside their computistical training. While computus is certainly not the only – or even the most important – part of the self-definition of monks in the late Anglo-Saxon period, it is important to recognize the role it played in articulating monastic identity both as a part of the curriculum and in many reformed manuscripts. When we begin to look at computus as constitutive of identity, then it might begin to explain why computistical material is so often defective, like the mess that is in Cotton Tiberius B.v, an otherwise richly decorated manuscript. If Patrick McGurk's date is correct, the Easter tables in that manuscript were some forty years out of date by the time the manuscript was copied.[64] Easter tables that are incomplete, inaccurate, or somehow unusable are quite common and perhaps reflect the extent to which Anglo-Saxon computus represents a medieval engagement with both monastic identity and man's place in the universe.

64 McGurk, *Eleventh-Century Anglo-Saxon Miscellany*, 33.

Hebrew Words and English Identity in Educational Texts of Ælfric and Byrhtferth

DAMIAN FLEMING

Language and identity are intimately connected; the relationship of speakers to their native language is often influenced by their experiences with a second language. The relationship of Anglo-Saxons to their native tongue as well as their adopted language, Latin, has long been studied.[1] The Greek language, while not widely known, certainly loomed large in the Anglo-Saxon imagination, having been brought to the island by Theodore and Hadrian and used as a source of erudite vocabulary among a variety of Anglo-Saxon ecclesiastics.[2] This study considers Hebrew, a language which most learned Anglo-Saxons knew about but had even less first-hand experience with.[3] Examining the particular triangulation of English, Latin, and Hebrew – respectively native, acquired, and distant languages – throws into relief Anglo-Saxons' attitudes towards language and appreciation of language difference. Both Ælfric of Eynsham and Byrhtferth of Ramsey wrote educational texts which reveal their senses of linguistic identity

---

1 Gneuss, "*Anglicae linguae interpretatio*" and "Study of Language in Anglo-Saxon England"; Dekker, "Pentecost and Linguistic Self-Consciousness"; Godden, "Literary Language."

2 Gneuss, "*Anglicae linguae interpretatio*," 118–23; Lapidge, "School of Theodore and Hadrian"; Bischoff and Lapidge, *Biblical Commentaries*; Bodden, "Evidence for Knowledge of Greek." The Venerable Bede also seems to have taught himself enough Greek to read the Acts of the Apostles; see Laistner, "Library of the Venerable Bede," 257; Dionisotti, "Bede, Grammars, and Greek"; Lynch, "Venerable Bede's Knowledge of Greek."

3 Keefer and Burrows, "Hebrew and the *Hebraicum*"; Fleming, "*Jesus*, that is *hælend*."

and particular interest in Hebrew. They discuss Hebrew at times when it is not immediately germane to their topic and leave their readers with the impression that they themselves could read Hebrew. These contemporary late Anglo-Saxon authors wrote texts in English which had otherwise been exclusively written in Latin: a Latin grammar and a commentary on computus.[4] Both of these texts are bilingual to a certain extent, and both of them engage with the idea of Hebrew on more than one occasion, but the effect of this engagement is quite different. Ælfric uses Hebrew within his Latin *Grammar* to connect his English-speaking students to a continuum of languages projecting back in time: English, Latin, Greek, and Hebrew. He shares his knowledge of Hebrew to help his students appreciate their own place in the history of Christianity as well as to appreciate the individuality of all languages. Byrhtferth likewise draws connections among English and the scriptural languages and, at times, projects an image similar to Ælfric's, connecting English through time to the languages of salvation history which preceded it. But Byrhtferth more often uses his linguistic skill – with Latin as well as Hebrew – to alienate at least some of his audience. He uses his advanced knowledge of languages to separate himself and those like him – namely Benedictine monks – from those readers who can only identify with English.

Both Ælfric and Byrhtferth grasp after Hebrew and in many ways embrace it; if not actually flaunting, they display their knowledge of Hebrew as if it were the most natural skill in the world. Neither of them thinks there is anything unusual about discussing Hebrew. Many educated Anglo-Saxons knew quite a bit about Hebrew, much of which can be traced back to the writings of the Venerable Bede, himself a champion of Jerome's insistence of the importance of Hebrew.[5] While there is no evidence to suggest any Anglo-Saxons actually read Hebrew, they were aware of the role of Hebrew in the textual history of salvation, and use that understanding to frame their appreciation of the role of translation in scriptural history. This is most clearly articulated in King Alfred's famous Preface to the *Pastoral Care*, where, lamenting the ignorance of Latin in his kingdom, he remembers that the Greeks had already translated the Bible from Hebrew, the Latins from Greek and Hebrew, and others had already translated

4 Zupitza, ed., *Ælfrics Grammatik*; Baker and Lapidge, ed., *Byrhtferth's Enchiridion*.
5 Fleming, "*Jesus*, that is *hælend*," 28–36.

important texts from Latin to vernaculars.[6] Ælfric and Byrhtferth work from a similar mindset, but with different results. Ælfric uses Latin and Hebrew as a means of including his students in a wider tradition of language. Especially in his discussion of interjections in his *Grammar*, he shows that some of the difficulties his students might have with Latin are ameliorated with reference to Hebrew; that is, stepping back to see the big picture helps make the differences between English and Latin seem less significant. Byrhtferth also draws Hebrew, English, and Latin together to a certain extent, by framing the place of English in linguistic scriptural history, but more often uses Hebrew as a means of exclusion to demonstrate his own linguistic superiority.

Ælfric of Eynsham is famous for his dedication to orthodoxy and clarity; he devoted his life to making the truths of the faith accessible to as wide an audience as possible.[7] This was primarily accomplished through his many homilies, translations, and adaptations of Latin texts.[8] But he was also a teacher, willing to use anything in his power to make his material intelligible to his audience.[9] Certainly this is the case in his *Excerptiones de Prisciano Anglice*, or *Grammar*, which was one of the most popular English texts of the eleventh and twelfth centuries, surviving in fourteen manuscripts.[10] This text holds the special distinction of being the first grammar of the Latin language written in any language besides Latin. As Ælfric explains in his Latin preface, his *Grammar* is a translation of an abbreviation of Priscian's *Institutiones grammaticae*, a surviving text which allows for careful source study revealing those sections that Ælfric has expanded or diminished.[11] Scholars have been most interested to follow up Ælfric's claim that his *Grammar* can be used to study Latin or

6 "Ða gemunde ic hu sio æ wæs ærest on Ebreisc geðiode funden, & eft, ða hie Creacas geliornodon, ða wendon hie hie on hiora agen geðiode ealle, & eac ealle oðre bec. & eft Lædenware swæ same, siððan hie hie geliornodon, hie hie wendon ealla ðurh wise wealhstodas on hiora agen geðiode. Ond eac ealla oðræ Cristnæ ðioda sumne dæl hiora on hiora agen geðiode wendon" (Sweet, ed., *King Alfred's West-Saxon Version*, 1:5–7).

7 Wilcox, ed., *Ælfric's Prefaces*, esp. 15–22.

8 Hill, "Ælfric: His Life and Works."

9 Hall, "Ælfric as Pedagogue."

10 Menzer, "Ælfric's English *Grammar*," 106; Hill, "Ælfric's Grammatical Triad."

11 Porter, ed., *Excerptiones de Prisciano*.

English grammar.[12] In conjunction with this, many have been struck by the text's distinctive Englishness, zeroing in on Ælfric's English tangents, or what Vivien Law calls "strong local colouring of the vocabulary and examples."[13] Ælfric exhibits his identity as an Anglo-Saxon and as a monk while providing his students with examples they can more readily relate to, replacing the model nouns found in his source, *Roma*, *Tiberis*, *urbs*, and *flumen*, with the Anglo-Saxon *Eadgarus*, *Adelwoldus*, *rex*, and *episcopus*.[14] He entirely displaces his source's discussion of Roman patronymics with details of how family names are formed in English, such as the *Pendingas* derived from *Penda* and *Cwicelmingas* from *Cwicelm*.[15] Under the names of peoples, he includes *anglus*: "englisc," alongside *graecus*: "grecisc," and *romanus*: "romanisc," and for place names he gives *lundoniensis*: "lundenisc" and *wiltuniensis*: "wiltunisc."[16] With these changes, Ælfric bolsters the status of English: details of English grammar are just as important as Latin ones or, in the case of patronymics, more important for his audience.

Hand in hand with "Englishing" is Ælfric's desire to Christianize his source: he makes a fifth-century pagan text more appropriate and relevant for tenth-century Christian monks and novices. An obvious example is when he changes *Pius Aeneas* to *Pius David rex*, supplanting Priscian's sense of Roman identity with his own sense of Judeo-Christian identity. A trickier example is when he replaces the example of a first declension masculine noun *poeta* with *citharista*, "cither-player," or as he translates it into Old English, *hearpere*, "a harper."[17] Scholars have taken this as an example of Ælfric inserting a distinctly Anglo-Saxon image into the text.[18] We can picture the harper, or *scop*, sitting in the middle of an Anglo-Saxon hall,

12 "In isto libello potestis utramque linguam uidelicet latinam et anglicam, uestrae teneritudini inserere interim, usque quo ad perfectiora perueniatis studia … Ne cweðe ic na for ði, þæt ðeos boc mæge micclum to lare fremian, ac heo byð swa ðeah sum angyn to ægðrum gereorde, gif heo hwam licað" (Zupitza, ed., *Ælfrics Grammatik*, 1–3). See Menzer, "Ælfric's English *Grammar*"; Gretsch, "Ælfric, Language, and Winchester," 120–1.

13 Law, "Anglo-Saxon England," 56; Hall, "Ælfric as Pedagogue," 198, similarly refers to Ælfric's "home-grown" examples.

14 Zupitza, ed., *Ælfrics Grammatik*, 8; Law, "Anglo-Saxon England," 56.

15 Zupitza, ed., *Ælfrics Grammatik*, 14–15.

16 Ibid., 13.

17 Ibid., 21.

18 See, e.g., Law, "Anglo-Saxon England," 57, "The prominent place given *citharista* … reflects the importance of the *hearpere* in Anglo-Saxon society."

ready to recite *Beowulf* – or something like it – to his mead-drinking audience. Or maybe not. In the writing of a monk who changed "Aeneas" to "David," who is the more likely harper: the *Beowulf*-poet, or King David, the psalmist?

In any event, through tracking these changes in his translation, we can begin to piece together a bit of Ælfric's sense of identity. Based on his presentation of Latin and English, the identity which emerges, not surprisingly, is one of a literate English Christian monk: exactly what Ælfric is. But he is also someone who is interested in language and languages. He reintroduces the image of a "harper" when he augments his source's list of adverbs derived from adjectives.

> Ða ðe habbað langne *e*, syndon *DIRIVATIVA*: *clarus* beorht and of ðam *clare* beorhtlice oððe beorhte; *pulcher* wlitig, *pulchre citharizat* fægere he hearpað; *faber* smið, *affabre* cræftlice; *anglus* englisc, *anglice* on englisc; *latinus* leden, *latine* and *latialiter* on leden; *graecus* grecisc, *graece* on grecisc; *ebraicus* and *ebraeus* ebreisc, *ebraice* on ebreisc.[19]

> [Those with a long *e* are derivatives: *clarus* bright and from it *clare* brightly *pulcher* beautiful *pulchre citharizat* he harps beautifully; *faber* smith, *affabre* skillfully; *anglus* English, *anglice* in English; *latinus* Latin, *latine* and *latialiter* in Latin; *graecus* Greek, *graece* in Greek; *ebraicus* and *ebraeus* Hebrew, *ebraice* in Hebrew.]

The list of language adjectives and adverbs has no parallel in his source material; however, these four languages – English, Latin, Greek, and Hebrew – frequently show up together in the corpus of Ælfric's writings. When Ælfric's mind drifts towards language, we find the languages that are on Ælfric's mind: his own English, his target language Latin, and the scriptural languages Greek and Hebrew. As in Alfred's preface, these languages represent the historical tradition of scriptural translation, from Moses right down to Ælfric's own day. When juxtaposed like this, they identify the English language and the English people as part of the Christian tradition.

The question of language and identity is even more to the fore in Ælfric's consideration of interjections, the eighth and final part of speech treated in his *Grammar*. This section reveals much about Ælfric's understanding of

19 Zupitza, ed., *Ælfrics Grammatik*, 235.

language and interjections' connection to linguistic identity. In discussing interjections – one of the most primal forms of communication, having only one quality, namely *getacnung* or "signification" – Ælfric demonstrates the interconnectivity of certain languages while at the same time revealing the fundamental individuality of every language. And he concludes his entire *Grammar* clearly focused on the English language.

From a strictly grammatical point of view, interjections are quite simple; they have no inflectional morphology and often do not even make it into the pages of modern Latin textbooks.[20] It is little surprise that they show up at the very end of medieval Lain grammars. Conceptually, however, interjections are fascinating.

> Interiectio is an dæl ledenspræce getaceniende þæs modes gewilnunge mid ungesceapenre stemne. *INTERIECTIO* mæg beon gecweden betwuxalegednys on englisc, forþan ðe he lið betwux wordum and geopenað þæs modes styrunge mid behyddre stemne. An þing he hæfþ: *SIGNIFICATIO*, þæt is getacnung, forðan ðe he getacnað hwilon ðæs modes blisse, hwilon sarnysse, hwilon wundrunge and gehwæt.[21]
>
> [The interjection is a part of Latin-speech signifying the desire of the mind in an unformed utterance. Interjection can be called "between-laid-ness" in English, because it lies between words and reveals the mind's feeling with an inarticulate [literally, "concealed"] voice. It has one thing: *Significatio*, that is signification, because it signifies sometimes the bliss of the mind, sometimes sorrow, sometimes astonishment and so forth.]

The externalization of emotional states which interjections represent seems to transcend individual languages, and Ælfric's discussion quickly reveals the slipperiness of interjections.[22] Like his *Grammar* itself, interjections can move between languages, "*hui* man cweþ on leden and ealswa on englisc: huig, hu færst ðu" (One says *hui* in Latin as well as in English:

20 Sauer, "Interjection, Emotion, Grammar, and Literature," "Ælfric and Emotion," and "How the Anglo-Saxons Expressed Their Emotions"; Hiltunen, "*Eala, geferan and gode wyrhtan*"; Cassidy, "Anglo-Saxon Interjection."

21 Zupitza, ed., *Ælfrics Grammatik*, 277–8.

22 Derolez, "Those Things Are Difficult to Express," 472–3.

huig, how do you do?).[23] Latin and English also share the onomatopoeias *haha* and *hehe*, "forðan ðe hi beoð hlichende geclypode" (because they are exclaimed [while] laughing).[24] Although Ælfric doesn't explicitly say as much, there seems to be something fundamentally human about the sounds of certain emotions, in any language. However, sometimes interjections suggest the exact opposite: some interjections are specific to a single language and thus utterly defy translation. Instead of offering an English or Latin equivalent, Ælfric can only suggest the emotional state which certain interjections "betoken" or imply: "Þes *heu* and *ei* getacniað wanunge ... *la* getacnað yrsunge, *e* gebicnað forsewennysse" (*heu* and *ei* show wailing ... *la* shows anger, *e* indicates contempt).[25] Again, showing his relative independence from his immediate source, he greatly expands its discussion of Latin *vae* – which only shows up in a list in the source – but is of course so very popular in the Bible.[26]

The linguistic peculiarities of interjections interest Ælfric so much that in the middle of his examples, he returns to its definition, "Þes dæl *INTERIECTIO* hæfð wordes fremminge, þeah ðe he færlice geclypod beo, and he hæfð swa fela stemna, swa he hæfð getacnunga, and hi ne magon ealle beon on englisc awende" (The part of speech interjection has the effect of a verb, though it is uttered quickly, and it has as many sounds as it has meanings, and they all cannot be translated into English), before introducing further biblical examples, which naturally have no place in his pagan source.[27]

> *Vah* getacnað gebysmrunge, and *racha* getacnað æbylignysse oððe yrre. *uah* and *racha* sind ebreisce *INTERIECTIONES*, and ælc þeod hæfð synderlice *INTERIECTIONES*, ac hi ne magon naht eaðe to oðrum gereorde beon awende.[28]

> [*Vah* denotes scorn and *racha* denotes indignation or anger. *Vah* and *racha* are Hebrew interjections and each people has separate interjections, but they cannot easily be translated into another language.]

23 Zupitza, ed., *Ælfrics Grammatik*, 278.
24 Ibid., 279.
25 Ibid., 278, 280.
26 Ibid., 278–9; Hall, "Ælfric as Pedagogue," 200.
27 Zupitza, ed., *Ælfrics Grammatik*, 279.
28 Ibid., 279.

Ælfric includes these Hebrew words as additional examples to make the *Grammar* more accessible to his English students. He knows that these Hebrew words, like the English patronymics above, will be readily recognizable to his monastic students. Although they were likely familiar from their scriptural usage, his students may not have realized that they were Hebrew. Ælfric, following in the footsteps of Bede and ultimately Jerome, regularly takes pains to point out the language of origin of Hebrew words. Ælfric gets both of these words from the New Testament; *racha* appears in Matthew 5:22, "ego autem dico uobis quia omnis qui irascitur fratri suo reus erit iudicio qui autem dixerit fratri suo *racha* reus erit concilio qui autem dixerit fatue reus erit gehennae ignis" (But I say to you, that whosoever is angry with his brother shall be in danger of the judgment. And whosoever shall say to his brother, *Raca*, shall be in danger of the council. And whosoever shall say, Thou Fool, shall be in danger of hell fire). *Racha* is one of the dozen or so Aramaic words preserved in the New Testament, most of which are attributed to Jesus (medieval writers do not generally distinguish between Hebrew and Aramaic). Its root seems to mean something like "empty" and it is generally understood as a term of abuse. Most medieval commentators follow Jerome in noting that it means *uanus* or *inanis* – though Eucherius of Lyon notes that the implication might be "without a brain" – or, like Ælfric, follow Augustine in simply stressing that it expresses indignation.[29]

Ælfric's second Hebrew interjection is probably not Hebrew or Aramaic. Although *uae* ("woe," a noun or interjection) appears over one hundred times in the Vulgate, *vah* appears only three or four times: twice in the Old Testament (Job 39:25; Is. 44:16, where it translates the Hebrew האח), and once each in the Gospels of Matthew and Mark, in the mouths of those mocking Jesus on the cross, "et praetereuntes blasphemabant eum mouentes capita sua et dicentes *ua* qui destruit templum et in tribus diebus aedificat" (And they that passed by blasphemed him, wagging their heads, and saying: Vah, thou that destroyest the temple of God, and in three days buildest it up again).[30] *Vah* here translates the Greek text's οὐά; Lewis and Short list *vah* as the Latin equivalent of οὐά, having been used in Latin since at least the time

29 Thiel, *Grundlagen und Gestalt*, 388–9.

30 Mark 15:29. Mt. 27:40: "et dicentes [uah] qui destruit templum et in triduo illud reaedificat salua temet ipsum si Filius Dei es descende de cruce"; *uah* is printed as a variant reading in Weber, ed., *Biblia Sacra*.

of Plautus.[31] Excepting the possibility of some intermediary source, it is likely Ælfric erroneously deduced that this word is Hebrew from its context. Used in a manner similar to *racha*, it appears just a few verses before Jesus calls out in Aramaic on the cross, "Heli Heli lema sabacthani."[32] Even though Ælfric is "wrong" about Hebrew in this instance, his discussion shows us where his mind is. As in the examples of adverbs above, when Ælfric thinks of languages, he naturally thinks of English and Latin but is just as likely to think of Greek and Hebrew, a group of languages always on the tip of his tongue – not because there is anything magical or mysterious about them, but because these are the languages of greatest importance in the textual history of scripture. Ælfric feels that awareness of even Hebrew is appropriate for all sorts of learners: even beginners, like the target audience of his *Grammar* – despite the fact that knowing about Hebrew interjections does not really help one learn to read Latin.

The second half of his comment also enlightens ideas of language and identity: "each people have separate interjections, but they cannot easily be translated into another language."[33] He reiterates the difficulty of translating interjections to justify his not providing translations for the Hebrew interjections *racha* and *vah*, following the example of the Gospels, which do not translate these words. This idea of the "untranslatable" words in scripture – especially interjections – is also found in Augustine's *De doctrina christiana*:

> hebrea verba non interpretata saepe inveniamus in libris ... quae in usum alterius linguae per interpretationem transire non possint. Et hoc maxime interiectionibus accidit, quae verba motum animi significant potius quam sententiae conceptae ullam particulam. Nam et haec duo talia esse perhibentur; dicunt enim *racha* indignantis esse vocem, *osanna* laetantis.[34]

> [We often find Hebrew words untranslated in the texts ... which just cannot be translated into the idioms of another language. This is especially true of

31 Lewis and Short, *Latin Dictionary*, s.v., "*vah*"; Sauer, "Ælfric and Emotion," 46.

32 Mark 15:34; Mt. 27:46.

33 As Gretsch notes generally on Ælfric's accomplishment in the *Grammar*, "Ælfric's metalinguistic reflections on the relationship between Latin and English ... are the first metalinguistic reflections to survive from, and on, any European vernacular" ("Ælfric, Language and Winchester," 119).

34 Green, ed., *Augustine: De doctrina christiana*, 73.

interjections, which signify emotion, rather than an element of clearly conceived meaning; two such words, it is said, are *racha*, a word expressing anger, and *osanna*, a word expressing joy.]

Some Hebrew words simply cannot be translated. Immediately after this comment, Ælfric lists more Latin interjections, and rather than translate them, gives their "signification" or their sense: "*la* getacnað yrsunge, *e* gebicnað forsewennysse, *euge* gebicnað blisse and bysmrunge" (*la* denotes anger, *e* indicates contempt, and *euge* indicates joy or derision), and he seemingly concludes his discussion of interjections with a translation of his source's final point, "Ealle hi sind *INTERIECTIONES,* ac heora sweg byð hwilon gescyrt and hwilon gelencged be ðæs modes styrunge" (All of these are interjections and their accent is sometimes shortened and sometimes lengthened, depending on the agitation of the mind).[35] But then he makes one more comment before the end of his entire *Grammar*, "*Afæstla* and *hilahi* and *wellawell* and ðyllice oðre sindon englisce INTERIECTIONES. Finiunt Partes Anglice" (*Afæstla* and *hilahi* and *wellawell* and other such words are English interjections. The *Parts [of Speech]* in English concludes).[36] Ælfric ends his Latin *Grammar* with seemingly superfluous information about English, which deserves attention: for one, these words are very odd.[37] Although Ælfric just throws them out there like the most natural examples of English, these words do not occur anywhere else in the corpus of Old English texts, which is an excellent reminder of the depth of our modern ignorance about Old English – especially spoken, colloquial Old English.[38] But for his Anglo-Saxon students, these words must have been very familiar; Ælfric allows them to stand for English, and this is how he chooses to end his Latin *Grammar*: with English. This final section of his *Grammar* offers insight into Ælfric's understanding of languages; they each have their own identity, and in this way, the English that his monastic students grew up speaking is not unlike the learned Latin they endeavour to learn, or even like the Hebrew spoken by Jesus himself.

35 Zupitza, ed., *Ælfrics Grammatik*, 280.

36 Ibid.

37 Sauer, "Ælfric and Emotion," 47.

38 Sauer notes that "Ælfric's *Grammar* is one of the rare witnesses (or even the only one) of some interjections which were perhaps frequent in spoken Old English. Thus we find traces of colloquial speech in a grammar" ("How the Anglo-Saxons Expressed Their Emotions," 173).

Byrhtferth of Ramsey, Ælfric's contemporary, shared a similar realistic conception of Hebrew as evidenced in his instructional text, his *Enchiridion*. While Ælfric's vernacular *Grammar* of the English language was genuinely innovative, Byrhtferth's *Enchiridion* is truly unique. In essence, it is a bilingual – English and Latin – commentary on computus: the texts which help one reconcile the Roman solar calendar with the Hebrew lunar calendar in order to determine the date of Easter and other moveable feasts.[39] Computus texts, like grammars, were otherwise exclusively written in Latin. However, Byrhtferth's *Enchiridion* is far from a simple translation of a computus; like many computus manuscripts, it is a compendium of useful knowledge, much of which bears little or no connection to the reckoning of time.[40] Nor can its complex intertwining of languages and registers within those languages be simply defined as either vernacular or bilingual. The overall structure gives the impression of being a bilingual text, with a passage in Latin followed by a more or less straightforward translation into Old English. However, some of the sections are written exclusively in Latin, and others are only in English. And, unlike Ælfric's *Grammar*, which is clearly aimed at introductory students of Latin, Byrhtferth's *Enchiridion* is intended for at least two distinct audiences: a clerical – but non-monastic – audience, which is primarily addressed in English, and a more learned audience of monks, who are instructed in Latin as well as English. Also unlike Ælfric's *Grammar*, the popularity of the *Enchiridion* is very difficult to assess; it survives in only one more or less complete copy.[41]

Rebecca Stephenson has convincingly delineated the multiple audiences of the *Enchiridion* and Byrhtferth's explicit concern with linguistic identity, showing how he endeavours to project monastic self-definition, which was necessary because of the lack of clear distinction between monastic and secular clergy in the late tenth century.[42] Byrhtferth accomplishes this through the use of different languages and different registers of these languages. The Latin sections of the *Enchiridion*, and especially those sections written in more difficult, "hermeneutic" Latin, "encoded in

39 Wallis, *Bede: The Reckoning of Time*, xviii–xxxiv.

40 Wallis, "Background Essay" (accessed 6 April 2012).

41 Baker and Lapidge, eds., *Byrhtferth's Enchiridion*, cxv–cxxiv.

42 Stephenson, "Scapegoating the Secular Clergy."

linguistic terms the division between monks and clerics."[43] He mocks the secular clergy in these Latin sections and bemoans the necessity of having to translate each of the Latin sections on their behalf. Byrhtferth uses the secular clergy as a "scapegoat," a caricature of lazy ecclesiastics in order to highlight the diligence and intelligence of the Benedictine monks. However, even some sections which are written entirely in English, such as the explanation of Latin figures of speech, discussed below, demand a thorough understanding of Latin to make any sense: "Both the untranslated Latin and the technical vocabulary of grammar indicate that this passage was written in English for a reader who had a fairly extensive knowledge of Latin, but who could understand some concepts better when explicated in English."[44] The spectre of the stupid cleric authorizes the translation of the text into English, which could then of course be read by monks as well as clerics. And monks alone, naturally, benefit from those sections written exclusively in English which nevertheless deal with complex Latin subjects, like schemes and tropes. Byrhtferth's use of Hebrew mirrors this dichotomy of the *Enchiridion* on the whole. He discusses Hebrew in the most straightforward English sections aimed at as wide an audience as possible in a way similar to Ælfric, connecting English to the global tradition of languages and biblical translation in particular. However, Byrhtferth also uses Hebrew in some of the most difficult sections of his text, which are intended exclusively for his fellow learned Benedictine monks. In these, Hebrew knowledge becomes another element in his specialized move to create a distinct monastic, intellectually superior identity.

Like Ælfric, Byrhtferth introduces a realistic conception of Hebrew in his most accessible sections – those sections which are translated into English and which would have been easily intelligible to both monks and secular clergy. For example, since Hebrew language and customs are central to the computus, Byrhtferth provides a summary of the Passover story – beginning with a gloss of the Hebrew word *Pascha* – in straightforward English. Like Ælfric, Bede, and Jerome, Byrhtferth uses the etymology of a proper Hebrew noun as a springboard for interpretation in

43 Ibid., 107. On hermeneutic Latin see Lapidge, "Hermeneutic Style," and his edition of *Byrhtferth of Ramsey: Lives*, xliv–lxv. Stephenson succinctly defines it as "a kind of Latin prose that affects an elevated register through importing poetic conventions into prose" (112).

44 Stephenson, "Scapegoating the Secular Clergy," 119.

English: "*Pasca* ys Ebreisc nama, and he getacnað **oferfæreld**. God ælmihtig **ferde** on Egiptena lande, hi sleande and alysende Israela bearn" (Pasch is a Hebrew noun, and it means "passage." God almighty passed into the land of the Egyptians, slaying them and freeing the children of Israel).[45] Like these authors, Byrhtferth can get carried away in his enthusiasm for sharing etymologies. Byrhtferth translates Exodus 12:1–11, which gives Yahweh's orders to Moses concerning the preparation of the Paschal meal, ending "*Est enim phase, id est transitus Domini*: hyt is witodlice Godes **færeld**" (It is *phase*, that is, the passing of the Lord: it is truly God's passage).[46] He begins his explication of the passage with yet another Hebrew etymology:

> Vton nu, la arwurðan gebroðro, us gegearwian þis lamb to etanne. We synt Abrahames bearn, and eac Israeles his sunu sunu bearn we synt getealde. Israhel ys gereht on Lyden *uidens Deum* and on Englisc God geseonde.[47]

> [O reverend brothers, let us now prepare to eat this lamb. We are the children of Abraham, and we are also considered the children of Israel, the son of his son. Israel means *uidens Deum* in Latin and "seeing God" in English.]

The first etymology – that of *Pasca* or *phase* – is immediately relevant and necessary for a proper understanding of the passage. The latter (of "Israel") is seemingly tangential – he has to really stretch to make it from Moses to Abraham to Israel – but reveals Byrhtferth's enthusiasm for Hebrew information in itself. Byrhtferth simply must share this information; Hebrew etymologies are useful information even for the most basic learners, in straightforward English.

In addition, since the whole purpose of the computus is to reconcile the Hebrew lunar year with the Roman solar year, the names and correspondences of the Hebrew months are essential information. In his *Enchiridion*, Byrhtferth includes a chart originally found in Bede's *De temporum ratione* showing the Hebrew, Egyptian, Greek, and Roman month names, as

45 Baker and Lapidge, eds., *Byrhtferth's Enchiridion*, 122–3. On comparable use of etymologies in Ælfric, see Hill, "Ælfric's Use of Etymologies," 35–44; Fleming, "*Jesus*, that is *hælend*," 37–44.

46 Baker and Lapidge, eds., *Byrhtferth's Enchiridion*, 122–3.

47 Ibid.

well as the pre-Christian Old English month names.[48] In a later, more miscellaneous, section of the *Enchiridion*, Byrhtferth provides a similarly practical series of alphabets: English, Latin, Greek, and Hebrew.[49] Like Ælfric's list of adverbs, these situate the English language in some impressive company, graphically demonstrating the continuity from the Old Testament to Byrhtferth's England.

Byrhtferth also uses his knowledge of Hebrew to demonstrate his own learning in both Latin and English sections of the *Enchiridion* that would have been comprehensible only to his advanced monastic students. In addition to Hebrew serving as part of the common inheritance of all Christians, Byrhtferth also uses it as part of his highly specialized linguistic toolkit, which helps create a sense of identity with his fellow learned monks by alienating the less educated clerks. At times, he uses it in such a specialized manner that it is hard to say if any of his contemporaries ever picked up on what he was doing.

In part 3 of the *Enchiridion*, Byrhtferth translates into English Bede's *De schematibus et tropis* – a handbook of rhetorical devices which Bede had composed to provide a school text, replacing the pagan quotations found in pre-Christian handbooks with biblical quotations. Bede's text had been glossed by Remigius, and some of Byrhtferth's translation decisions strongly suggest that he was using such a glossed version.[50] Ironically, for a teacher like Byrhtferth who regularly chides the ignorance and laziness of students – especially for their lack of understanding Latin – he makes the mistake of reading only the first element of a word's definition. Following Bede, Byrhtferth mentions the *Iliad* and *Odyssey* as examples of "mixed" compositions; then, following Remigius's gloss, he provides etymologies for the titles of Homer's works: "Ilias, þæt beoð gewyn, and Odissia beoð gedwyld, swa Omerus on þære bec recð" (*Ilias* means strife, and *Odyssey* means wandering, as Homer tells in that book).[51] As Lapidge and Baker note, Byrhtferth was probably looking at the Remigian commentary which explains that "ILIAS: **subuersiones** Troiae and ODYSSIA

48 Ibid., 24. On Bede's original lists of months, see Wallis, *Bede: The Reckoning of Time*, 285–7.

49 Baker and Lapidge, eds., *Byrhtferth's Enchiridion*, 186–8; commentary on 334–5. See also Wallis, "2. Computus Related Materials: 11. Runic, Cryptographic and Exotic Alphabets," in her *The Calendar and the Cloister* (accessed 6 April 2012).

50 Baker and Lapidge, eds., *Byrhtferth's Enchiridion*, lxxxi; Kendall, ed., *Bede: De arte metrica*, 148.

51 Baker and Lapidge, eds., *Byrhtferth's Enchiridion*, 162–3.

id est **errores** Vlixis" (ILIAD: the destruction of Troy and ODYSSEY: that is the wanderings of Ulysses).[52] Byrhtferth has erroneously extracted only the first half of each gloss, leaving out the actual root of the word he defines, rendering his definition of each term almost laughable.

For the most part, Byrhtferth's translation of Bede's work provides illustrative quotations for a variety of rhetorical devices which would have been comprehensible to a monastic student. Although this section is written in English, it requires a substantial understanding of Latin, without which none of the examples would make sense. As Stephenson shows, this is one section where the idea of an incompetent clerical readership authorizes English translation which in fact will benefit only Byrhtferth's monastic students.[53] His example of paronomasia is indicative of the difficulty of this section, even in English.

> Fægere þis hiw geglengde Isaias se witega þa he þus giddiende cwæð: *Expectaui ut faceret iudicium, et ecce iniquitas; et iustitiam, et ecce clamor.* Þas word swyðe fægere geþwærlæcað on Ebreiscre spræce, swa we þæt her willað þam rædere geswutelian. *Iudicium* on Lyden and on Englisc dom and on Ebreisc *mesaphaat*; *iustitia* on Lyden and on Englisc *rihtwisnys* and on Ebreisc *sadaca*; *iniquitas* on Lyden on Englisc ys gecweden unrihtwisnys and on Ebreisc *mesaphaa*; *clamor* on Lyden on Englisc ys hludnys and on Ebreisc ys gereht *suaca.* Fægere he gemetegode þæra namena gelicnyssa. Iudicium he genemde mesaphaat, and iniquitas mesaphaa, and iustitia sadaca, and clamor suaca.[54]
>
> [Isaiah the prophet elegantly adorned this figure [paronomasia] when he said in his song, "I looked that he should do judgment, and behold iniquity; and justice, and behold an outcry." These words correspond very elegantly in the Hebrew language, as we will here explain to the reader. *Iudicium* in Latin is judgment in English and *mesaphaat* in Hebrew; *iustitia* in Latin is called righteousness in English and *sadaca* in Hebrew; *iniquitas* in Latin is called iniquity in English and *mesaphaa* in Hebrew; *clamor* in Latin is loudness in English and is called *suaca* in Hebrew. He elegantly regulated the resemblances among these nouns. He called justice *mesaphaat*, and iniquity *mesapha*, and righteousness *sadaca*, and outcry *suaca*.]

52 Ibid., 328–9.

53 Stephenson, "Scapegoating the Secular Clergy," 119.

54 Baker and Lapidge, eds., *Byrhtferth's Enchiridion*, 166–7.

There are a number of interesting things at play here; the most obvious, of course, is that Byrhtferth is casually throwing around Hebrew words in the middle of an English text – perhaps giving his audience the impression that he could deal with the Hebrew text of the Bible. Of course he could not; he has lifted this from Bede, who – also not really knowing Hebrew – ultimately got the information from Jerome.[55] Byrhtferth goes out of his way to make the Hebrew, and his use of Hebrew, more central to the passage, using the word *ebraisc* five times compared with just once in Bede. He also more forcefully insists on the beauty of this example: "Fægere þis hiw ... Þas word swyðe fægere ... Fægere he gemetegode." Byrhtferth may just be overly enthusiastic about this example, but he may also be attempting to refute another reader who was less impressed. In Remigius's commentary on *De schematibus et tropis* – which almost certainly accompanied Byrhtferth's copy of Bede – we find this scholion:

> Super haec non accurrit figura, id est paranomasia apud Hebraeos quia paene idem sunt in sono, apud Latinos uero nec sensu nec litteratura.[56]
>
> [The figure, that is paronomasia, doesn't occur with these words because in Hebrew they barely sound the same, but in Latin neither the sense nor the spelling works.]

Remigius is right: in many ways it is not a very good example of paronomasia, especially if we are looking for unambiguous clarity in an educational text. Bede himself seems to have gotten carried away here, bringing in Hebrew based on his own enthusiastic interest in Hebrew and thorough knowledge of Jerome's commentaries. This example is a bit abstruse and would not be particularly helpful for students trying to learn the application of rhetorical devices in Latin. But if they have something else on their minds, like talking about Hebrew for its own sake or as a means of demonstrating one's own brilliance, it is an excellent example. Byrhtferth, like Bede, enjoys the engagement with Hebrew for its own sake and sees the value in being able to connect his advanced students directly to the Hebrew past. More subtly, this passage could be seen to bolster the status of English by showing how even the Latin translation of scripture is deficient. Readers

55 See Kendall, ed., *Bede: De arte metrica*, 147–8; the immediate source for Bede is Jerome: Adriaen, ed., *S. Hieronymi in Esaiam*, 68.

56 Kendall, ed., *Bede: De arte metrica*, 140.

need to return all the way to the original Hebrew to appreciate the wordplay here, which one might as well do in English as in Latin.

Byrhtferth also turns to Hebrew for some of his most purposefully difficult passages in the whole *Enchiridion*. The final major section of the *Enchiridion* is for advanced Latin-reading students only. He begins with a long section on the meanings of numbers, or arithmology. This section is one of Byrhtferth's most original and innovative as he attempts to provide, for the first time, a Christian handbook of number symbolism.[57] It is the most difficult section of the *Enchiridion*, written entirely in dense, flowery, hermeneutic Latin. Although this section begins with a fairly extensive English gloss, this is rather quickly reduced to a trickle of Latin glosses and ceases altogether less than halfway through. As Stephenson argues, Byrhtferth uses a section like this to highlight the learning of the monks in contrast to the secular clerics who cannot even read it. And while Byrhtferth will happily share his knowledge of Hebrew with a general audience, he is also able to employ it in some of the showiest moments in the whole text. His introduction to the number eight is typical of his style in this section.

> Post septenarium exsurget regali potentia fretus ipse octonarius. Ipse enim uerus est octonarius, qui crimina tulit mundi. Ipse primus, ipse octauus, ipse ultimus. Ipse sic erit ultimus ut sit perpetuus. Ipse angelica uisitatione festiuus, et redemptoris aduentu sacratissimus; ipse resurrectione saluatoris sabbatissimus; ipse aduentu paracliti celeberrimus; et, peracto iudicio, cum fuerit celum nouum et terra noua ipse erit, ut prephati sumus, sempiternus.[58]

> [After the number seven, the number eight arises, sustained by royal might. For he is the true eight, who "taketh away the sins of the world." He is first, he is eighth, he is last. It will be the last that it may be everlasting. It is celebrated by an angelic visitation, and it is sanctified by the saviour's advent; it is most Sabbath through the saviour's resurrection; it is most renowned through the advent of the Holy Ghost; and, as we have said, it will be eternal following the day of judgment, when there will be a new heaven and a new earth.]

Although the syntax of this particular passage is not very difficult, it exhibits a number of the characteristics of Byrhtferth's Latin, such as polysyllabic

57 Baker and Lapidge, eds., *Byrhtferth's Enchiridion*, lxxiii.
58 Ibid., 212–13.

names for numbers, anaphora ("ipse ... ipse ... ipse ..."), Greek-influenced spelling ("prephati"), and seemingly unnecessary superlatives ("sabbatissimus," "celeberrimus").[59] Of course he is discussing God here, so a superlative is not completely out of place, but I would draw particular attention to the first of them, "sabbatissimus," which appears to be a coinage of Byrhtferth himself. While Grecisms are standard, if not *de rigueur*, in hermeneutic Latin, this new coinage of Byrhtferth's is a Hebraism, formed on the Latin from the Hebrew loanword *sabbat*. This is the only case of such a Hebrew-based neologism I am aware of in the body of Anglo-Latin texts. Furthermore, like the Hebrew-based example of paronomasia above, the educational value of this new word is dubious. What, exactly, would "most Sabbath" mean? As Lapidge has suggested, Byrhtferth seems to have been attracted to polysyllabicity for its own sake; this word additionally takes the conventions of hermeneutic Latin a step further to include Hebrew.[60]

His most extraordinary employment of Hebrew, however, occurs slightly earlier in this section and exemplifies how Byrhtferth uses his learning to draw a line between the *cognoscenti* monks and the rest of his audience. After concluding a lengthy section on the number four, Byrhtferth provides the following transition sentence: "De quaternario Galileam faciamus ad quinarium" (From four let us make a Galilee to five). This seemingly nonsensical sentence is only rendered intelligible by a gloss which explains "Galileam id est transmigrationem."[61] Byrhtferth has attempted to make the Hebrew proper noun *Galilee* stand in place of its etymology, extending the reach of erudite vocabulary to include Hebrew proper nouns. Of course, Byrhtferth is not unique in his knowledge of these interpretations. As I have discussed before, Hebrew etymologies of proper nouns were a popular source of exegetical material since the time of Jerome and before.[62] Gregory the Great uses them in his homilies, as does Bede, and Ælfric, all with great enthusiasm. The difference is that these authors use Hebrew etymologies in order to aid in the explication of biblical texts in which a given Hebrew word appears. But this is not what Byrhtferth is doing at all – he is trying something new: turning to Jerome's definitions of Hebrew names as fodder for his vocabulary. Again, I know

59 See Lapidge, ed., *Byrhtferth of Ramsey: Lives*, xliv–lxv.
60 Lapidge, ed., *Byrhtferth of Ramsey: Lives*, xlvi–xlvii.
61 Baker and Lapidge, eds., *Byrhtferth's Enchiridion*, 203.
62 Fleming, "*Jesus*, that is *hælend*," 26–8.

of no other author turning to Jerome's etymologies for vocabulary, especially for something as mundane as this. He returns to his Hebraism again at the conclusion of the section on arithmology. Having explained fifty, he declares further,

> Fiat, precor, Galilea (id est transmigratio) de morte ad uitam, de corruptione ad incorruptionem; de pena ad gloriam <licet> nobis transire: quasi quinquagenarium relinquentes assumere mereamur sexagenarium uel epinicion, quod nomen palmam siue triumphum possumus appellare. De sexagessimo et septuagessimo et octuagesimo necnon et nonagesimo, supersedimus hoc in loco sermocinari, ne forte <perturbemus> audientes.[63]

> [Let there be, I pray, a Galilee (that is a crossing), from death to life, from corruption to purity; it is fitting for us to proceed from suffering to glory – as if, abandoning fifty, we deserve to acquire the sixty or the *epinicion*, which we render "palm" or "triumph." We omit to discuss the numbers sixty, seventy, eighty and ninety at this point, lest we aggravate our audience.]

Byrhtferth was so pleased with his first attempt at using a Hebrew proper noun in running prose that he tried it out again, here with rhetorical flourish for the conclusion to his discussion of numbers. Byrhtferth suggests a way of making simple prose almost into a cipher, which would only be understood by those who had access to the exegetical tradition of Jerome and Bede. Byrhtferth apparently came up with this idea late in his production of the *Enchiridion* and does not develop it further. One does not get the sense that he was confident that his readership would understand what he was doing – both times he uses it, the word *Galilee* is explained in glosses which may very well have been written by Byrhtferth himself. But he has done something truly innovative here; he is trying, as it were, to speak a little Hebrew.[64] He has moved beyond the conventions of his fellow learned Benedictines who relied on Greek-Latin glossaries for their arcane vocabulary. For Hebrew, the only such available lists were Jerome's lists of proper nouns, and Byrhtferth has, at least with this one word, tried to use it. Of course, we have no evidence that anyone ever followed his innovation, but such is the case for the entirety of Byrhtferth's eclectic text.

63 Baker and Lapidge, eds., *Byrhtferth's Enchiridion*, 226–7.
64 Cf. Fleming, "*Rex regum*," 242–50.

If we cannot speak to the lasting influence of Byrhtferth, we can speak of what he represents: he is emblematic, in many ways, of Anglo-Saxon intellectual attitudes towards Hebrew – a language never forgotten or perceived as utterly unattainable. Rather Byrhtferth, like many of his countrymen, makes Hebrew palpable and tangible by sharing the months' names, the alphabet, and the superfluous etymologies; at the same time, Hebrew serves to reaffirm his and his fellow monks' sense of intellectual superiority. Ælfric, too, feels that Hebrew is close: it is a language which can be known, to a certain extent at least, and should be known by all Christians because of its historical importance in the transmission of scripture. But Ælfric never uses it to alienate his audience, rather to raise his audience up by showing them some of the Hebrew they already know: New Testament words like *racha* and *vah*. Furthermore, Ælfric's discussion of Hebrew interjections authorizes him to widen the scope of his *Grammar* to discuss not only Latin but languages generally, and in doing so is able to place English on an international historical stage.

Oswald's *versus retrogradi*: A Forerunner of Post-Conquest Trends in Hexameter Composition

LESLIE LOCKETT

Only one Anglo-Saxon poet is known to have composed retrograde verse, that is, poetry that is metrically and syntactically viable when read both forwards and backwards, word by word. This poet names himself "Osuuoldus" in a brief work of twenty-one dactylic hexameters, which begins with the words "Centum concito" and survives only in Cambridge, University Library, Gg.5.35.[1] These hexameters appear to be unremarkable, and their retrograde nature is betrayed only by the final line of the poem, which instructs the reader, "Versa uertice iosum scandens perlege susum" (Scanning downwards with the top turned down, read upwards).[2] Immediately following "Centum concito" in the manuscript is another composition in retrograde verse. These four elegiac couplets in praise of God, which begin "Terrigene bene nunc laudent," do not advertise their retrograde nature or name their author.[3] Michael Lapidge proposes that the author of both poems was Oswald the Younger of Ramsey, first a student and then a monk at Ramsey in the decades before and after the year 1000, as well as the nephew and namesake of St Oswald of Worcester, archbishop of York (972–92).[4]

In this essay I take up the authorial identity of this Oswald in a different sense. My objective is neither to corroborate nor to challenge Lapidge's conclusions about his individual identity but rather to explore what sort

1 On this manuscript, see Rigg and Wieland, "Canterbury Classbook."

2 Quotations and translations of "Centum concito" follow Lapidge, "Hermeneutic Style," 144–5.

3 "Terrigene bene nunc laudent" is edited and translated into German by Dronke, Lapidge, and Stotz, "Die unveröffentlichten Gedichte," 67–8.

4 Lapidge, "The Hermeneutic Style," 132–3, and "Oswald the Younger."

of intellectual and aesthetic genealogy Oswald embraced when he chose to compose in an extremely unusual metrical form. In the past, study of the vocabulary and syntax of Oswald's two poems has underscored affinities with the "hermeneutic style" that was especially favoured by authors working within the milieu of English reformed Benedictine monasticism from the mid-tenth century through the early eleventh. However, with respect to metrical structure, Oswald's "Centum concito" departs radically from the classical and Aldhelmian norms that govern the hexameter compositions of other practitioners of the "hermeneutic style" in England. My metrical analysis of Oswald's retrograde verses suggests that Oswald is better understood as an early adopter of Carolingian versification practices that did not flower in England until after the Conquest.

Oswald's Retrograde Elegiacs and Their Antecedents

Oswald's "Terrigene bene nunc laudent" is metrically interesting in its own right, but it offers little insight into the poet's metrical models and artistic affiliations, so my discussion of the poem here will be brief. A rigid metrical pattern governs all four elegiac couplets; the variable feet of each hexameter scan DDSS, and the variable feet of each pentameter scan DS.[5] Even more striking, the positions of word-breaks remain largely unchanged from one line to the next, as becomes clear when the hexameter lines are printed together, followed by the pentameter lines, as in table 9.1.[6]

One might suppose it would be easy to identify metrical models for such an idiosyncratic performance. In fact, it is not difficult to compare Oswald's poems with all of their relevant antecedents, because the corpus of surviving retrogrades from antiquity and the early Middle Ages is quite small, and because only a few of those surviving retrogrades consist of bidirectional hexameters and elegiac couplets, the rest being written in unusual metres, such as a bidirectional sotadean or an iambic trimeter that

5 The elegiac couplet consists of a dactylic hexameter and a pentameter. In a dactylic hexameter, the first four feet may be either dactylic (D) or spondaic (S), while the fifth is typically a dactyl and the sixth necessarily a spondee or trochee. The pentameter line consists of two units of two and a half dactyls, separated by a caesura; spondees are admitted in place of dactyls prior to the caesura. For a concise introduction to the scansion of classical Latin hexameters and elegiac couplets, see Raven, *Latin Metre*, 90–9 and 103–6.

6 Though rearranged, the text follows Dronke, Lapidge, and Stotz, "Die unveröffentlichten Gedichte," 67–8.

Table 9.1. Structure of retrograde elegiac couplets

Hexameters	4 syllables	2	1	variable	3	2
Oswald 1	Terrigene	bene	nunc	laudent ut	condecet	almum
Oswald 3	Celigenam	patre	de	celo for	gaudia	mundi
Oswald 5	Omnipotens	habet	hic	nomen hoc	fungitur	actu
Oswald 7	Verbotenus	fore	sunt	que fecit	robore	grandi
"neoterici"	Icarium	Notus	ut	confidens	flamine	tranat
Optatian 15	perpetuis	bene	sic	partiri	munera	saeclis
Sidonius	Praecipiti	modo	quod	decurrit	tramite	flumen

Pentameters	3 syllables	variable	1	2	4
Oswald 2	uocibus	excelsis	sic	sibi	perplacitis
Oswald 4	debita	soluentem	que	pia	perficiat
Oswald 6	uiribus	eternis	est	iugis	altithronus
Oswald 8	omnia	subsistunt	ut	regit	omnipatrans
"neoterici"	caerula	uerrentes	sic	freta	Nereides
Optatian 15	sidera	dant patri	et	patris	imperium
Sidonius	tempore	consumptum	iam	cito	deficiet

becomes a dactylic pentameter when reversed.[7] I am aware of only four compositions in retrograde elegiacs that antedate Oswald's. One of these may be swiftly eliminated from the pool of Oswald's possible models: this is a poem consisting of eight retrograde couplets plus their reversed readings, now numbered carmen 28 among the works of the fourth-century panegyrist Publilius Optatianus Porfyrius.[8] Carmen 28 is excluded from all surviving manuscripts of Optatian's series of panegyrics; it survives

7 Flores and Polara, "Specimina di analisi," 113–15. On the comparatively large corpus of later medieval retrogrades, see Lockett, "Composition and Transmission." In that essay I prematurely claimed that very few retrograde poems of more than two lines are known to survive; however, I have since uncovered a number of previously unedited retrograde poems of various metres and lengths. Editions of these poems will appear in my book (in progress) on the history of retrograde verse from antiquity through the early modern era.

8 Polara, ed., *Publilii Optatiani carmina*, 1.109.

only in the Codex Salmasianus, which Oswald is unlikely to have seen.[9] Furthermore, Optatian succeeded in introducing some degree of metrical variety into his elegiacs, which Oswald would presumably have imitated had he known this poem.[10]

Each of the remaining three specimens consists of an individual retrograde couplet: one, attributed to the "neoterici," is reported by the late antique grammarians Diomedes and Aphthonius;[11] a second appears amid other retrograde metres in Optatian's carmen 15;[12] and Sidonius Apollinaris composed a couplet to illustrate the mechanics of retrograde verse.[13] But as table 9.1 shows, all three couplets are structured identically to one another and to "Terrigene bene nunc laudent," so it is impossible to say which of them lent inspiration to Oswald. Setting aside the possibility that Oswald had access to a model of continuous retrograde elegiacs that has not survived, the simplest explanation for "Terrigene bene nunc laudent" is that Oswald took note of a single retrograde couplet in Optatian's carmen 15 or a Latin grammar, and he replicated its metrical structure four times in succession.

Oswald's Retrograde Hexameters

Oswald opens "Centum concito" with exuberant praise for the poet who is capable of writing retrograde verse: "the resplendent scansion confers the bounty of praise on the poet: let this poet by all means be called Vergilian" (lines 4–5). Although he adopts a more humble posture in lines 9–13 and 17–18, Oswald twice expresses a longing to be included among

9 On the separate transmission histories of Optatian's panegyric series and carmen 28, see Polara, ed., *Publilii Optatiani carmina*, 1.viii–xix and 1.xxviii. Recent scholarship favours an origin in central Italy in the late eighth or early ninth century for the Codex Salmasianus (Paris, Bibliothèque nationale de France, lat. 10318 [CLA 5.593]); see Spallone, "Il Par. lat. 10318 (Salmasiano)."

10 In carmen 28, hexameters scan DDDS and DDSS, and pentameters scan DD, DS, SD, and SS before the caesura. Hexameters begin (and pentameters end) with four- and seven-syllable words; hexameters end (and pentameters begin) with two- and three-syllable words.

11 Diomedes, *Ars*, *GL* 1.221–529, at 1.517; Aphthonius, *De metris* (printed as part of Marius Victorinus, *Ars*), *GL* 6.31–173, at 6.114.

12 As a whole, carmen 15 is the metrical equivalent of a needlework sampler, in which each row displays a different ornamental stitch. Optatian, carmen 15, lines 9–10; in Polara, ed., *Publilii Optatiani carmina*, 1.62.

13 Sidonius Apollinaris, ep. 9.14.4, in Loyen, ed., *Sidoine Apollinaire*, 3.172.

the ranks of the intellectual elite (7–8 and 14–16). Despite his profession of humility, above all Oswald desires that his audience appreciate his poetic virtuosity.

Metrical exigencies undeniably constrain the composer of retrograde hexameters and elegiacs. To cobble together a single retrograde epigram might constitute a modest word-game, but to compose continuous retrogrades served to display the author's intellectual and artistic agility in the face of extreme formal constraints. Therefore in the opening lines of "Centum concito," Oswald advertises not only the quality of his retrograde verses but also their quantity, as well as the efficiency with which he produced them: "He who knows how to compose quickly a hundred lines in this manner." (line 1) deserves abundant praise. Oswald's rhetoric has proven persuasive to modern readers: Lapidge characterizes Oswald's retrograde hexameters as a "fiendishly difficult form" in which to compose.[14]

However, I would locate Oswald's virtuosity in the innovative structure of his retrograde hexameters rather than in the inherent difficulty of his medium. "Centum concito," like "Terrigene bene nunc laudent," adheres throughout to a metrical pattern that greatly eases the challenges of composing quantitative retrograde verse. In the case of "Centum concito," the pattern permits some metrical variety and, importantly, it seems to be a pattern of Oswald's own devising. The most efficient way to illustrate this pattern is to print the text with space introduced after the second and fourth foot of each hexameter, as I have done below.[15]

Centum concito	sic qui nouit	condere uersus
nullo crimine	commaculatos,	ordine gratos,
sensu denique	confertos et	cursibus aptos –
laudis munera	dat dictanti	scansio lucens:
Virgilianus	hic dicetur	maxime uates.
Ingeniosis	ars hec paret	nescia mismet:
experientis	sensum exercet	sepius ipsam,

14 Lapidge, "Oswald the Younger."

15 Note that in Gg.5.35, metrical segments are *not* spatially separated. Aside from the spacing, the text and translation printed here follow Lapidge, "Hermeneutic Style," 144–5, with the sole exception that at line 17 he prints "lectos" and I read "lector." The scribe either wrote *–s* and corrected to *–r* or vice versa, but the reading "lector" is supported by the interlinear gloss, "s[cilicet]. O," meaning that the glossed form is vocative.

doctilogorum nam socium dat doctificando.
istos texuit Osuuoldus, qui est nescius artis;
tantum nomine cognoscit hanc nescius actu.
ob hoc cernuus omnipotentem deprecor orans
idem quatinus haud omittat criminis ergo
perpetuali infaustum subdi segnitiei.
mentem tangere is dignetur pneumate sancto
prudens utpote prudens dicar nomine statim;
concopulari necnon doctis quiuero post hinc.
lector cernere qui dignaris, corrige, uersus,
radens noxia uatis, delens crimina noxȩ:
restituentur perpetualia premia facto!
uatis gloria stat rectori maxima digne.
uersa uertice iosum scandens perlege susum.

[He who knows how to compose quickly a hundred lines in this manner, marred by no fault, pleasing in their arrangement, and then full of meaning and suitable in their cadences – [why,] the resplendent scansion confers the bounty of praise on the poet: let this poet by all means be called "Vergilian." This unwitting skill of mine obeys the intellectuals: it often taxes the mind of someone experiencing it, for by its intellectualizing it provides a companion for the verbally learned.

Oswold, who is ignorant of the art [of composition] composed these lines; he knows this art by name only and is ignorant of its workings. For that reason, praying as a suppliant, I beseech omnipotent God that he not permit (?) unfortunate me – for the sake of an error – to be subjected to perpetual sluggishness. If he deign to touch my mind with the Holy Ghost, I shall straightway be called wise in the true sense of the word; henceforth I'll also be able to associate with learned men.

You who deign to examine my select verses, correct them, stripping off the poet's peccadilloes, deleting the errors of his [metrical] offence: let perpetual rewards be returned for this deed! The greatest glory of the poet justly accrues to his corrector.

Scanning downwards with the top turned down, read upwards [i.e., the poem can be read upside-down or downside-up].]

As this arrangement of the text reveals, Oswald has not fashioned twenty-one integral retrograde hexameters; instead, he has composed sixty-three self-contained retrogradable segments of two feet apiece, which are juxtaposed to resemble hexameters.

Each of the three segments in Oswald's hexameters follows a particular formula that ensures the retrogradability of the entire line. The final segment constitutes an adonic (i.e., a dactyl plus a spondee); Oswald fills this segment with a single pentasyllable or with a trisyllable followed by a disyllable, to ensure that the line will open with a long syllable when it is scanned backwards.[16] This adonic is mirrored in the first segment: here Oswald employs either a pentasyllable that scans as an adonic, or a spondaic disyllable and a dactylic trisyllable, either of which will supply the required fifth-foot dactyl when the line is reversed. The final adonic and the initial "mirror adonic" elements pivot around a central segment that need not have any short syllables in it; the easiest way to ensure its proper scansion in both directions is to fill the segment with four long syllables (e.g., "dat dictanti") or a single word that fills both feet (e.g., "perpetualia"). Oswald uses one of these two methods to fill the middle segment everywhere except line 8 ("nam socium dat"). This tripartite formula greatly simplifies the task of composing bidirectional hexameters, enabling the poet "to compose quickly a hundred lines in this manner."

Evaluating "Centum concito" as a Hexameter Composition

The few retrograde hexameters that antedate "Centum concito" occur in the same types of texts that supply the elegiac couplets considered above: three of them are cited by late antique grammarians, and one forms part of Optatian's verse "sampler" in carmen 15. However, none of these earlier retrograde hexameters is a free-standing epigram. Aside from the bidirectional hexameter by Optatian,[17] all are "accidental" retrogrades that occur in the course of Vergil's *Eclogues* and *Aeneid*. Aphthonius quotes *Eclogues* 8.96 and *Aeneid* 1.8 to exemplify the bidirectional hexameter;[18]

16 In retrograde verse, prepositions that immediately precede their objects often act as proclitics: "post hinc" in line 16 remains "post hinc" when the line is reversed, and the same is true of "ob hoc" in line 11.

17 Optatian, carmen 15, line 9; in Polara, ed., *Publilii Optatiani carmina*, 1.62.

18 Aphthonius, *De metris*, *GL* 6.113–14.

Diomedes similarly adduces *Aeneid* 1.8;[19] and in his commentary on the *Aeneid*, Servius observes that 7.634 is retrograde as well as a spondaizon (i.e., the fifth foot is a spondee rather than the expected dactyl).[20]

Ecl. 8.96:	ipse dedit || Moeris, || nascuntur | plurima ponto	DSSS
Aen. 1.8:	Musa, mihi || causas || memora quo | numine laeso	DSSD
Optatian 15:	alme pater || patriae, || nobis te, | maxime Caesar	DDSS
Aen. 7.634:	aut leuis ocreas || lento || ducunt argento	SDSS+SS

Unlike the hexameters of "Centum concito," which are divided into three equal parts by virtue of diaeresis after the second and fourth feet, these lines exhibit the medial caesuras that are expected to occur in ordinary Latin hexameters: trihemimeral and penthemimeral caesuras in the first three examples, and penthemimeral and hepthemimeral caesuras in *Aeneid* 7.634.[21] Whereas Oswald could have modelled "Terrigene bene nunc laudent" on any of the earlier retrograde elegiacs except Optatian's carmen 28, he could not have modelled "Centum concito" on any of the bidirectional hexameters known to have been available to him.

I would emphasize that the four retrograde hexameters with which I have compared "Centum concito" are structurally unremarkable. That is, "Centum concito" is metrically at odds with these four retrogrades because Oswald contravenes the norms of classical and medieval hexameter composition. To illustrate the idiosyncrasy of Oswald's hexameters, let us compare their structure with that of a few hexameter compositions that were held to be authoritative models for Anglo-Saxon poets: the works of Vergil, the biblical epic *Euangelia* of Juvencus (fl. ca. 330), and the works of Aldhelm (ob. 709/710).

As illustrated above, the tripartite structure of each of Oswald's hexameters results from the repeated use of diaeresis to separate the second foot from the third and the fourth from the fifth. In traditional hexameters, diaeresis may appear frequently between the fourth and fifth feet:

19 Diomedes, *Ars grammatica*, *GL* 1.516–17.

20 Maurus Servius Honoratus, *In Vergilii carmina commentarii*, in Thilo and Hagen, eds., *Servii Grammatici commentarii*, 2.175.

21 Caesura (here marked ||) is a break between words that occurs in the middle of a foot; diaeresis (here marked |) is a break between words that coincides with a break between feet.

diaeresis at this position occurs at a rate of roughly 52.5 per cent in Vergil, 50.0 per cent in Juvencus, and 67.5 per cent in Aldhelm.[22] Oswald, however, employs diaeresis at the end of the fourth foot 100 per cent of the time in "Centum concito."

Oswald also places diaeresis at the end of the second foot in twenty of his twenty-one lines.[23] Classical and early medieval hexameter poets habitually minimized diaeresis in this position, to the extent that diaeresis at the end of the second foot is not typically accounted for in statistical studies of caesura and diaeresis.[24] To supply comparative data, I calculated the frequency of diaeresis at the end of the second foot in passages of the same length at the start of other hexameter compositions. In the opening twenty-one lines of Vergil's *Aeneid*, diaeresis occurs at the end of the second foot only once; it occurs once in the opening twenty-one lines of Juvencus's *Evangelia*, and it does not occur at all in the opening twenty-one lines of Aldhelm's *Carmen de virginitate.* It is also instructive to consider the overall density of diaeresis in these passages. A maximum of five diaereses may occur in a hexameter line; Oswald employs diaeresis at most of the available positions, such that an average of 3.95 diaereses occur per hexameter in "Centum concito," a rate that far exceeds that of standard hexameters. In the opening twenty-one lines, diaeresis occurs at a rate of 1.52 per line in the *Aeneid*, 1.71 per line in Juvencus, and 2.38 per line in Aldhelm's *Carmen de virginitate.*

The unusually high occurrence of diaeresis in "Centum concito" goes hand in hand with the frequent absence of the medial caesura, which classical principles prescribe must be present. Standard hexameters typically exhibit a caesura in the third foot, either a strong caesura after the first syllable (known as the penthemimeral caesura) or a weak caesura after the first short syllable of a dactyl (a trochaic caesura). In the absence of a penthemimeral caesura, a strong caesura should appear in the second and fourth feet (the trihemimeral and hepthemimeral caesuras).[25] Among Vergil's hexameters, only 2.5 per cent lack a caesura in the third foot

---

22 These figures are drawn from Orchard, *Poetic Art*, 92–3; the diaeresis after the fourth foot is called "C2" in table 6. Orchard has rounded off the data in this table to the nearest 2.5 per cent.

23 Elision prevents diaeresis after the second foot in line 13: "perpetual(i) in | faustum."

24 Orchard, *Poetic Art*, 92–3.

25 See further Raven, *Latin Metre*, 95–8.

(either penthemimeral or trochaic), and Juvencus and Aldhelm virtually never fail to include a caesura in the third foot.[26] In stark contrast, 57.1 per cent of the lines in "Centum concito" lack a caesura of any kind in the third foot.

Oswald's metrical idiosyncrasies might seem inconsequential, but they alter the rhythm and the sound of his hexameters so radically that to the ear (or the mind's ear) of the tenth- or early eleventh-century reader, "Centum concito" could scarcely have sounded like hexameters at all. The omnipresence of diaeresis in "Centum concito," along with the correspondingly low rate of caesuras per line, effectively increases the coincidence of natural stress-accent with the first long syllable of each foot – a coincidence that classical and early medieval hexameter poets sought to minimize in the first four feet of each verse in order to keep the rhythm from becoming overly sing-song.

The preference for caesura over diaeresis, especially in the first half of each hexameter, was ingrained in early medieval students of Latin literature as part of their elementary training. Bede teaches that the most praiseworthy sort of hexameter exhibits "conjoined scansion," which admits no diaereses at all, as in the opening line of Juvencus's *Euangelia*: "inmor- | tale ni- | hil mun- | di con- | page te- | netur." At the other end of the spectrum, a hexameter exhibits "districtive scansion" if every break between feet coincides with a break between words. "You will find this very rarely" in the authoritative hexameter poets, according to Bede, who further specifies that such a line cannot be reckoned viable ("ratus haberi uersus nequit") if it does not have a penthemimeral or hepthemimeral caesura.[27] "Centum concito" clearly does not conform to Bede's prescriptions. Eight of twenty-one lines in "Centum concito" contain no medial caesura; six lines contain no caesura whatsoever; and four of its lines are entirely districtive, that is, every break between feet coincides with a break between words.

Weighing "Centum concito" against the standards of classical hexameter composition necessarily leads to a negative judgment that Oswald's formula for composing "a hundred such verses quickly" was achieved at

26 Orchard, *Poetic Art*, 92–3.

27 Bede, *De arte metrica* 1.12; ed. Kendall, CCSL 123A, 116.

the expense of traditional metrical viability. His metrical idiosyncrasies make it difficult to localize Oswald's literary niche among the poets of tenth- and early eleventh-century England, whose hexameters and elegiac couplets staunchly aspire to the metrical standards of the curriculum authors. I have been unable to find evidence that any poet writing in England during this period shared Oswald's inclination towards experimental or innovative metres.[28] Several of Oswald's contemporaries and predecessors in England engaged in the composition of acrostics and figural poems, an endeavour whose roots stretch back to the panegyrics of Optatian, but by metrical criteria, the acrostics of tenth-century England are quite conventional.[29]

In sum, if vocabulary and syntax dictate that Oswald's literary niche was among the poets of the reformed Benedictine milieu in England, then metrical idiosyncrasies make Oswald's small oeuvre something of a strange footnote to the history of a compositional tradition dominated by Aldhelmian norms. Evaluating "Centum concito" on its own terms, however, rather than against Aldhelmian models and Bedan prescriptions, brings to light a different intellectual genealogy that better explains Oswald's choice of metrical form.

Evaluating "Centum concito" as an Innovative Compound Metre

I suggested above that the high rate of diaeresis in "Centum concito" fundamentally alters the sound of the lines, so that their rhythm is radically different from hexameters with the expected medial caesuras. In fact, the rhythm of "Centum concito" bears a much stronger resemblance to that of continuous adonics, such as these which Alcuin of York, writing ca. 800 at Tours, composed in six-line stanzas: "Haec pia uerba / uirgo fidelis, / ore caneto / ut tua mitis / tempora Christus / tota gubernet."[30] The structural similarity between hexameters and continuous adonics was

---

28 Discussion of the pertinent texts may be found in Lapidge, "Hermeneutic Style" and "Tenth-Century Anglo-Latin Verse Hagiography."

29 Gwara, "Three Acrostic Poems"; Lapidge, "Hermeneutic Style," 134 (on Dunstan's "O pater omnipotens").

30 Alcuin, "Te homo laudet," lines 25–30, MGH PLAC 1.303.

occasionally amplified by those scribes who copied continuous adonics three to a line.[31] Now, the composition of continuous adonics has been shown to be very rare in the English Benedictine milieu of the tenth and early eleventh centuries: Michael Lapidge identifies the *Responsio discipuli* associated with Æthelwold's circle in Winchester as the only surviving Anglo-Saxon composition in continuous adonics.[32] Moreover, the structural similarity between continuous adonics and hexameters was not exploited by pre-Conquest Anglo-Latin poets. However, continuous adonics, as well as innovative compound metres that employed adonics as building-blocks of longer quantitative forms, were popular among post-Conquest authors in England.

The evolution of adonics into tripartite hexameters is well illustrated by the *Epigrams* of Henry of Huntingdon (c. 1088–c. 1154). Henry casts his sixteen-line poem "On England's Troubles" in a quantitative metre equivalent to two adonics per line: "Garrula puri uenula fontis, / Sorde repleta reddere priscas / Gurgite presso abnuit undas."[33] Shortly thereafter follows an epigram in adonic hexameters: "Qui tenerorum uulnus amorum non reueretur / Innumerorum tela dolorum perpetuetur."[34] Henry's epigrams also exemplify the fact that in the post-Conquest period, rigidly segmented forms of the hexameter were cultivated primarily in order to facilitate rhyme, not retrogradability. Segmented rhymed hexameters flourished throughout the later Middle Ages: *dactylici tripertiti* and adonic hexameters, which require diaeresis at the ends of the second and fourth feet of each line, as well as leonines and *trinini salientes*, which require that medial caesuras recur in the same place in each line.[35] Adonic hexameters

31 For instance, Alcuin's "Te homo laudet" is copied without line breaks at the ends of verses in St Gall, Stiftsbibliothek 269 (s. x, St Gall), pp. 475–6, with the result that sections of the poem are written with precisely three adonics to the line: see the digital facsimile at www.e-codices.unifr.ch./en/csg/0269/.

32 Lapidge, "Three Latin Poems," 263, and "Authorship of the Adonic Verses 'ad Fidolium,'" 827.

33 Henry of Huntington, epigram 1.19, lines 1–3, in Greenway, ed., *Henry of Huntington*, 794. Epigram 1.5, though incomplete, also employs a compound metre of two adonics per line (ibid., 784).

34 Henry, epigram 1.25; in Greenway, ed., *Henry of Huntington*, 802. See also Rigg, "Henry of Huntingdon's Metrical Experiments," 61–2.

35 On these verse types, see Norberg, *Introduction*, 59–62.

and *dactylici tripertiti* would also appear amid the polymetry of several Anglo-Latin authors of the thirteenth and fourteenth centuries.[36]

Oswald was not the only English author to recognize how easily tripartite hexameters could be made retrogradable. An English manuscript of the thirteenth century contains a copy (already thoroughly corrupted) of an anonymous treatise that begins "Hec est forma componendi uersus retrogradientes [*sic*]" (This is a model for composing retrograde verses). Two pages' worth of original retrograde hexameters and elegiacs conclude with tripartite hexameters that are reminiscent of Oswald's:

Doctor strenue, mores corrige discipulorum,
mentes instrue, libros discere philosoforum.[37]

Although these retrogrades exhibit rhyme and a tendency towards rhythmic rather than quantitative scansion,[38] their author's technique for ensuring retrogradability is nearly identical to that which Oswald devised.

Oswald's unrhymed tripartite hexameters thus represent an early incarnation of versification techniques which would flourish after the Conquest but were yet absent from England in his day. To identify the influences that prompted Oswald to develop his unrhymed tripartite hexameters, I propose that we look to the Continent, where already in the ninth and tenth centuries, poets were experimenting with quantitative adonics and building innovative compound metres that approximated the dactylic hexameter.

Polymetry and Compound Metres among the Carolingians

Versification manuals that support the study and composition of quantitative metres other than the dactylic hexameter and the elegiac couplet were

36 For tripartite hexameters in John of Garland, see his *Parisiana poetria*, ed. Lawler, 186–7; in Michael of Cornwall and Robert Baston, see Rigg, *History of Anglo-Latin Literature, 1066–1422*, 319–21; and in the Prophecy of John of Bridlington, see ibid., 265.

37 Oxford, Bodleian Library, e Mus. 96, pp. 456–7; a second (and even more corrupted) copy survives in London, Lambeth Palace Library, 120, fols. 200v–201r (s.xiv). This unedited treatise receives detailed attention in my forthcoming history of retrograde verse.

38 E.g., "philosoforum" has a short first syllable and therefore is not a quantitative adonic.

widely available in western Europe before the Carolingian period;[39] however, unusual quantitative metres came to be more intently studied and more frequently emulated as the Carolingians became increasingly interested in two important polymetric works: Boethius's *De consolatione philosophiae* and Martianus Capella's *De nuptiis Philologiae et Mercurii*. The pre-Carolingian manuals typically defined long quantitative metres in terms of their constituent segments, and this practice was adopted in the ninth and tenth centuries by Lupus of Ferrières, Remigius of Auxerre, and many anonymous scholiasts who commented on the poems of Boethius and Martianus.

Lupus's treatise *Genera metrorum in librum Boetii*, which circulated widely alongside the *Consolatio*,[40] identifies (albeit erroneously) the metre of Boethius's second *metrum* of book 1 as the dactylic tetrameter, which according to Lupus "constat spondeo dactilo catalecto item dactilo spondeo" (consists of a spondee, a dactyl, a catalecton, then again a dactyl and a spondee).[41] The word *item* marks a fixed boundary between the two segments of the line – a penthemimere and an adonic respectively. Some scribes graphically reinforced the mental habit of conceptualizing long quantitative metres according to their constituent segments by introducing space between the shorter elements within each line of a compound metre. Thus in St Gall, Stiftsbibliothek 844, in which the *Consolatio* is supplemented with marginal glosses based on Lupus's treatise, the so-called dactylic tetrameters of the second *metrum* of book 1 are laid out in distinct segments:[42]

Cernebat rosei   Lumina solis ·: –
Visebat gelidae   Sidera lunae ·: –

39 Kendall, CCSL 123A, 60–72, provides descriptions of ninety-six manuscripts of Bede's *De arte metrica*; works with a more circumscribed dissemination include Mallius Theodorus's *De metris*, Servius's *Centimetrum*, and possibly treatises on the metres of Horace by Aphthonius and Servius.

40 Virginia Brown counts sixteen known copies of Lupus's treatise: see "Lupus of Ferrières," 63.

41 Lupus of Ferrières, "Genera metrorum in libro Boetii," in Peiper, ed., *Anicii Manlii Severini Boetii Philosophiae consolatio*, xxv. As Brown observes, this *metrum* is more properly described as a dactylic trimeter catalectic followed by an adonic ("Lupus of Ferrières," 74).

42 Boethius, *De consolatio philosophiae* 1 m 2, lines 8–12, transcribed from the digital facsimile of St Gall, Stiftsbibliothek 844, p. 17, at www.e-codices.unifr.ch/en/csg/0844/. I have silently incorporated scribal corrections and expanded abbreviations.

Et quecumque vagos	Stella recursus ·: –
Et exercet uarios	Flexa per orbes ·: –
Comprensam numeris	Victor habebat ·: –

The study of the metres of Boethius and Martianus stimulated Carolingian interest in imitating these authors' unusual metres in their own polymetric compositions and in using metrical building-blocks to devise new quantitative metres.[43]

I suspect that the habit of conceptualizing long quantitative metres according to their constituent segments also instigated a notable shift in the conceptualization of the dactylic hexameter, which had previously demanded integration and balance across the whole length of the line as well as metrical variation across a series of lines. Within the context of innovative polymetric compositions, lines that superficially resemble the hexameter could be constructed out of smaller metrical units whose boundaries remained fixed from one line to the next. The scope of the present essay does not permit thorough consideration of the numerous Carolingian poets who shared the new enthusiasm for polymetry and unusual, rigidly segmented metres (e.g., Heiric of Auxerre's *Vita sancti Germani* and the mnemonic verses on compound metres attributed to Walahfrid Strabo),[44] but the pertinent features of this trend and its effects on hexameter composition are usefully exemplified in Odo of Cluny's *Occupatio*.

Odo composed the seven books of this long theological poem in traditional dactylic hexameters, but each of the eight prefatory poems displays a different quantitative metre, each comprising two or three distinct segments.[45] Furthermore, the rigid segmentation of these prefatory metres is emphasized by their layout in the only surviving manuscript of the *Occupatio*: a small red capital (represented by bold type in the quotations of the *Occupatio* below) and vertical alignment mark the beginnings of the

43 See Klopsch, *Einführung*, 93–9.

44 Heiric, *Vita sancti Germanii*, ed. Ludwig Traube, MGH PLAC 3.421–527; on the mnemonic verses attributed to Walahfrid, see Huemer, "Zu Walahfrid Strabo."

45 Odo of Cluny, *Occupatio*, ed. Swoboda, xxii; on the overall character and content of the *Occupatio*, see Rosé, *Construire une société seigneuriale*, 320–4. A new edition of Odo's *Occupatio* with extensive commentary is now being prepared by Christopher A. Jones, to whom I am grateful for answering many questions about the poem and sharing his microfilm images of the manuscripts.

first and second segments within each line.[46] For instance, in the preface to book 3, each line contains a pair of adonics, which are arranged on the page in this fashion:[47]

Iam proto gibra	Marcet in umbra
Ceu tenebrosus	Nube reatus
Frixerat ardor	Ille polosus
Irruit algor	Demoniosus

Pertinent to our understanding of Oswald's endeavours, Odo also used short metrical segments to build metres that resemble hexameters. The preface to book 1 of the *Occupatio* consists of one minor archilochian followed by a dactylic trimeter catalectic in two syllables;[48] to put it another way, the segments add up to a dactylic hexameter which lacks the second half of the third foot. Again, the scribe underscored the segmentation of the line:[49]

Vita bonumque simul	Morsque malumque locatur
Ante hominem quod ei	Forte placet datur illi
Lex moysea refert	Hoc sophus ille fatetur

Similarly, Odo's preface to book 2 consists of hexameters that all scan DDS | DDS and are split by diaeresis between feet 3 and 4:[50]

En manus illa creatrix	De nichilo omnia finxit
Tale quid et dedit esse	Quod uigeat ratione
Scemate regis honorum	Cognitione beatum

The recurrent diaeresis diminishes the opportunity for a strong medial caesura in this prefatory poem; in fact, none of its ten lines contains a penthemimeral caesura, and only one line compensates for that lack by

46 The *Occupatio* survives in a single copy that is now split into two parts: Paris, Bibliothèque de l'Arsenal 903, fols. 1r–52r; and Paris, Bibliothèque Sainte-Geneviève 2410, fols. 174r–229v (s. x ex. or xi in., Canterbury?); see Gneuss, *Handlist*, number 903.

47 Odo, *Occupatio*, 3 *praef.* 1–4; transcribed from Arsenal 903, fol. 19r.

48 Swoboda, ed., *Odonis abbatis Cluniacensis Occupatio*, xxii.

49 Odo, *Occupatio*, 1 *praef.* 1–3, transcribed from Arsenal 903, fol. 1v.

50 Odo, *Occupatio*, 2 *praef.* 1–3; transcribed from Arsenal 903, fol. 8v.

supplying both trihemimeral and hepthemimeral caesuras.[51] For Odo, the lack of medial caesura did not vitiate this brief poem; he deliberately set aside the required medial caesura in order to devise a six-foot dactylic line that is rhythmically and graphically distinct from the traditional hexameters that follow in book 2. Perhaps Odo himself conceived of this preface not as ten hexameters, all with diaeresis at the end of the third foot, but as twenty dactylic trimeters catalectic in two syllables, paired up two to a line.[52]

In the same way, Oswald must have conceived of "Centum concito" not as a series of faulty hexameters but rather as a compound metre consisting of three dactylic dimeters per line. Odo's *Occupatio* exemplifies some Continental trends that may have prompted Oswald to devise such a compound metre, but in order to understand why Oswald decided to employ this compound metre in the composition of continuous retrogrades, we must return to the panegyrics of Optatianus Porfyrius.

"Centum concito" and Optatian's carmen 13

The scholia that circulated with Optatian's series of panegyric poems offer this explanation of the metre of carmen 13: "In hac pagina uersus est ex dimidio iambico et dimidio trochaico constans, qui dum fit reciprocus trochaicam partem in iambicam uertit et iambicam in trochaicam" (On this page, each verse consists of half an iambic line and half a trochaic line; when it is reversed, the trochaic part becomes iambic and the iambic part becomes trochaic).[53] To illustrate how this metre operates, I print here the first three lines of the poem, separated into metrical segments:[54]

– –	⏑ – ⏑	⏑ ⏑ –	⏑ – ⏑	– x
Princeps	beate,	placido	sub axe	iamnunc
iustis,	serene,	populis	fauente	mundo
uictor	triumpha	tribuens,	salubre	numen.

51 For the full text of the preface to book 2, see Swoboda, ed., *Odonis abbatis Cluniacensis Occupatio*, 14.

52 This is in fact Swoboda's identification of the metre (ibid., xxii).

53 Scholia to Optatian, carmen 13, in Polara, ed., *Publilii Optatiani carmina*, 1.54. While the last six syllables clearly follow a trochaic rhythm (– ⏑ – ⏑ – x), the iambic rhythm of the first half of the line is less obvious, because (as classical norms permit) the first iamb is replaced by a spondee, and the long syllable of the third iamb is resolved into two short syllables.

54 Optatian, carmen 13, in Polara, ed., *Publilii Optatiani carmina*, 1.55.

While the scholiast conceived of Optatian's metre as a bipartite one, it is equally accurate to regard it as tripartite. The first segment, consisting of two and a half iambs (¯¯|˘¯|˘), is a mirror image of the final segment consisting of two and a half trochees (˘|¯˘|¯x). The middle segment (˘˘|¯), in theory, provides half an iamb and half a trochee, but in practice, it merely sits still in its place while the rest of the line is inverted around it.

This is precisely the structural principle that underpins "Centum concito": the adonic of the final two feet and the "mirror adonic" of the first two feet pivot about the central segment, which Oswald made readily retrogradable by filling it with four long syllables or a single five- or six-syllable word. By adapting Optatian's structural principle to the dactylic hexameter, Oswald generated a verse form that his countrymen were more likely to appreciate, given that Anglo-Latin poets rarely composed in quantitative metres other than the hexameter and the elegiac couplet. A slavish imitation of carmen 13 was unlikely to impress an Anglo-Saxon readership: unless the reader comprehends lyric metres, Optatian's carmen 13 looks like an artificial metre that exists solely for the sake of facilitating continuous retrogrades, whereas Oswald's retrogrades are recognizable hexameters on the page, even if they sound unusual by Aldhelmian and Bedan standards.

Conclusions

Our view of the intellectual and artistic identity that Oswald claimed through his two retrograde poems depends upon which characteristics of his verse we understand to be the most indicative of his intellectual genealogy and artistic intentions. Both poems exhibit a restrained enthusiasm for the erudite vocabulary and obscure syntax associated with the reformed Benedictine milieu of pre-Conquest England, yet Oswald certainly did not aim to match the outlandish diction of (for instance) Frithegod, Dunstan, and Byrhtferth, so I hesitate to identify Oswald's mildly recherché language as the defining feature of his poetic style.[55]

---

55 Some of Oswald's compounds are common coin in late antique and medieval literature (terrigena, altithronus), while his more unusual compounds are nonetheless utterly transparent in meaning ("doctificando," "celigena," "omnipatrans," and "doctilogos," a Greek-Latin hybrid). Oswald's other Grecism ("pneuma") and grammatical archaisms ("mismet"; "ergo" as a preposition with the genitive) can be traced to mundane sources such as Priscian's *Institutiones*, Isidore's *Etymologiae*, and Ælfric's bilingual *Grammar*. Given the metrical parallels between the prefatory poems of Odo's *Occupatio* and

Of course our assessment of Oswald's artistic affiliations cannot gloss over the fact that he is the only Anglo-Saxon author known to have composed in retrograde metres. This choice must have been influenced at least partly by Optatian's series of panegyric poems, which suggests a link with Abbo of Fleury, who arguably consulted Optatian's carmina 2, 14, and 24 as models for the acrostic figural poems that he addressed to Dunstan while residing at Ramsey during the years 985–7.[56] Perhaps Oswald and his readers understood the decision to write in retrograde metres to signify affiliation with the sizeable group of Anglo-Saxon and Carolingian practitioners of acrostics and figural poems.[57] However, for Oswald's readers to have made this connection, they would have had to possess a more thorough familiarity with Optatian's whole panegyric series than we can reasonably presuppose, given the extreme rarity of new retrograde compositions in England and on the Continent during the early Middle Ages.

With respect to Oswald's poetic genealogy, the key characteristic of his small oeuvre is not simply that both poems are retrograde but that Oswald devised a way to generate continuous retrograde hexameters with great efficiency by segmenting the hexameter into three self-contained retrogradable units. Outside of "Centum concito," the practice of devising new compound metres – especially metres that resemble dactylic hexameters but circumvent classical prescriptions about the positioning of caesuras – was a distinctly non-English practice prior to the Conquest, while many Carolingian poets made compound metres a part of their polymetric repertoires already in the ninth and tenth centuries. Oswald appears to have been the first poet working in England to produce segmented hexameters; the first to incorporate into his own writings the segmented approach to long quantitative metres found in Lupus's treatise on the metres of Boethius; and the first to emulate Carolingian poets, such as Odo of Cluny, who put adonics to use in longer compound metres and who devised new metres that superficially resemble the classical dactylic hexameter.[58]

Oswald's "Centum concito," it may be significant that Odo and Oswald share the rare, archaic forms "iosum" and "susum" (*Occupatio* 1.206 and 4.293; "Centum concito," line 21); see Lapidge, "Hermeneutic Style," 133n3.

56 Gwara, "Three Acrostic Poems," 209–10.

57 Ibid., 210n32.

58 The international profile that emerges of our "Osuuoldus" is entirely compatible with Lapidge's proposition that he was Oswald the Younger of Ramsey, who studied under Abbo of Fleury and travelled at length among centres of Benedictine learning on the Continent, chiefly Fleury, where Optatian's panegyrics were available.

German Imperial Bishops and Anglo-Saxon Literary Culture on the Eve of the Conquest: *The Cambridge Songs* and Leofric's Exeter Book

ELIZABETH M. TYLER

Two impressively large poetic collections, one Latin (Cambridge, University Library, Gg.5.35) and the other English (the Exeter Book, Exeter 3501), survive from late Anglo-Saxon England. The close literary and social ties which connect these two manuscripts during and immediately after Edward the Confessor's reign (joint king with Harthacnut 1041–2, sole king 1042–66) illustrate a newly dynamic relationship between Latin and the vernacular in mid-eleventh-century England. Both Latin and English texts were fully a part of new developments in European literary culture evident on both sides of the Channel.[1] This relationship between Latin and English was unlike that of the tenth and earlier eleventh century when England's extensive, and from a Continental perspective unusual, use of the written vernacular enabled a difficult style, unintended to communicate beyond elite Benedictine reformed circles, to dominate the Latin written in England (though not, of course, the Latin circulating in England).[2] Standing outside the Anglo-Saxon literary canon defined by *Beowulf*, Ælfric, and difficult Latin, and seemingly about to be swept away by the Norman Conquest, the literary history of the Confessor's reign (and the years just following) has not seemed worthy of attention.

Recent work on the continuity and vitality of written English into the twelfth century, on Goscelin's hagiography, and on history-writing in

1 O'Donnell, Townend, and Tyler, "European Literature."

2 Lapidge, "Hermeneutic Style" and "Poeticism," 336; Tyler, "From Old English to Old French," 168, and Stephenson, "Byrhtferth's *Enchiridion*." Difficult Latin is also a feature of tenth-century Continental and Continentally educated writers (for example, Rather of Verona, Liudprand of Cremona, Abbo of St Germain des Près, Lantfred, and Frithegod) but does not dominate in the way it does in England.

Latin and English has begun to build up the story of literary culture in mid- and late eleventh-century England.[3] *The Cambridge Songs*, a collection of Latin poems brought together in Germany and found in Gg.5.35, and the vernacular Exeter Book, donated by Bishop Leofric to Exeter in 1072, also testify to the richness of the literary culture of the Confessor's reign. This richness disappears from view if we fail to look at pre-Conquest England as fully integrated within Europe and if we cast the Normans as the prime agent of Europeanization, rather than seeing a more complex interaction between England, northern France (including Normandy), Flanders, and the German Empire. The twenty-five years of the Confessor's reign might seem short in medieval literary history, especially given the scales we are accustomed to use for Anglo-Saxon England. However, across western Europe, the middle of the eleventh century, often seen as the beginning of the Twelfth-Century Renaissance, saw a quickening in the development of literary culture.[4] *The Cambridge Songs* and the Exeter Book, taken together, illustrate how the vital literary culture of the Confessor's reign created bridges between new Latin poetry from the Continent and a long-established vernacular poetic tradition.

I

The Cambridge Songs comprise an anthology of Latin verse ranging from poems composed in medieval Germany, France, and Italy back to excerpts from classical and late antiquity.[5] Alongside a predominance of religious poetry, the political, classical, humorous, and love poetry of this

3 Mary Swan and Elaine Treharne's edited collection (*Rewriting Old English*) was instrumental in focusing attention on Old English after the early eleventh century: see also Treharne, "Categorization, Periodization," *Living through Conquest*, and "Production and Use." For historical writing, see Orchard, "Literary Background"; Tyler, "Fictions of Family," "Talking about History," and "*Vita Ædwardi*"; and Baxter, "MS C." For Goscelin, see Rosalind Love's editions: *Three Eleventh-Century Anglo-Latin Saints' Lives* and *Goscelin*.

4 Of the studies of the Twelfth-Century Renaissance, most relevant to this current chapter, with its focus on poetry, the German Empire, and England are Tilliette, "*Troiae ab oris*" and Thomson, "England and the Twelfth-Century Renaissance" and "Place of Germany." The now classic strong articulation of the view that the Conquest brought England into Europe is Southern, "Place of England."

5 Ziolkowski, ed., *Cambridge Songs*. All the songs will be cited by the number assigned by Ziolkowski.

generically diverse collection evinces an investment in the secular experience of men and women. Metrical diversity and a strong interest in music – thematically, theoretically, and in practice (many of the poems are neumed) – also mark this rich collection.[6] Their most recent editor, Jan Ziolkowski, describes *The Songs* as "the most varied and substantial assemblage of Medieval Latin lyrics ... extant from the centuries between the Carolingian corpora of the ninth century and the *Carmina burana* of the thirteenth."[7] The presence among *The Songs* of six poems (carmina 3, 9, 11, 16, 17, and 33) celebrating German emperors immediately draws attention to the court of Henry III (1039–56), for which the collection is likely to have been compiled.[8] The position of the first of the two poems about Conrad II (father of Henry III) on the first folio of the collection, just after twelve introductory lines which enjoin the praise of Christ and the Father though music, ensures that the reader approaches *The Songs* within a clearly articulated Imperial context.[9]

The twelve surviving folios of *The Cambridge Songs* are found at the end of Gg.5.35, which was copied at St Augustine's, Canterbury in the mid-eleventh century. *The Songs* follow and are dwarfed by a very extensive collection of poetry. This collection comprises 431 folios which, even without the addition of *The Songs*, makes Gg.5.35 by far the largest anthology of Latin poetry surviving from Anglo-Saxon England, if not western Europe. These first 431 folios encompass the staples of the early medieval canon, including late antique biblical verse, Prudentius's *Psychomachia*, Lacantius's *De ave phoenice*, Boethius's *De consolatione philosophiae*, epigrams, the *Disticha Catonis*, riddles, Carolingian verse, and Anglo-Latin verse dating from the seventh to the eleventh centuries. The latest poem, written in a difficult Latin and a complex metre, is by Oswald, a Benedictine monk of Ramsey and nephew of the reforming bishop, Oswald.[10] Peter Dronke, Michael Lapidge, and Peter

6 Ibid., xxxix–xliv.

7 Ibid., xviii.

8 Bulst, "Zur Vorgeschichte"; Dronke, Lapidge, and Stotz, "Die unveröffentlichen Gedichte," 56–8; and Ziolkowski, ed., *Songs*, xxxii–xxxiii.

9 Ibid., 36–8.

10 For a full list of the contents of the "reference work," see Rigg and Wieland, "Canterbury Classbook," 120–9 (but see Dronke et al., "Die unveröffentlichen Gedichte," 55–6 for corrections), and Irvine, *Making of Textual Culture*, 358–71. On the identity of Oswald: Lapidge, "Hermeneutic Style," 132–3 and 144–5.

Stotz have characterized this collection as a "Nachschlagewerk" (reference work).[11]

The appearance of *The Songs* in England has been seen as accidental and irrelevant to Anglo-Saxon literary culture more broadly. This perspective of a disjunction between the two parts of the collection characterizes both work on the first part of the manuscript by Anglo-Saxonists and on *The Songs* by scholars of Continental literature. However, *The Songs*, which were copied by two scribes who were responsible for much of the "reference work" section of Gg.5.35, are not a mere appendix to this large manuscript.[12] When we look at *The Songs* in the context of the Continental ties of the eleventh-century Anglo-Saxon court, their presence at St Augustine's reveals the participation of England in new developments in European literature. As they sought to create an ostentatiously monumental and comprehensive collection of poetry, the monks of St Augustine's saw no conflict between old Anglo-Saxon traditions and new European horizons, even though modern scholars have struggled to see the two parts of Gg.5.35 as coherent.

In contrast to the common practice of considering the two parts of Gg.5.35 as the products of different literary cultures, this chapter will keep the manuscript context of *The Cambridge Songs* firmly in view. From this starting point, I will situate the songs in respect to other Latin and vernacular texts from mid-eleventh-century England. In Latin, the *Encomium Emmae Reginae* and the *Vita Ædwardi Regis* are key.[13] In Old English, the poems of the Exeter Book act as revealing comparanda.[14] These comparisons serve not only to contextualize *The Songs* but also to open up new ways of thinking about the place of Old English verse in

---

11 Dronke et al., "Die unveröffentlichen Gedichte," 56, and Lapidge, "Study of Latin Texts." For the view that the manuscript is a "classbook," see Rigg and Wieland, "Canterbury Classbook." Irvine steers a middle course, considering it a "reference text of the canonical poems read in the grammatical curriculum" (*Making of Textual Culture*, 360).

12 Ziolkowski articulates this position (*Songs*, xxx–xxxi and xxxix), but it is implicit in other scholarship on Gg.5.35 which rarely crosses the two collections it contains (Rigg and Wieland, "Canterbury Classbook," 113; Irvine, *Making of Textual Culture*, 358–71; and Gneuss and Lapidge, *Anglo-Saxon Manuscripts*, number 12, where only the earlier reference work section is detailed). On the scribes: Rigg and Wieland, "Canterbury Classbook," 115 and Ziolkowski, ed., *Songs*, xxvi.

13 Muir, ed., *Exeter Anthology*.

14 Campbell, ed., *Encomium Emmae*; Barlow, ed., *Life of King Edward*.

very late Anglo-Saxon England. Throughout, all of these texts will be considered in light of the tight social networks within which they demonstrably made their meaning and which linked them together. My aim is to open up the shifting and distinctive place of Latin literature in England in the decades between the Benedictine Reform and the Conquest. These decades saw the cultivation of new types of Latin texts as part of the expression of the West Saxon court's full engagement with recent developments in western European literature.[15]

II

There are many points of contact between *The Songs* and Latin texts composed in mid-eleventh-century England. Both the *Encomium* and the *Vita Ædwardi* reveal that the royal court was an important centre for the cultivation of literature in this period. The *Encomium Emmae Reginae* is an account of the Anglo-Danish dynasty which Queen Emma commissioned likely from a monk of St Bertin in St Omer (Flanders) for Harthacnut's and then Edward's courts. The *Vita Ædwardi Regis*, a life of the Confessor, commissioned by Edith, was written across the Conquest, for a court audience, with strong connections to the royal nunnery at Wilton. The imperial panegyrics among *The Cambridge Songs* bring to mind the importance of this mode to the *Encomium*. Like Cnut, the emperors are remembered as pious Christian rulers and heirs of Rome. The mix of lamentation with praise in the poems marking the deaths of the emperors Henry II and Conrad II (carmina 9, 17, and 33) will be matched in the poetry of the *Vita Ædwardi*, which also shares *The Songs*' attention to King David (carmina 3, 81, and 82). Kings and literary culture had a long history of association in England, as elsewhere in Europe, as we see most notably with Alfred and Edgar. What is different in the mid-eleventh century is prominent queenly patronage and the orientation of Latin literature towards dynastic politics.

Classicism is a strong feature of both the *Encomium* and the *Vita Ædwardi*. The Encomiast figures himself as Vergil, Emma as Octavian, and

15 Unless otherwise stated, discussion of the *Encomium* and the *Vita Ædwardi* draws on my articles "Fictions of Family," "Talking about History," and "*Vita Ædwardi.*" Work cited in these articles will not be cited here and these articles will not be cited again. This work is developed further in my forthcoming *England in Europe*; see also O'Donnell, Townend, and Tyler, "European Literature," 619–21.

Cnut as a second Aeneas. The Anonymous author of the *Vita Ædwardi* explicitly uses the *Aeneid*, the *Thebaid*, the *Civil War*, and Ovid's poetry as interpretative frameworks for the political crises which ended the West Saxon dynasty. Henry III's court experienced an intensification of Imperial emulation of classical Rome. The classical past makes its mark too on *The Cambridge Songs*.[16] Carmen 11, celebrating the three Ottos, is overtly classicizing. Opening with the words "Magnus cesar Otto," it quotes Horace in its final lines which announce that praise of the Ottos would have exceeded even the power of Vergil.[17] Carmen 33, Wipo's religious lament for Conrad II, occurs in the midst of secular laments from classical poets. The voices of two mourning women from Statius's *Thebaid* precede Wipo's poem (carmina 31, 32, and 33), after which the manuscript returns immediately to classical verse as Aeneas recounts his sorrow over the death of Hector, "spes o fidissima Teucrum" (O trustiest hope of the Trojans), to Dido (carmen 34).[18] This juxtaposition of contemporary and classical is a defining feature of the *Vita Ædwardi*.

The presence of excerpts from the *Thebaid* deserves special emphasis. This compelling account of fratricide, set in train by a father (Oedipus), was among the Latin poems that the Muses of Wipo's *Tetralogus* claim to have inspired (alongside Vergil, Horace, Lucan, and Ovid). The *Tetralogus*, a straightforward poem, was written to educate the young Henry III.[19] The *Thebaid* also fascinated the Anonymous author of the *Vita Ædwardi*. He presents the story of Thebes to Edith, Edward's wife and then widow, as a framework for understanding the destructive warring of her brothers Harold and Tostig Godwineson (who did, in effect, kill each other, as Eteocles and Polynices did). The Anonymous uses Statius's account of Thebes, intermingled with Lucan's *Civil War*, to represent Harold and Tostig's rivalry as igniting civil war.[20] However, although Statius's *Thebaid* was part of the school curriculum in the eleventh century and evidence survives of several copies from pre-Conquest and Conquest England, it was not yet a well-known text, only gaining in popularity in the twelfth

16 Jaeger, *Origins of Courtliness*, 122.

17 Ziolkowski, ed., *Songs*, 201.

18 See now Newlands, *Statius*, 127–31. This appeared in print after this chapter was finished; however, sections on Statius benefit from discussion with Carole Newlands.

19 "Ex notris monitis callebat Statius auctor / Thebanos miseris iuvenes discernere flammis." Wipo, *Tetralogus*, lines 58–9, in Bresslau, ed. *Wiponis Opera*.

20 Barlow, ed., *Life of King Edward*, 20–1, 26–9, 58–61, and 84–91.

century. It appears that copies originated from northern France, to which manuscripts from both England and the Empire, where the poem was more popular in the tenth and eleventh century than it was in France and Italy, can be traced. Conrad of Hirsau's meagre grasp of only part of the *Thebaid*'s plot in his summary of the text for his *Dialogus super auctores* illustrates that even some of the better educated in this period did not know it first hand.[21] The Anonymous's use of Thebes as a framework which he expects his secular audience to understand is thus one of the most breath-taking aspects of the *Vita Ædwardi* – one which demands that we step back and reimagine the literary culture of Edward's court. A century later, the popularity of Statian poetry would contribute to the emergence of courtly romance. Thebes was the first of the classical legends to move into written vernacular romance, when a poet associated with the Angevin court of Henry II and Eleanor of Aquitaine produced the *Roman de Thèbes*.[22] Earlier in the twelfth century, Orderic Vitalis saw Thebes as a story which laypeople, including Robert Curthose, used themselves to understand their experiences.[23] Thebes as an intertwined literary and political language was already current in both the Imperial and Anglo-Saxon courts in the eleventh century.

The inclusion of the neumed opening lines of each of the Metres of Boethius at the end of *The Cambridge Songs* draws us back to Edward's *Vita*, in which we find dialogues between the Muse (who bears a striking resemblance to Queen Edith) and the Poet, which are knowingly based on the exchanges between the prisoner and Lady Philosophy in the *Consolatio*. In their metapoetic sophistication these prologues point forward to the reworkings of Boethius that we find in more philosophical poems of the twelfth century. The Loire poet Hildebert of Lavardin and also Adelard of

21 Reeve, "Statius," 394–6; Irvine, *Making of Textual Culture*, 356–8; Munk Olsen, "Production of the Classics," 3; Wetherbee, "From Late Antiquity," 125. We know of two copies of the *Thebaid* in English libraries before the Conquest: a copy dating from the second half of the tenth century and copied in Canterbury (perhaps at St Augustine's) and a fragment of a glossed copy, perhaps originating in France, that survives from Worcester (Gneuss and Lapidge, *Anglo-Saxon Manuscripts*, numbers 497 and 766). A third copy, a glossed Statius, likely to be or include the *Thebaid*, appears in Leofric's booklist (see below, p. 194). For a comprehensive list of manuscripts see Munk Olsen, *L'étude des auteurs classiques latins*, 2.2:520–67, and Anderson, *Manuscripts of Statius.*

22 Ziolkowski, ed., *Songs*, 263; for an introduction to the romances of antiquity, Baswell, "Marvels of Translation." See now Newlands, *Statius*, 131 and 133.

23 Chibnall, ed., *Ecclesiastical History*, 3.100–1, 4.122–3, and 6.86–7.

Bath, Bernard Silvestris, and Alan of Lille, all of whom modern literary scholars recognize as working at the forefront of new literary developments, framed their prosimetra with imaginative transformations of Lady Philosophy.[24] Like Thebes, Boethius already had a currency in the royal courts of both England and Germany in the eleventh century.[25]

A final point of connection between *The Songs* and eleventh-century Anglo-Saxon literary culture lies with the interest they evince in the lives of queens and nuns: they include a poem celebrating the recovery of an unnamed queen from illness and a number of poems, many of which are humorous, which take nuns as their subject (carmina 20, 26, 28, and 41).[26] Queens very obviously figure centrally in the *Encomium* and *Vita Ædwardi*. In addition, Goscelin's writing for the royal nunnery at Wilton, especially his life of the princess-saint Edith (King Edgar's daughter), also fits in here.[27] The *Vita Ædwardi* too is preoccupied with Wilton and was probably composed there or completed there after Edith's retirement from court on the death of the Confessor. In both England and Germany, royal or Imperial nunneries, which often educated high-status women, were not cut off from the court, but played central roles in keeping dynastic history.

24 Dronke, *Verse with Prose*, 46–53; Balint, *Ordering Chaos* (especially chapters 1 and 2).

25 Boethius's *Consolatio* was, of course, an important text in medieval schools, and we find the full text (not just the Metres) in the "reference work" section of Gg.5.35. The neumed Metres, few of which are complete, of *The Cambridge Songs* are presumably included in Gg.5.35 for their musical value. Neumes appear widely in *The Cambridge Songs*, which throughout display a strong thematic and metapoetic interest in music. A musical as well as literary study could be made of their place in Anglo-Saxon England. Perhaps Goscelin, who was not only later in life a monk of St Augustine's but also celebrated as a musician by Reginald of Canterbury, should be seen as an inheritor of *The Cambridge Songs* or at least as a member of the foundation who would have appreciated the collection's musicality (Liebermann, "Raginald," carmen 15, 542–4; Rigg, *History*, 24–30).

26 Many royal and aristocratic women in eleventh-century England were educated in royal nunneries and would thus have a particular interest in nuns (my "*Vita Ædwardi*" provides further references). William of Malmesbury's *Gesta Regum Anglorum*, begun in the early twelfth century at the behest of another Wilton-educated queen, the Anglo-Scottish Edith/Matilda (daughter of the Anglo-Saxon princess Margaret and King Malcolm III of Scotland), also shares the enjoyment of scurrilous stories about clerics, including one about a nun (said to be the sister of Emperor Henry III), that we also find in *The Cambridge Songs*; we should not imagine such material distancing the text from a court audience in which women played a central role in the reception of Latin literature. Mynors, Thomson, and Winterbottom, eds., *William of Malmesbury: Gesta Regum*, 1:340–3.

27 Wilmart, ed., "La légende de Ste Édith" (trans. Wright and Loncar, "Goscelin's Legend of Edith").

There are, of course, very significant differences that make it a mistake to homogenize *The Cambridge Songs* with other Latin literature circulating in eleventh-century England. Many facets of the poetic collection do not find correspondents. Non-riddling erotic verse and proto-fabliaux, for example, are not present in other contemporary Anglo-Saxon manuscripts. Despite the demonstrable parallels between them and *The Songs*, the classicism of the *Encomium* and the *Vita Ædwardi* shows greater affinities with the poetic culture emanating from Reims (in whose archdiocese St Omer lay) and the Loire Valley than with the Empire. The extensive presentation of Emma in the *Encomium* as a literary patron in the mould of Vergil suggests ties to Reims.[28] The poetry of the *Vita Ædwardi*, meanwhile, should be studied in connection with that of a group of poets, including Hildebert of Lavardin, Baudri of Bourgueil, and Godfrey of Reims (often called the "Loire School"), whose work is marked by an ostentatious Ovidianism and increasingly philosophical metapoetic exploration which we do not find in later eleventh-century poetry from the Empire (as the nature of the classicism of Sextus Amarcius's poetry, for example, reveals).[29] The *Encomium*, the *Vita Ædwardi*, and *The Songs*, viewed together, however, warn against viewing the literary culture which flourished in eleventh-century northwestern Europe through the lens of modern nationalizing literary history. Some of the contemporary *Songs* come from southern France, perhaps a literary consequences of Henry III's second marriage to Agnes of Poitou, as well as from within the Empire (Germany *and* Italy).[30] For its part, the *Vita Ædwardi*, for all its literary affinities with northern France, is alert to the prestige of Imperial political power, recording Edward's kinship with Henry III.[31]

III

Attention to the social networks which bound the Anglo-Saxon and Imperial courts together compellingly strengthens the case, thus far made on literary grounds, for the integral place of *The Cambridge Songs* within English literary culture. The presence of Wipo's poem (carmen 33) memorializing

28 Haye, "*Nemo Mecenas.*"

29 Manitius, ed., *Sextus Amarcius*, esp. 26–7; Tilliette, "*Troiae ab oris*"; and Ziolkowski, ed., *Songs*, xliv.

30 Ibid., xxxvi–xxxviii.

31 Barlow, ed., *Life of King Edward*, 16–17.

the death of Conrad II in 1039 among *The Songs* suggests that political alliances and dynastic ties between the English and Imperial courts played an important role in their arrival in England. The poem, probably the latest chronologically in the collection, mourns not only Conrad but also Gunnhild.[32] The daughter of Cnut and Emma, Gunnhild married Henry III as part of a political alliance between the Anglo-Danish and Imperial dynasties. An exchange of letters shows not only how the Imperial court was a magnet for learned clerics but also that that magnetism may have been known to the Anglo-Saxon court. A letter reports that Azecho, bishop of Worms (known for its cathedral school), consoled Gunnhild with almonds to alleviate her homesickness. That same letter also recounts that Gunnhild and her mother corresponded after the young woman's departure from England, providing solid evidence of communication between the two courts.[33] After Gunnhild's death, Edward's continuation of the alliance with his brother-in-law Henry III provides a context for understanding how a collection of poems which came together in the German court should come to be preserved in an Anglo-Saxon monastery.[34]

As Michael Lapidge pointed out in his article on the transmission to England of the Romano-German pontifical, Ealdred, bishop of Worcester and later archbishop of York, is an obvious route for *The Cambridge Songs* to have found their way to England.[35] From this perspective, ecclesiastical networks and dynastic concerns combine to bring *The Songs* to England. In 1054, the childless Edward sent Ealdred to Germany to arrange for the return of Edward the Exile, son of Edmund Ironside, banished as an infant at the time of the Danish Conquest. Ealdred spent a year in Cologne as the guest of both the archbishop, Hermann, and Henry III. William of Malmesbury's report that Ealdred attracted many presents, including a sacramentary and psalter which Cnut and Emma had sent to Conrad a generation earlier, illustrates that his visit entailed the exchange of books whose symbolic value explicitly resided in the direct link they forged between emperors and kings.[36] The twelfth-century Chronicle of the Archbishops

32 Carmen 33 and Ziolkowski, ed., *Songs*, xxvi.

33 Bulst, ed., *Die ältere Wormser Briefsammlung*, letter 5:3, 20–2. See my "Crossing Conquests," 181 for full references.

34 Barlow, *Edward the Confessor*, 98–9 and 215; Campbell, "England, France, Flanders and Germany," 194–7.

35 Lapidge, "Ealdred," 464.

36 Winterbottom and Thomson, eds., *William of Malmesbury: Saints Lives*, 40–1; Lapidge, "Ealdred," 460–5; Nelson, "Rites," 126–7.

of York leaves a vivid portrait of Ealdred intent on remembering the ecclesiastical practices he encountered in Cologne so that they could be observed in England.[37] Why would he not also remember the literary culture which flourished in the court of the learned Henry III?[38]

Although Ealdred's chief interest lay with liturgical texts, the place of poems about or mentioning bishops, and indeed archbishops of Cologne (carmina 7, 16, and 25), within *The Songs* might well have appealed to him, projecting a model of court culture in which bishops featured centrally. The prominence of bishops within *The Songs*, alongside their mix of secular and sacred themes, opens up to view Ealdred's exposure to the powerful religious and temporal roles bishops played within the Empire. In conjunction with their spiritual responsibilities, Imperial bishops, who were in constant contact with the Emperor, were charged with political, military, and diplomatic duties. For these highly educated men, literary and artistic activities were integral to their wielding of power: it is in just this context that Ealdred may possibly have acquired *The Cambridge Songs*.[39] It is worth noting that courtier bishops are a European rather than a German phenomenon and Anglo-Saxon bishops too could have court formations and careers: Dunstan and Oswald were raised at court, and Wulfstan II of York was key counsellor to both Cnut and Æthelred.[40] But the splendour of the Anglo-Saxon courtier bishops did not rival that of their Imperial counterparts, whose wealth and political power were unparalleled.[41] Hermann, son and then brother of the powerful Ezzonid counts palatine of Lotharingia, was a close advisor to Henry III and was especially well placed to impress Ealdred. Frank Barlow, meanwhile, singles out Ealdred as the only Anglo-Saxon "Prince-Bishop," not only on account of his political influence but also on account of the magnificence of his episcopate, which contrasted with the more ascetic manner of his contemporary and subordinate St Wulfstan, bishop of Worcester.[42]

37 Raine, ed., "Chronicle," 2, 345; Nelson, "Rites," 126.

38 Schmidt, "Heinrich III"; Jaeger, *Envy of Angels*, 200–2; Wolfram, *Conrad II*, 22 and 141.

39 The key study of the imperial church remains Fleckenstein, *Hofkappelle.* See also Parisse, "L'évêque d'Empire," and Jaeger, *Origins*, 19–48.

40 Ibid., 25–6; Reuter, "Imperial Church System"; and Giandrea, *Episcopal Culture*, 47–50 and 61–6.

41 Barlow, *English Church*, 133–4; Reuter, "Imperial Church System," 348; and Brühl, "Sozialstruktur," 44–5.

42 Barlow, *English Church*, 86–95; Lewald, "Ezzonen."

A further feature of Ealdred's career as a diplomat may also account for *The Songs*' St Augustine's provenance. The foundation was known for its close ties to the Godwines, as evidenced by the promotion of their cause in the E version of the Chronicle, which was kept at St Augustine's in the mid-eleventh century.[43] Although Ealdred went to Cologne on Edward's mission, he began his career as an ally of Edward's oftentimes enemy, Godwine. Reconciled with Edward, Ealdred maintained close ties with the Godwines, thus playing a critical role in negotiating the bitter factionalism which constantly threatened to destabilize the kingdom.[44] The Godwines, though frequently in conflict with Edward, were a mainstay of his court, where Edith (Godwine's daughter) was queen. That the *Vita Ædwardi*, written under her patronage, walked a fine line between the Godwines and Edward (like Ealdred himself) testifies to how mid-eleventh-century factionalism shaped the literary as well as political culture of the court.

Although Ealdred is a likely conduit for *The Songs*, he is far from the only possibility. Edward's Imperial connections were extensive and the poems could have travelled with any one of the numerous Imperial clerics who came, alongside Norman and French counterparts, to England and found preferment as bishops in Edward's kingdom. In raising court chaplains to bishops, he deliberately modelled his church on Imperial practice. Although the royal chapel was long established as a route to a bishopric, between 1050 and 1066 this progression intensified, with half the bishops appointed having served at court.[45] These royal chaplains included Hermann, Leofric (English or Cornish but educated in the Empire), Giso, and Walter. These men all subsequently became bishops in the southwest. Another royal chaplain, Regenbald, whose name suggests Imperial origins, served as Edward's chancellor and held the status of a bishop, although he remained a priest.[46] The Anglo-Saxonist habit of referring to this group of clerics as Lotharingian, rather than Imperial (or German), while understandable in a post-war context, masks the very real influence of the Empire on eleventh-century England, in favour of looking for Norman or French connections.[47]

43 Most recently, Baxter, "MS C," 1189–90.

44 Nelson, "Rites," 127, and Giandrea, *Episcopal Culture*, 65–6.

45 Barlow, *English Church*, 134, and Reuter, "Imperial Church System," 347.

46 Keynes, "Regenbald," 195, 197, and 209, and "Giso," 212; Jaeger, *Origins*, 21.

47 Lewis, "French in England."

More important than the specific person who carried *The Songs* is the wider context. Whoever brought *The Songs* to England brought them to a kingdom where the court and ecclesiastical elite were interested in the latest Imperial developments: we can see an audience as well as a transmission route.[48] The speed with which *The Songs* travelled to England – they were copied in the mid-eleventh century and the latest poem could be no earlier than 1039 – points to an active desire to acquire them, as do Imperial influences in other areas of cultural production.[49] The architects of Edward's Westminster Abbey may have looked to Imperial churches like Speyer, a Salian cathedral and mausoleum begun by Conrad II, as well as to Normandy.[50] Edward's seal and some of his coinage followed Imperial models.[51] Revealing a specifically royal focus within Ealdred's Imperially based liturgical innovations, Janet Nelson argues that the Third English Ordo, which may have been used for the coronation of both Harold and William in 1066, was written by Ealdred based on an Imperial ordo found in the Romano-German Pontifical he brought back from Cologne.[52] The Continental diplomatic of Regenbald left its mark on the charters of Edward's reign.[53] The royal nunneries of Wessex bear a strong resemblance to Imperial foundations such as Quedlinburg and Gandersheim, where Gunnhild and Henry III's daughter, Beatrice, became abbess.[54] Imperial connections were not the preserve of the West Saxon dynasty but were more widely cultivated at court. Harold's collegiate foundation at Waltham included one Adelard. Born in Liège and educated in Utrecht, he was chosen by Harold for his experience of the life of a regular canon more common in the Empire than England.[55]

In this context, it would be surprising indeed if there was no interest in the literary culture which the Salians, under the guidance of their courtier bishops, so ostentatiously cultivated. Edward, raised in Normandy and England, does not appear to have been learned, unlike his

48 Keynes, "Giso," 212.

49 Ziolkowski, ed., *Songs*, xxvi.

50 Gem, "Romanesque Rebuilding," 46 and 52–3; Fernie, "Edward the Confessor's Westminster Abbey," 150.

51 Barlow, *Edward the Confessor*, 184–5, and Keynes, "Regenbald," 216–17. Keynes points also to French models for the seals.

52 Nelson, "Rites," 126–8.

53 Keynes, "Regenbald."

54 Tyler, "Crossing Conquests," 182 and 188.

55 Watkiss and Chibnall, eds., *Waltham Chronicle*, 28–9.

Imperial counterparts. However, the *Encomium*, whose promotion of the Anglo-Danish dynasty was aimed at Edward and Harthacnut in particular as well as the court (including the Godwines) more generally, shows that the active role Latin literature played in eleventh-century politics and royal image making did not rely on the personal Latin literacy of the king or his noblemen. *The Cambridge Songs* make sense in connection with an Anglo-Saxon court which sought out and contributed to the latest developments in Latin literature, whether they originated in the Empire or from the more ecclesiastical networks connected to Reims.

IV

Does this love of Continental literary culture at court, and more widely in elite circles, drive a wedge between the literature of mid-eleventh-century England and that of previous decades and centuries? In making Gg.5.35, the monks of St Augustine's created continuity between the new Latinity of the eleventh century and the Latinity which had been built up over the centuries since the conversion of Anglo-Saxon England and which was in any case largely a western European inheritance. But what of the impact of this new Latinity, and its place at court, on the distinctive place of the vernacular within Anglo-Saxon literature? Was this threatened or pushed aside? In recent years, scholars, most especially Elaine Treharne, have persuasively argued for the continued vitality of English into the twelfth century.[56] Did this also hold true, in the second half of the eleventh century, in court and episcopal circles increasingly oriented towards the Empire as well as northern France? Looking at *The Cambridge Songs* alongside the Exeter Book reveals a close and dynamic interface between literature in English and a desire to be part of the newest developments in Latin literary culture in this period.

That there are close ties between the Exeter Book and the "reference work" section of Gg.5.35 has long been recognized. The Exeter Book includes vernacular versions of Lactantius's *De ave phoenice* and a few of Symphosius's *Enigmata*, poems which appear in the earlier part of Gg.5.35 and which can be traced back to the sixth century *Anthologia Latina*, the ancestor of many medieval poetic anthologies.[57] Other poems which are

56 See above, note 3.

57 Boutemy, "A propos d'anthologies poétiques"; Rigg, "Medieval Latin Poetic Anthologies (I)"; Irvine, *Making of Textual Culture*, 360; Miles, "*Anthologia Latina.*"

not direct translations also illustrate the connection between the first section of Gg.5.35 and the Exeter Book. Genre and theme link *Judgment Day I* with Bede's *De die iudicii* and *Precepts* with *Disticha Catonis*. The Boethian expressions of transience, which mark *The Ruin* and *The Wanderer*, find their counterpart in the Latin *Consolatio* included in full early in Gg.5.35. Meanwhile, the listing together of the Exeter Book and *The Old English Boethius* in Leofric's Donation list of 1072 may suggest that the bishop himself closely associated the two.[58] The three Christ poems, brought together to create a substantial piece, which begin the Exeter Book, echo the place of New Testament biblical epic at the start of Gg.5.35. These ties between the Exeter Book and Gg.5.35 illustrate the very tight link between the vernacular manuscript and a European anthologizing habit and show what a strong influence Latin literature exerted on Old English vernacular poetry. The Exeter Book, whose compiler's choices were shaped by Latin anthologies, represents a substantial portion of surviving Old English poetry.

Strikingly, when *The Cambridge Songs* are considered along with the "reference work" section, the connections between Gg.5.35 and the Exeter Book become stronger.[59] *The Songs* take a greater interest in courts than did the earlier part of Gg.5.35. This concern is also evident in the Exeter Book, though convention has us speak of the hall, not the royal court, when we look at poems like *Maxims I* and *The Gifts of Men*. *Widsith* is most obviously court oriented and, by referring to poetry from a wide geographical and chronological range, performs what *The Cambridge Songs* themselves do. *The Cambridge Songs* also share the Exeter Book's interest in women's voices and love poems. Carmen 40 recalls *The Wife's Lament* not only in the sentiments expressed and in the depiction of the woman's relationship to nature, but also in the multiplicity of possible interpretations – as Ziolkowski writes:

> the poem lends itself to a host of possible constructions. To cite only a few, the woman could suffer from unrequited love for a man; the woman could love a man who shares her sentiment but who is absent or dead; the woman

58 Robertson, ed., *Anglo-Saxon Charters*, 228–9; and discussed further below. We do not know if Leofric's *Old English Boethius* included the metres.

59 My consideration of the relationship between Gg.5.35 and the Exeter Book benefits from discussions had while supervising Kirsten Armstrong's 2009 University of York MA dissertation in Medieval Studies.

> could be a nun suffering from wistfulness for the secular world; or the "woman" could be an allegorical representation of the soul that longs for God.[60]

Excerpted from the *Thebaid*, carmina 29/32, Argia's lament for her dead husband, killed by his brother, bring to mind both *The Wife's Lament* and the woman ensnared in the strife of her husband's family in *Wulf and Eadwacer*.[61] Turning to the affections felt between lord and retainer, the appearance of Hector in a dream to Aeneas from the Trojan's famous lament to Dido (carmen 34) evokes aspects of *The Wanderer*. Both classical excerpts moreover require, like *Deor*, an audience who knows the larger myth or legend to which allusion is made. *Deor* also illustrates that, after the addition of *The Songs*, both manuscripts contain pagan material, whether from the Germanic or Roman story-world. Finally, Latin and vernacular meet in both manuscripts, which each contain macaronic verse. In the Exeter Book, the Latin of the final lines of *The Phoenix* conforms to the metre of the Old English, while in contrast, in *The Songs*, the German half-lines of *De Henrico* (carmen 19) conform to a Latin metrical scheme.[62] Macaronic verse of the type found in *The Phoenix* and in *De Henrico* and *Clericus et Nonna* (carmen 28) is rare, and it is possible that these two German poems reveal the influence of insular models.[63] Although *The Cambridge Songs* came to England from the Continent, they are part of a larger two-way exchange of literary culture.

Without overstating the commonality of Gg.5.35 and the Exeter Book, the links between the two manuscripts suggest that the Exeter Book, copied in the late tenth century from an earlier tenth-century exemplar which contained poetry perhaps as old as the seventh century, was far from old-fashioned in the eleventh century. As Elaine Treharne has discussed, vernacular literary culture from the years after the Benedictine Reform into the twelfth century consisted largely in the reproducing of earlier texts, an activity that modern literary history tends to exclude.[64] This culture of reproduction characterizes both Latin and vernacular literary cultures in the early Middle Ages, with the majority of manuscripts copied being older

60 Ziolkowski, ed., *Songs*, 288.

61 See now Newlands, *Statius*, 127.

62 Ziolkowski, ed., *Songs*, 234; Cain, "Phonology and Meter," 281–2; Schneider, "Latein und Althochdeutsch," 299.

63 Schneider, "Latein und Althochdeutsch," 309–11.

64 Treharne, "Categorization," 249–52.

prose and verse texts. Both sections of Gg.5.35, like many earlier poetic anthologies, largely comprise older poetry, which is put in relation with later poetry in a process that the St Augustine's monks extend up to their own time – much as the compiler of the Exeter Book had done a century earlier. Looking at the Exeter Book in light of Leofric's other books and his ties with the Empire shows him treating the vernacular codex in a strongly analogous manner: he too sought to maintain the place of older poetry within contemporary literary culture.

Leofric's donation list, inventorying the lands, treasure, and books that he left to Exeter Cathedral on his death, makes even starker the up-to-date character of the Exeter Book in late Anglo-Saxon England. The inclusion of the inventory both in his Latin and his English Gospel books requires us, moreover, to think across both languages in order to understand the place of the Exeter Book in the late eleventh century.[65] Joyce Hill and Elaine Treharne have recently shown that Leofric developed a carefully bilingual program for carrying out his liturgical and pastoral duties as bishop of Exeter. Hill's study of Cambridge, Corpus Christi College 190, a compilation originally made by Archbishop Wulfstan, shows Leofric deliberately expanding an already bilingual, episcopal manuscript so that, broadly speaking, what was available in Latin was likewise available in English. As an Imperially educated cleric unfamiliar with the ecclesiastical use of the vernacular, he needed to take a more systematic approach to English than did his vernacular-trained contemporaries. Treharne persuasively argues that the flourishing of writing in English at Exeter in the third quarter of the eleventh century is specifically attributable to Leofric's efforts to promote the vernacular. Of particular relevance for our discussion of *The Cambridge Songs*, his Latin and English additions to Corpus Christi 190 show him keen to use English to promote Imperial practice for the regulation of secular clerks. Leofric's status as a secular cleric likely made Imperial models especially attractive. Unlike in England, France, and Italy, the German church drew its bishops from cathedral chapters rather than monasteries. Essential to Leofric's activities at Exeter was the establishment of a reformed community of canons, following practices more Imperial than English, as William of Malmesbury pointed out. His inventory includes a "Regula Canonicorum," and among the surviving manuscripts copied at Exeter is a bilingual *Enlarged Rule of Chrodegang*

65 For a detailed discussion of the booklist, see Gameson, "Origin of the Exeter Book."

(Cambridge, Corpus Christi College 191) to which he submitted his clergy. His sacramentary (Oxford, Bodleian Library Bodley 579, usually called the "Leofric Missal") shows that he had or had access to a Romano-German Pontifical, while his collectar is based on a Liège model. Leofric emerges as a man endeavouring to behave like an Imperial bishop but doing it in English.[66]

Leofric's Imperial expectations for the role of a bishop are evident in the inclusion of poetry within his booklist. Richard Gameson emphasizes how very ordinary the contents of the list are. He argues that Leofric, in taking over the impoverished see of Crediton and in moving it to Exeter, had to acquire the most basic liturgical, paraliturgical, and reading texts. In this endeavour, he may not have been in a position to be choosy, rather having to accept what was available.[67] Christian biblical poetry held an important place within the early medieval grammatical curriculum, and the copies of Prudentius, Sedulius, and Arator found in Leofric's list fit squarely into this context.[68] However, our sense that the poetry in the inventory exceeds what might be expected in such a basic library is confirmed by the presence of two classical Latin poets: Persius and Statius. Persius, a moral satirist easily appropriated to Christianity, found his way into early medieval libraries.[69] Statius, whose manuscripts are rare before the twelfth century, has always, in contrast, seemed out of place, extravagant even.[70] Likewise, if we look back at the non-ecclesiastical vernacular books in Leofric's inventory, the Exeter Book seems similarly out of place. Indeed, Hill sees it as an unimportant book left to the end of the list of books containing English.[71]

---

66 Winterbottom and Thomson, eds., *William of Malmesbury: Gesta Pontificum*, 314–15; Treharne, "Producing a Library" and "Bishops and Their Texts"; Hill, "Two Anglo-Saxon Bishops" (I am grateful to Joyce Hill for sending me a copy of this article in typescript); Barlow, "Leofric and His Times," 10; Parisse, "L'évêque," 97; and Orchard, ed., *Leofric Missal*, 1:207–8.

67 Gameson, "Origin," 143 and 147.

68 Lapidge, "Study of Latin Texts," 470–94, and "Versifying the Bible."

69 Gameson, "Origin," 151.

70 The inventory lists "glose Statii," which is likely to refer either to a glossed *Thebaid* or a glossed *Thebaid* and *Achilleid*. The *Achilleid* (incomplete and thus short) circulated with the *Thebaid* or as part of other poetic anthologies (as a survey of Munk Olsen's catalogue reveals: see above, note 21).

71 Hill, "Anglo-Saxon Scholarship," 15.

Consideration of Leofric's inventory alongside our earlier comparison of Gg.5.35 (which included Prudentius, Sedulius, and Arator alongside excerpts from Statius's *Thebaid*) and the Exeter Book illustrates that the Latin and English poems of Leofric's list belong together. From this perspective, the Exeter Book does not look like a random gift to a provincial diocese but a considered and well-made choice. With regard to the Old English ecclesiastical texts, Treharne has shown that, although most of the items contained within the Exeter list are ordinary, the collection is deliberately shaped by Leofric's needs and instructions.[72] I would argue that his shaping hand also accounts for the inclusion of the Exeter Book, a book whose own monumentality – it is the "mycel ... boc" in Leofric's list – cannot but remind us of the size of Gg.5.35. Statius, meanwhile, alerts us to the literary ambitions of Leofric, who wanted to have the latest Latin learning represented in his library. Leofric's Imperial training ensured that he also saw the cultivation of poetry as part of the dignity of being a bishop, alongside the pastoral duties which Hill and Treharne have demonstrated Leofric took very seriously.[73] He turned to the Exeter Book – a handsome book containing some of the best Old English verse – in order to be able to project that dignity fully in English as well as Latin. Leofric's Imperial formation has also intervened in the transmission and survival of Old English verse. Leofric's taste is a filter though which the most important manuscript of Old English poetry passed and thus has had a profound influence on the modern canon of Old English literature.

Although it is not certain where within Lotharingia Leofric was trained, Toul and Liège have both been suggested. Each would have enabled him to gain access to poetic learning and news of the Imperial court, with its powerful learned bishops. The bishop of Toul when Leofric would have been there was Bruno, kinsman of Conrad II and Henry III and royal chaplain, who was thus well connected in the Imperial court. With Henry III's support, he became the reforming pope Leo IX.[74] It was from Leo IX that Leofric sought and gained permission to move his see from the rural Crediton to the *civitas* of Exeter, a move in line with Continental practices

72 Treharne, "Producing a Library," 158 and 163.

73 Ibid., and Hill, "Two Anglo-Saxon Bishops."

74 Parisse, "L'évêque," 98, and Wolfram, *Conrad II*, 286. For recent collection of essays on Leo IX, see Bischoff and Tock, eds., *Léon IX et son temps*.

of situating bishoprics in urban environments.[75] Eleventh-century Exeter's substantial Roman remains, particularly in the area of the Saxon minster which would become the cathedral, could well have recommended the town to Leofric.[76] Indeed, the bishop may have been an especially appreciative reader of *The Ruin*: a vernacular *encomium urbis* commemorating a past *Romanitas* still present in the landscape. *The Ruin* is yet one more reminder of the attractiveness of the Exeter Book to a man familiar with the increasing classicism of contemporary Latin literary culture. Toul itself, especially the monastery of St Evre, enjoyed rich library resources, including an impressive collection of classical and Christian poetry. Among the poets included in its booklist of 1084 is Statius. Meanwhile, *Waltarius*, which shares the same Germanic story-world as *Deor* and *Widsith*, was also found in the library.[77] The poet of the *Ecbasis captivi*, an innovative beast fable probably of the eleventh century, meanwhile, may have been educated at Toul.[78]

Strong links between Liège and Exeter in liturgical manuscripts make it more likely that Leofric was educated there rather than Toul.[79] Indeed, Liège was known for attracting students from far away and it was a hothouse for training clerics who went on to become, like Leofric, bishops elsewhere.[80] In the early years of the 1020s, Egbert of Liège composed a long poem, the *Fecunda ratis*. Comprising 2373 hexameters and indebted to the *Disticha Catonis* and Avianus's fables, it was designed to teach the trivium in the cathedral school. Egbert's poetry contains allusions to a wide range of classical and Christian authors, though we do not know if he knew these directly or through *florilegia*. Comparison of the *Fecunda ratis* to the Exeter Book simultaneously shows the earlier vernacular collection to be the richer and more complex of the two and reminds us of poetry's prominence within the Liège curriculum which Leofric may have

75 Barlow, "Leofric," 2, and Hill, "Anglo-Saxon Scholarship," 11 and "Two Anglo-Saxon Bishops," 150.

76 Henderson and Bidwell, "Saxon Minster," 148–9.

77 Becker, ed., *Catalogi bibliothecarum antiqui*, 152; Glauche, *Schullektüre im Mittelalter*, 94–6; Riché, *Écoles*, 68–9.

78 Riché, *Écoles*, 68; Zeydel, ed., *Ecbasis cuiusdam captivi*, 6–7.

79 Drage, "Bishop Leofric," 143 and 282; Orchard, *Leofric Missal*, 1:208.

80 On the schools of Liège see Riché, *Écoles*, 164–77; Kupper, *Liège et l'église imperiale*, 377–83; and Renardy, "Les écoles liégeoises."

followed.[81] Meanwhile, Anselm of Liège's *Gesta episcoporum Leodensium* depicts bishops and schoolmasters, in the decades before Leofric returned to England, as players in the Imperial court.[82] Writing later in the eleventh century, Gozechin, then archbishop of Mainz, reminisced about the school at Liège. Gozechin, who refers to classical poets with real knowledge as he asserts the superiority of Christian writers, taught in the cathedral school just after Leofric's return to England.[83] At Liège, where he was perhaps taught in the classroom of Egbert or the famous Wazo, Leofric would have learned that Imperial bishops were cultivated men who kept up with and drove new developments, secular as well as sacred, in literary culture.

Leofric's social networks within England are more securely known than where he spent his time on the Continent. These networks, which included Edward and Ealdred alongside a number of Imperial clerics, draw together even more tightly the worlds of *The Cambridge Songs* and the Exeter Book. Leofric returned to England with Edward in 1041 and served as his chaplain until he was named as bishop of Devon and Cornwall in 1046. As chaplain, he was an obvious person to translate and explicate the *Encomium* for Edward, including discussing its presentation of Cnut as an Aeneas figure. Leofric may well have met the Encomiast, who wrote not only for, but from within, the Anglo-Danish court to which Edward returned. Meanwhile, if St Omer, Bibliothèque municipale 202, a manuscript that moved from St Bertin to England and back to St Bertin, is the homiliary detailed in Leofric's booklist, we also see connections with Flanders and indeed with the same monastery whose monks likely wrote the *Encomium* and the *Vita Ædwardi*. This manuscript also contains the *Evangelium Nichodemi* and the *Vindicta saluatoris*, vernacular versions of which were produced at Exeter, again emphasizing the bilingual character of Leofric's library.[84] Although the place of Imperial material in his sacramentary (the "Leofric Missal") underscores Leofric's primary formation, the inclusion of material from southern France and Normandy shows his receptivity to wider influences, including, perhaps, the literary culture of

81 Voigt, ed., *Egberts von Lüttich*, liii–lvii; Brunhölzl, *Histoire*, 260. I am grateful to Julia Smith for suggesting this connection.

82 Koepke, ed., *Anselmi Gesta episcoporum*, 189–234 (Anselm's account is critical of the court values of bishops); Jaeger, *Envy of Angels*, 202–10.

83 Ibid., 56 and 349–75 (discussion and translation of the letter); Latin text: Huygens, ed., *Gozechin*, 11–43.

84 Chapters by Cross and Crick (31–5) and by Cross (82–4) in Cross, ed., *Two Old English Apocrypha*.

the Encomiast.[85] Not incidentally, given the neumes of *The Songs*, the Leofric Missal, along with other Exeter manuscripts, show the bishop's own interest in music. Susan Rankin argues that Leofric himself was among the scribes responsible for musical notation in Exeter manuscripts.[86] The sacramentary adds further to our understanding of Leofric's approaches to old books. Although he could have had a new one made, he chose an old one, which belonged to Dunstan and earlier archbishops of Canterbury, thus creating a link between his reformed community of canons and the earlier Benedictine Reform. Such a man is unlikely to have been an accidental or antiquarian owner of the Exeter Book.

Leofric's experience of court literature in England, alongside his Imperial formation, may have shaped the aspirations that stand behind his copy of Statius. The charter recording the consecration of Exeter cathedral asserts Leofric's continuing close ties with king and queen, describing Edward leading Leofric, on his right arm, and Edith, on his left arm, to the altar.[87] Throughout Edward's reign, Leofric, though he did not attend the king as closely as some prelates, continued to move in court circles, as his presence in charter witness lists attests. Those same witness lists show Leofric together with the other Imperial bishops of the southwest.[88] Finally, Leofric probably had an Imperial cleric within his own household; when he petitioned Pope Leo IX to move his see to Exeter, he sent his chaplain Landbert, whose name invokes the patron saint of Liège.[89] The prevalence of Imperial clerics among Edward's chaplains and their subsequent preferment to sees in the southwest meant that Leofric's Imperial inclinations – liturgical and literary – should not be seen as taking place in isolation on the fringe of Wessex.

Links between Leofric and Ealdred drive home the connections between the mid-eleventh-century world of the Exeter Book and that of *The Cambridge Songs*. Ealdred likely shared Leofric's West Country origin, and their careers brought the two men into frequent contact, as the number of charters where they are both among the witnesses attests.[90]

85 Orchard, *Leofric Missal*, 207 and 234.

86 Rankin, "From Memory to Written Record," esp. 100 and 104.

87 S 1021. Charters are cited by Sawyer number. Texts can be found in the Electronic Sawyer website: www.esawyer.org.uk.

88 S 1023, 1024, 1025, 1026, 1027, 1031, 1033, 1034, 1036, 1037, 1038, 1040, 1041, 1042, 1043.

89 Barlow, *English Church*, 84.

90 S 1012, 1020, 1022, 1025, 1026, 1027, 1031, 1033, 1036, 1037a, 1038, 1040, 1041, 1042, 1043; and post-Conquest: Bates, ed., *Regesta*, numbers 254 and 286.

When Bishop Lyfing died, they jointly succeeded him: Leofric in Cornwall and Devon and Ealdred in Worcester. Moreover, as Lapidge has argued, Cotton Vitellius E.12, which contains the Romano-German Pontifical that he suggests Ealdred brought to England, was later added to at Exeter. Lapidge, identifying the hand of the additions as one which copied other Exeter manuscripts from the period of Leofric's pontificate, concludes that "an Anglo-Saxon scribe who had been a member of Ealdred's household found employment in the household of Leofric and … he took Vitellius E.xii with him to Exeter."[91] Connections to Ealdred also brought Leofric into contact with Worcester, where written English was extensively used and from whose library he may have acquired Wulfstan's episcopal collection discussed earlier.[92] Ealdred's own investment in Old English extended beyond his time at Worcester, as witnessed by the compilation of the "D" version of the Anglo-Saxon Chronicle, the most court-centred of all the Chronicles for this period and likely produced in Ealdred's entourage when he was archbishop of York.[93] The inclusion within the "D" text of a poem commemorating the death of Edward the Confessor brings the kind of royal panegyric missing in the Exeter Book but so present in *The Cambridge Songs* into the frame. Meanwhile, Ealdred's Worcester also held a glossed copy of Statius's *Thebaid* (Worcester, Cathedral Library, Q.8, fols. 165–72) – a text excerpted in *The Cambridge Songs*, invoked in Queen Edith's *Vita Ædwardi*, and donated to Exeter by Leofric. Creative and sustained engagement with Statius emerges as a defining feature of eleventh-century Anglo-Saxon literary culture, in which regard it was at the cutting edge of European literary developments. Both Ealdred and Leofric, who experienced, first hand, the turmoil created by the strife between Harold and Tostig, would have found much of interest in Statius, suggesting that part of the *Thebaid*'s popularity in mid-eleventh-century England was the result of its political topicality.

Situating the Exeter Book and *The Cambridge Songs* in a literary culture common to both court and cathedral does not require that we imagine Ealdred and Leofric poring over the Exeter Book and *The Cambridge Songs* together or even that Ealdred himself brought *The Songs* back from Henry III's court. Both men were English bishops with first-hand

91 Lapidge, "Ealdred," 465–6.

92 Hill, "Two Anglo-Saxon Bishops," 160.

93 Cubbin, ed., *Anglo-Saxon Chronicle: Manuscript D*, lxxviii–lxxxi; but see Stafford, "Archbishop Ealdred."

knowledge of the Empire and close connections to Edward's court. Their close association forms part of a larger picture in which Edward's court and church actively sought to forge political, liturgical, architectural, and literary ties with Imperial Germany. In the process, Imperial influences were brought in alongside the French ones evident in the *Encomium* and the *Vita Ædwardi.* Critically, this openness to new trends in European Latin literary culture did not threaten the distinctive Anglo-Saxon use of the written vernacular. On the contrary, the books of Leofric's inventory show that English kept pace with and was a part of these new developments. *The Cambridge Songs*, viewed within their manuscript and social contexts, reveal that on the cusp of the Conquest there was no conflict between the old and new Latinities evinced in Gg.5.35 – and likewise no conflict between Latin and vernacular poetics.

We might still see Leofric and English as a dead end and imagine that, when he died in 1072, the Exeter Book was locked in a cupboard, as French replaced English as an elite language. But Leofric lets us see something different. He was an example of an Anglo-Saxon looking at the written vernacular with fresh, even Continental, eyes, assessing very shrewdly its potential, and from this perspective deciding to promote it vigorously. Leofric did not find a desperate, second best, limited pastoral language. Rather he sought out, and wanted to be associated with, the best vernacular poetry in a handsome book. He was an insider/outsider whom we can almost watch assessing English – a language and a mode (the vernacular) which he did not find wanting.

We can, however, be more specific about Leofric's Continental linguistic experience. His education in Toul or Liège means that he is likely to have been a French, rather than a German, speaker.[94] Thus he is an example of what a Francophone (as well as an Anglophone) learned from the use of written English. Equally, he is a reminder that French was a language not solely associated with the Normans or the French but was an elite vernacular which enabled communication across the boundaries of counties, duchies, kingdoms, and even the Empire. In the eleventh century, it was also the language of the Flemish court and of the western reaches of the Empire, as well as of the French principalities and Normandy.

94 Haubrichs, "Volkssprache und volkssprachige Literaturen" and "Von *pêle-mêle* zum *vis-à-vis*"; Parisse, "Lotharingia."

Given that the long experience of English as a written language was an important stimulus to the writing of French in the early twelfth century, what Leofric did with English matters for both English *and* French.[95] Indeed, Leofric, who witnessed charters of William the Conqueror, as he had the Confessor, can be seen as a figure for the multifaceted relationship between English and French.[96] English on the cusp of the Conquest emerges not as backward-looking but as flexible, intellectually and artistically alive, and capable of teaching French a trick or two. Leofric leads us away not only from setting Latin and the vernacular up as binaries but also from seeing a simple hierarchy of Latin, French, and English after the Conquest.[97]

95 Short, "Patrons and Polyglots"; Tyler, "From Old English to Old French."

96 Bates, ed., *Regesta*, numbers 138, 181, 213, 254, and 286.

97 The research for this article was supported by the Centre for Medieval Literature, funded by the Danish National Research Foundation and located at the University of Southern Denmark and the University of York (project number DNRF102ID). Versions were read at the International Medieval Congress (Leeds) and the universities of Oxford, Cambridge, Frankfurt, and Pennsylvania. I am grateful to audiences in all these places for comments and to the editors of this volume for their insightful suggestions. This chapter also benefits from discussion with Rita Copeland, Christian Høgel, Lars Boje Mortensen, Carole Newlands, Thomas O'Donnell, Felicitas Schmieder, Matthew Townend, and George Younge.

Writing Community: Osbern and the Negotiations of Identity in the *Miracula S. Dunstani*

KATHERINE O'BRIEN O'KEEFFE

At some point between 1076 and March 1077 one Ægelward ("Ægelwardus"), an English brother of the monastic community of Christ Church, lost his mind while assisting Archbishop Lanfranc at mass.[1] The severity and length of his suffering, with its florid behaviour and uncanny threats, made Ægelward's affliction the concern of the entire community and beyond, as the unusual number of competing accounts of the event attest. In a letter written to John, archbishop of Rouen, Lanfranc (one of the principals in Osbern's account) alludes to John's having heard rumours of the experience of a young monk at Christ Church but chooses not to commit an account to writing, electing instead to have the bearer of the letter brief the archbishop on what Lanfranc had witnessed.[2] It is likely that this "euentum" is Ægelward's breakdown. Lanfranc's discreet refusal to write contrasts strikingly with Osbern of Canterbury's decision to record the story in a disproportionately lengthy chapter (cap. 19) of his *Miracula S. Dunstani*.[3] Osbern's half-apology, "latius fortasse quam opus esset hoc miraculum scripsimus"

1 Clover and Gibson, eds., *Letters of Lanfranc*, 91n3, date Ægelward's breakdown to this period, i.e., between the appointment of Prior Henry and the consecration of Gundulf as bishop of Rochester. C.N.L. Brooke (in Knowles, ed., *Monastic Constitutions*, rev. Brooke, xxviiin1) reviews arguments for the dating of Prior Henry's promotion and finds the evidence inconclusive. It is often dated to 1076. Searle, *Ononmasticon*, 57 lists him as "Æþelweard." The name does not appear in the Prosopography of Anglo-Saxon England (PASE) database.

2 Clover and Gibson, eds., *Letters of Lanfranc*, letter 15 (88–91) at 90.

3 BHL 2345. For Osbern's *vita* and *miracula* of Dunstan see Stubbs, ed., *Memorials of Dunstan*, 67–161. The miracle of Ægelward's healing is cap. 19 (pp. 144–51). Eadmer treats the incident, though somewhat more briefly: Turner and Muir, eds., *Eadmer of Canterbury*, cap. 19 (pp. 182–9). The anonymous *Vita Gundulfi* makes Bishop Gundulf

(perhaps we have written of this miracle more extensively than necessary),[4] invites attention to this oddly told miracle and its mixed functions within a text that seeks to make a community by writing it. As Osbern makes his Latin prose the vehicle for writing the new identity of his house, his account of this miracle lays bare the ambivalences haunting his negotiation of dissociations more far reaching than Ægelward's breakdown.

In the decade between the Conquest and Ægelward's collapse, the community at Christ Church had experienced a number of disruptions, not least of which was the burning of virtually all its structures and most of its books in the fire of 1067. Towards the end of his life, and with the objective distance of more than fifty years, Eadmer could ascribe the fire of 1067 to carelessness: "contigit ciuitatem Cantuariam ex incuria quorundam sua minus caute curantium igne succendi" (it happened that the city of Canterbury was burned through the negligence of certain men who cared for it not so carefully).[5] Osbern, by contrast, attributes the fire not to chance but to Dunstan's quitting the cathedral in disgust: "Quotiens etiam in nocturna visione visus est fratribus de ecclesia exire! quem cum exeuntem retinere vellent, 'Non possum,' inquit, 'ibi manere propter foetorem pagani pueri, licet initiati, in hac ecclesia sepulti'" (How often in nightly visions was he seen by the brothers to leave the church, and when they wished keep him from leaving he said, "I cannot stay here because of the stench of the pagan child buried, although unbaptized, in this church").[6] Osbern's account makes the fire and its destruction an object lesson on the folly of ignoring the will of the saint.[7]

---

hero of the incident: see Thomson, ed., *Life of Gundulf*, cap. 11 (pp. 33–4). For a late treatment of the miracle see Gibson, ed., "Vita Lanfranci," 710–11.

4 Stubbs, ed., *Memorials of Dunstan*, cap. 19, p. 151. Further page references to cap. 19 of Osbern's *Miraculi* in Stubbs's edition will be included in the text. This chapter's length flouts Osbern's promise to write the miracles in the collection "quantum possumus breviter atque dilucide" (130) (as briefly and clearly as we can). All translations are my own.

5 Scholz, "Eadmer's Life of Bregwine," 144. Eadmer adds that almost all the books were burned as well. Scholz dates the writing of the *vita* to 1123 (131).

6 Stubbs, ed., *Memorials of Dunstan*, cap. 16, p. 142. On the meaning of "initiatus" see *DML*, s.v. (2) *initiatus*, "not christened, or ? *f[alsa] l[ectio]*."

7 It would appear that Dunstan was additionally provoked by the refusal of the prior to credit the account of a young boy who reported Dunstan's dissatisfaction at the saint's command: "sed ille infideli mente nunciata parvipendebat" (142) (but he [the prior] with a faithless mind discounted what had been told to him). Stubbs, ed., *Memorials of Dunstan*, 142n2, indicates that London, British Library, Harley 56 and London, British Library, Cotton Titus D. iv substitute a clause for "propter ... sepulti"

The wretched physical conditions after the Christ Church fire were only the most dramatic of sharp breaks with the past, marked as well in the personnel and practices of the monastery following the Conquest. The Norman ascendancy was accompanied by a substantial replacement in the ranks of the English clergy.[8] By the end of William's reign, most of the English Benedictine monasteries were ruled by Norman abbots bent on the reform of those Anglo-Saxon houses.[9] While violent disruptions (between 1087 and 1090) at St Augustine's led to the removal of its rebellious monks, by comparison the inmates of Christ Church seemed accepting or at least resigned. Indeed, Teresa Webber infers from the tolerance of different styles of script in Christ Church in the early post-Conquest period that there was no "politics of script" in that community.[10] There was, however, a politics of reform, as Norman abbots updated and renewed the texts and practices of English monastic houses they considered hopelessly backward. These are the anxious circumstances of the community of Christ Church in the first decades of Norman rule as loss and change produced what can only be described as a state of "between-ness" for both Anglo-Saxon and Norman inmates. While the Normans might console themselves for their dislocation by remaking their newly acquired house, the Anglo-Saxon brothers were left to accommodate to those changes as best they could. Osbern's writings model a complex form of that accommodation.

In assessing Archbishop Lanfranc's years in Canterbury leading up to the composition of his *Decreta*, C.L.N. Brooke points to a fundamental between-ness – "the ambivalence of his attitudes" to various elements of pre-Conquest tradition at Christ Church.[11] But ambivalence about life at Christ Church could not have been Lanfranc's alone amid the cascading changes in the conditions of its monastic life in the two decades following

---

not found in his base text: "propter spurcitias malorum morum et reorum in ecclesia sepultorum" (because of the filthiness of the evil practices and crimes of those buried in the church).

8 Of course, Edward the Confessor had, in a sense, begun the process, but his imposition of two foreign prelates – Roðulf, a Norwegan relation who was appointed abbot of Abingdon in 1050, and Robert of Jumièges, who was appointed archbishop of Canterbury – had been very unpopular. See O'Brien O'Keeffe, ed., *Anglo-Saxon Chronicle: MS C*, s.a. 1050 and 1052.

9 Knowles, *Monastic Order in England*, 111–13.

10 Webber, "Script and Manuscript Production," 156.

11 Knowles, ed., *Monastic Constitutions*, rev. Brooke, xxxvii–xxxviii.

the Conquest. The canonically inadequate Stigand (who had held plural sees and had never taken up monastic life) was likely responsible for the laxity in the practice of monastic life which Lanfranc (appointed archbishop in 1070) would address in his tenure.[12] Whatever the degree of Lanfranc's well-rehearsed ambivalence over the sanctity of Sts Ælfheah and Dunstan, he was firmly decisive about reforming and managing the house's monastic life.[13] While Norman superiors were brought in to administer and reform, most of the brothers of the community, like Osbern, Ægelward, and Eadmer, were Anglo-Saxons.[14] Godric, the dean of Christ Church (mentioned by Osbern as a sympathetic figure when he was a boy), was replaced by Prior Henry (appointed probably in 1076), who seems to have been personally unsympathetic to Osbern.[15] The Norman Ernulf became the schoolmaster and brought changes to the curriculum.[16] The *Decreta*, a work dedicated to Prior Henry which outlined the kind of religious life Lanfranc was shaping for the community, emerged from the archbishop's early years of reacting to and dealing with monastic life at Christ Church as it was before the Conquest.[17] In this period as well,

12 Brooks, "Anglo-Saxon Cathedral Community," 32. Eadmer censures the laxity of life at Christ Church and ascribes the terrible events of Ægelward's madness to the kindly correction of Christ "quos ... cessante disciplina, in saeculari uidebat conuersatione ultra quam debebant iacere" (who saw that they (viz. the monks) had fallen into secular life more than they should have when regular discipline ceased). Turner and Muir, eds., *Eadmer of Canterbury*, 184. On the "demoralizing" years of Stigand's rule see Knowles, *Monastic Order in England*, 79.

13 Pfaff, "Lanfranc's Supposed Purge," finds no "purge" of the Anglo-Saxon Calendar. Ridyard ("*Condigna veneratio*," 200–4) argues that events before 1089 prepared for a "Norman assimilation" of Christ Church's major saints. It is the case, however, that Dunstan's feast did not appear in Lanfranc's *Decreta* (Ridyard, "*Condigna veneratio*," 202).

14 See Southern, *Saint Anselm and His Biographer*, who describes the monks from Bec and Caen accompanying Lanfranc to Christ Church as "a small addition to a predominantly English community ... likely ... marked out for future promotion" (246).

15 See Stubbs, ed., *Memorials of Dunstan*, cap. 11, p. 128. On Prior Henry see Cowdrey, *Lanfranc*, 150–1. Rubenstein, "Life and Writings of Osbern," 33–4, speculates that Prior Henry was the unnamed antagonist in the lawsuit Osbern describes in *Miracula S. Dunstani*, cap. 25.

16 Gibson, "Normans and Angevins," 41.

17 Knowles, ed., *Monastic Constitutions*, rev. Brooke, xxviii. According to Brooke, Henry was prior from sometime between 1070×1076 and 1096, when he became abbot of Battle. While the *Decreta* is variously dated to c. 1077, post-1079, and before 1083, Brooke finds c. 1077 the most probable date.

Lanfranc undertook the building work which required the destruction of what was left of the pre-Conquest foundation and the moving of the relics of the saints, including those of St Dunstan, to temporary quarters in the refectory.[18] If historians infer a successful integration of Anglo-Saxon cult from the altars of Sts Dunstan and Ælfheah in the cathedral that St Anselm would build, we must remind ourselves that such an outcome was never guaranteed in the preceding decades.[19] Ensuring the continuing veneration of Anglo-Saxon saints under the Norman dispensation, an act of shoring up fragments against the ruins, required careful negotiation and anxious management. Osbern's writings, particularly the *Miracula S. Dunstani*, offer striking illustration of the costs of such negotiation, as he uses the social form of the miracle story to write the present of his house and shape the future.[20]

In her compelling analysis of English miracle collections, Rachel Koopmans has persuasively argued that miracle stories themselves did not create the "social bond" they are often credited with, but rather "the telling of stories, and not the miracles per se ... acted as the bonding device."[21] Continuing veneration of a saint thus depended on *process*: the sharing of wonderful stories about the intervention of a saint itself constituted the cult. One would be "within" the cult of a saint by seeking, receiving, or telling stories of where the saint had intervened in the lives of those devoted to him or her. This emphasis on the intimately social underpinnings of a saint's cult brings us to a central point of difficulty for the community of Christ Church seeking the preservation of its major saints. For the pre-Conquest saints of Christ Church – pre-eminently Ælfheah and Dunstan – the sharing of such stories, and hence the creation and continuation of cult, would have been in Old English.[22] Preserving their position in the wake of the Conquest necessarily meant extending the cults beyond the

18 For the "new Continental ways" of Lanfranc's architectural project see Klukas, "Architectural Implications," 151.

19 Southern, *Saint Anselm and His Biographer*, 250–1 and n2. For a review of the cult over time see Ramsay and Sparks, "Cult of St Dunstan."

20 Osbern was precentor, a position that put him in charge of books and music. For the responsibilities of contemporary precentors see Licence, "History and Hagiography," 523.

21 Koopmans, *Wonderful to Relate*, 26. Koopmans suggests that the Anglo-Saxon saints of Christ Church were "loci of integration" (89).

22 There are two surviving Latin hagiographical works on Dunstan, those by "B" and by Adelard, both of which Osbern knew. For these early writings on Dunstan see Winterbottom and Lapidge, eds., *Early Lives of Dunstan*, lxiv–cxxii and cxxv–cxxxv.

vernacular and thus, critically, changing the language of exchange. This is the task that Osbern took on himself in his hagiographical works.

The writing of these works dates to after his return from Bec, where he had been sent for education and discipline. In his role as hagiographer, the re-formed Osbern offers a provocative, early view of the textual interactions between the two post-Conquest cultures and an example of the first accommodations of writing on the Anglo-Saxon past to the political realities of its newly subaltern context. Of Osbern himself very little is known, though Jay Rubenstein has coaxed the few mentions about him into a suggestive biography.[23] Osbern was an Anglo-Saxon oblate of Christ Church, Canterbury before the Conquest. Although the circumstances are very unclear, it would appear that for some fairly serious transgression Lanfranc sent Osbern for discipline and study to his own former monastery of Bec in Normandy, probably between 1076 and 1080. There he studied with and became a protégé of St Anselm.[24] It would appear that Osbern returned to Canterbury in 1080 and remained there until he died, perhaps in 1093. His surviving texts, the *passio* and *translatio* of Ælfheah and the *Vita* and *Miracula* of Dunstan, though undateable, must post-date Osbern's return from Normandy in 1080.[25] Osbern's life in both communities (Bec and Christ Church), his reformation following study with Anselm (attested by his appointment as precentor after his return), and perhaps his Latin style itself, refined by his study in Normandy, all produced him as a negotiator, linguistically and culturally, between the two ethnic communities, bearing in his own person the conflicts and compromises of the go-between.

The *Vita* and *Miracula* of Dunstan, written somewhat after the works on Ælfheah, have a more ambitious aim – quite literally to write an idealized version of the blended community at Christ Church by gathering all within the cult of Dunstan. And we see this goal marked by a strategic shift in Osbern's prologue for the *Miracula*. The prologue to the earlier *passio* of Ælfheah focuses on language as the issue to be negotiated in vouching for the trustworthiness of his vernacular sources. Quite a

23 Rubenstein, "Life and Writings of Osbern," 28–31.

24 A number of letters of St Anselm mention Osbern and appear to promote his rehabilitation. See Schmitt, *Anselmi Opera*, vol. 3, ep. 39, 58, 66, 67, and 182.

25 Rubenstein, "Life and Writings of Osbern," 38, has speculated that the *vita* and *miracula* of Dunstan were written following Lanfranc's death in 1089, but there is little conclusive evidence for this argument.

different problem confronted Osbern in composing a *vita* of Dunstan: a liturgical work and at least one *vita*, both in Latin, already existed. In his preface to the *vita* of Dunstan, Osbern transforms this plenitude into a double lack: Adelard's liturgical text lacked detail, and "B"'s hermeneutic Latin, though detailed, lacked elegance because it was written in a pompous style.[26] And, he adds, although better Latin writings were burnt in the fire of 1067, Old English translations of these incinerated texts had survived. These are the works his senior (presumably Norman) interlocutors wish him to rescue for them: "aliqua in patrium id est in Anglicum sermonem translata supersunt, ex quibus id quod petimus elicere, et in Latinam denuo poteris linguam Deo suffragante transferre" (70) (others survive translated into the ancestral, that is, English language, from which you [scil. Osbern] will be able, God willing, to draw out what we seek and translate it again into the Latin language). When Osbern claims that these seniors urge him to write a *vita* of Dunstan better suited to the tastes and abilities of his contemporary readers, the issue of this preface, then, becomes the style and not the truth of language.[27] In representing his *vita* of Dunstan as a back translation, Osbern implies that those commissioning the work had already accepted that the Old English writings Osbern identifies as trusted sources of Dunstan's life could yield a more suitable *vita* than the previous Latin writings from Christ Church's Anglo-Saxon past. The work of Osbern's Latin prose, re-formed in the schoolroom at Bec, is thus cast as restoration – of a *vita* appropriate to the saint – and its amelioration in a language (and style) suited to a discerning, linguistically blended audience. In this positioning of his audience(s), writing the present in Osbern's Latin is at once a sacrifice of the vernacular of both saints' cults and a strong move to unite both parts of the house in a language that both and neither owned. For Osbern, writing the present is writing its identity.

The second piece of the argument for Dunstan's cult structures the prologue to the *Miracula* as it makes a claim to truth and a demand for belief. Unlike with the *vita* of Dunstan, Osbern identifies himself as the first to

26 Stubbs, ed., *Memorials of Dunstan*, 70, "in illud dicendi genus quod suffultum [?recte "sufflatum"] Romanae princeps eloquentiae vocat" (in that kind of style the prince of Roman eloquence calls "suffultum"). "Suffultum" is likely an error for Cicero's "sufflatu[m]." For an analysis of Osbern's appeal to audience in this preface see Townsend, "Anglo-Latin Hagiography," 397. Townsend identifies the reference to *Rhetorica ad Herennium* IV.x.15.

27 Townsend, "Anglo-Latin Hagiography," 397, identifies this as a "classicizing style."

commit the saint's miracles to writing. For this reason, he must establish the trustworthiness of his account, claiming that he writes only those things "done in our time" and only a very few miracles told to him by the most credible of men. In a related gesture within the *Miracula* proper, Osbern pronounces two miracles to be of uncertain etiology (i.e., possibly effected by other saints of the house [cap. 22]) and declines to include four other stories lest he strain the credulity of his readers.[28]

Osbern fashions the *Miracula* as a history of events in "our" day that demands belief from a specific group of future readers, the "Angligenae": "propositum habemus ea narrare, quae, post depositionem corporalis sarcinae, felix spiritus ejus in hoc saeculo dignatus est operari, ut omnes futuri temporis Angligenae populi agnoscant quid tanti nominis viro honoris ac reverentiae debeant" (129) (I intend to recount those things which, after the burial of his fleshly burden, his blessed spirit deigned to perform in this age, that all the English people of future time will recognize what honour and reverence they owe to the man of so great a name). "This age" contrasts the "now" of the text with an imagined future that mirrors a desired present. In the decades immediately following the Conquest, the word "Angligenae," literally, those born in England, stood in binary contrast to "Francigenae," those born in France.[29] Although there is a very early example, according to George Garnett, of politically calculated "Angligenae" applied by William the Conqueror to his own troops at his coronation,[30] overwhelmingly, careful distinctions were made between the "French" (and Normans were very early included in the appellation) and the "English," in vernacular writs as well as Latin writing. We see the distinction of "Angligenae" and "Francigenae" in Lanfranc's letter on the

28 Stubbs, ed., *Memorials of Dunstan*, cap. 26, p. 160: "Videtis quibus abstineo, propterea quod aestimationem audientium supergredi nolo; quae tamen si commemorarem, incredibilis esse non deberem, propterea quod nihil est difficultatis ubi Dominus Christus auctor est operis" (You see what I abstain from because I do not want to exceed the appraisal of my audience; still, if I were to record those things, I ought not to be unworthy of belief, because nothing is difficult when the Lord Christ is the doer). Among these rejected miracles is Dunstan's hanging his robe on a sunbeam.

29 *DML*: "English born, English," 86, s.v. "angligena." Lanfranc refers to Normans as "Francigen[ae]" in Clover and Gibson, eds., *Letters of Lanfranc*, letter 53 (pp. 166–7). Clover and Gibson date this letter between 19 March 1077 and 28 May 1089. For studies of the two language communities see Clark, "People and Languages," and Short, "*Tam Angli quam Franci.*"

30 Garnett, "'Franci and Angli,'" 113 cites the *Laudes regiae*: "Angligenis turmis" (English-born armies) refer to William's own army.

canonical status of women in English convents.[31] When, in a letter written early in his reign as archbishop of Canterbury, Lanfranc wishes to refer to his own status as now living in England, he uses "nouus Anglus," suggesting that "Anglus" was sufficiently neutral to indicate English status by emigration.[32] And the base-word "genae" overwhelmingly refers to those born in the country.

The "Angligenae" of Osbern's day, pointing as the word does to a community of native-born English, hardly needed convincing about the importance of Dunstan's cult. In the context of a Latin work extending that cult to a different language community, however, Osbern's reference to those born in England only makes sense if it refers to future generations no longer distinguished by difference of native language and united in their having been born in England. For this imagined future readership, then, Osbern defines the critical issue as the challenge of believing what they themselves have not seen. Of course the trick of this appeal is that by contrast with this imagined future readership, Osbern constructs his *present* readership – Anglo-Saxons and Normans alike – as a single community of belief, the "we" who have seen and believed. In constructing two readerships, one of the present (divided by language and custom) and one of the future (blended by birth in a common land), Osbern sutures the two contemporary language groups, English and French, in reverence for the great patron of their house. Osbern's Latin prose becomes the means of uniting the present community, giving them a common non-native language for belief and constructing them in collegial opposition to the doubting readership of the future. Osbern's "nos" is slippery: it both refers to himself as author and also to the community of Christ Church in their devotion to their powerful patron, Dunstan.[33] "We" believe these miracles and demand belief of those Englishmen of future times.

The very structure of Osbern's *Miracula* is calculated to build such belief by establishing a foundation of "standard" miracles before moving the reader to the more personal interactions witnessed by members of the community. The first thirteen narratives of miracles show Dunstan to be

31 Clover and Gibson, eds., *Letters of Lanfranc*, letter 53 (pp. 166–7). Clover and Gibson date this letter between 19 March 1077 and 29 May 1089. Searle, "Women and the Legitimisation of Succession," 165, would date the letter to "the mid or late 1070s."

32 Clover and Gibson, eds., *Letters of Lanfranc*, letter 2 (pp. 38–9).

33 Later, in cap. 24 and 25, in accounts of miracles affecting him, Osbern lays "nos" aside and refers to himself in the singular. He also writes in the singular in his conclusion (cap. 26).

imitating Christ: there are healings of the blind individually and in groups (cap. 2, 3, 6, 7, 11); of paralytics (cap. 4, 9); of a mute who is also a cripple (cap. 5); of a demoniac (cap. 8); and of various crippled individuals (cap. 12, 13, 14), some carefully supplied with names and locations.[34] Thus these otherwise generic miracles are particularized by association with individuals and places in addition to the shrine itself. Osbern reports witnessing the healing of a crippled young woman (cap. 12) after her distraught mother begged him and another boy for help at the steps of the altar. Following the miracle at Dunstan's tomb, Osbern reports "accurrimus, vidimus, flevimus, et facto mane cum exultatione totius urbis, Dominum Deum nostrum Jesum Christum laudavimus" (139) (we ran, we saw, we wept, and when morning came along with the rejoicing of the entire city, we praised our Lord God, Jesus Christ). Such personal witness lends veracity to the earlier miracles reported by others, just as identifying the Anglo-Saxon boy of the community who had a vision of St Dunstan (cap. 15) as "nunc vero reverendae aetatis senior" (but now a senior monk of venerable age) is meant to strengthen belief. The miracles in the collection to this point are pre-Conquest: cap. 16 (recording the fire of 1067) marks the beginning of the present-day miracles. Osbern introduces this shift in the following chapter by observing "horum ruina in melius commutata est" (142) (their destruction was changed for the better), while noting that this change required moving the relics of the saints at Lanfranc's order. Thereafter the miracles make a claim on the contemporary community by involving Archbishop Lanfranc in increasingly personal ways. In cap. 17 Lanfranc witnesses a miracle involving Abbot Scotland of St Augustine's following the removal of the Christ Church saints' relics to the oratory. And the next miracle (cap. 18) shows Lanfranc himself to be victorious in a lawsuit against Odo of Bayeux after he sought Dunstan's help. These miracles establish the saint's power to dispose the outcome of political and legal events and portray the powerful Lanfranc within Dunstan's cult.[35] But the incorporation of Lanfranc in Osbern's narrative was, it appears, a mixed blessing.

34 For miraculous healing in general, Matt. 15:30; in particular: healings of the possessed, Matt. 8:16; of the blind, Matt. 20:30–4; of the crippled, Luke 13:11–13; of a deaf mute, Mark 7:32–7.

35 In cap. 24 Osbern recounts how Dunstan aided him in the prosecution of a legal case. For a discussion see Koopmans, *Wonderful to Relate*, 18–25.

Ægelward's healing (cap. 19), in effect, pits Lanfranc and Dunstan against each other in resolving a case of demonic possession. It is a curious handling of a miracle in a collection whose purpose is to write community and cement belief. But as Walter Pohl has trenchantly observed, "the rhetoric of concord often is a sure sign of conflict."[36] And the narrative of this strange chapter reveals the disquiet lying beneath the placid surface of Osbern's hagiography. As it is cast here, this miracle bespeaks a politics of *patrocinium* in the monastery, where Lanfranc, portrayed as a devotee of Dunstan, becomes the foil to show Dunstan's power.

The unfortunate subject of the miracle, Ægelward, a *iuvenis*, is likely to have been substantially formed as a monk under the rule of the secular Stigand. His breakdown into madness coincides with a time of maximal disruption to the community, when Lanfranc had ordered the destruction of the oratory housing the relics of Christ Church's saints. Osbern understands Ægelward's breakdown as an instance of demonic possession arising from some uncleanness on Ægelward's part and his neglect of confession. Its hagiographical frame places the story squarely in the struggle for the identity of this ancient English foundation in the aftermath of the Norman Conquest. Especially unusual in the account, and where Osbern's otherwise careful rhetorical control slips into between-ness, is its awkward combination of two narrative strands: the first dealing with Lanfranc and the efficacy of confession, the second with the attempts to cure the possessed man by expelling his demon. Both strands thematize speech acts, but their combination into a single miracle narrative produces an unintended result. In cap. 19, acts of confession, the compulsive, obscene rantings of the demoniac (portrayed as the consequence of his failure to confess), and the intercessory prayers of the community are connected through Archbishop Lanfranc's exercise of the abbot's power.[37] And these instances of speech contrast with the silent power of Dunstan, called "communis pater" (father of us all) by the healed demoniac returned to wholesome speech by the saint. There is another, awkward contrast, as the otherwise unsuccessful intercessory prayers of the community are

36 Pohl, "Construction of Communities," 6.

37 On Lanfranc's equation of bishop and abbot see Knowles, *Monastic Order*, 622. The fifth step of humility in the *Regula Benedicti* (=*RB*) requires a monk to confess sinful thoughts and deeds to the abbot. See *RB* 7.44–8. The procedures for accusing individuals of sins and administering punishment are outlined in Lanfranc's *Decreta*, cap. 99–100 and 106 (Knowles, ed., *Monastic Constitutions*, rev. Brooke, 146–53 and 164–7).

balanced against the fruitful prayer of an unnamed monk especially devoted to Dunstan. These narratives cross at the level of abbatial and episcopal power, where Lanfranc is shown to fail in his efforts to exorcise the demon, and Dunstan, former abbot and archbishop, effects the cure.

There are four moments when confession of a hidden sin checks the power of the devil. Lanfranc, functioning as abbot, begins by ordering Ægelward to confess the sin that made it possible for the devil to possess him ("praecepit illi culpam confiteri propter quam a tam saevo daemone potuisset invadi" [145–6]); but the man cannot speak because the demon prevents him from framing the words. When Lanfranc forces the demon to permit him to confess the specific sin that occasioned the possession, the suffering monk gains some relief. But after the chapter meeting, though the monk is temporarily calm after ritual chastisement, his affliction returns, and he threatens to reveal what each of the monks around him has done in secret. In particular, one young monk (identified only as an "adolescens") receives specially threatening attention from the demoniac.[38] To protect the unnamed young monk from this terrible fate, Lanfranc urges the youth to confess "ut si quid in illo peccati lateret in vera Deo confessione ediceret" (146) (that if there were any sin hiding in him he should declare it to God in a true confession), and he does so copiously. Once again, when the demoniac rages against the brothers, threatening to reveal the secret sins of each of them, full confession is shown to be the corrective.[39] In the final moment, though, the demoniac once again rages at the "adolescens," but is shown to be unable to recognize him and thus unable to know his secret deeds. Lanfranc explains that this outcome is due to the efficacy of confession (148). Yet confession has been shown to be ineffectual for the demoniac.

This narrative strand about speech and confession is complicated by another about Lanfranc's own efforts to exorcize the demon. After the first attempt, Ægelward's rages return and increase. Then Lanfranc orders him brought to Dunstan's tomb, where the archbishop performs an exorcism; after this the man remains quiet for a day. But his madness returns with behaviour so florid that Lanfranc orders him brought back to Dunstan's tomb and orders the whole community to pray for his healing ("communis

38 Rubenstein, "Life and Writings of Osbern," 30, speculates that the young man is Osbern himself.

39 Stubbs, ed., *Memorials of Dunstan*, 147: "Caeterum de iis qui peccata sua confessi fuerant omnino nihil improperando potuit efferre."

omnium supplicatio" [147]). Yet Ægelward only gets worse, unable to say the words of the Creed and assaulting those present with spittle and curses instead of reciting the Lord's Prayer.[40] Finally, he is bound to his bed as the demon grows in strength.

While the demoniac's madness is increasing, the relics of Dunstan are removed from their tomb as Lanfranc completes plans to destroy the old foundation to build the new church (148–9). Osbern stages a meeting between the holy and the obscene while Dunstan's relics are being moved and Ægelward is being carried out still bound to his heavy bed. At the sight of Dunstan's coffin, the demon rages and blasphemes, and he appears to move about within the suffering brother as if a little dog were inside him. Finally, when the relics are settled in the place prepared for them, the demoniac is laid before Dunstan's remains. While the entire community begs for Dunstan's help, a monk especially devoted to the saint places on the demoniac the banner which had once been carried before Dunstan in episcopal rituals, and prays fervently for the saint's help. Immediately the demon is expelled. This time the demon is gone for good: "liberatus est monachus ab omnimoda daemonum vexatione, multisque annis postea vixit, et sancto fine ultimum diem clausit" (150–1) (the monk was freed from all kinds of demonic vexation, and he lived afterwards for many years and finished his final day with a holy end).

Such a staging of the miracle story shows Lanfranc's temporal power as abbot – he urges confession on his monks, he initially commands the demon to leave, he orders the community to call on Dunstan – but it also shows its painful limits. Ægelward and other monks have not been dutiful about confession; Lanfranc's efforts to exorcize the demon are only modestly successful; the physical chastisement designed to provide satisfaction for sin (and outlined at length in the *Decreta*) has no lasting result; the hapless community makes several fruitless efforts to invoke Dunstan's help. At the same time, Osbern's narrative shows that Dunstan is the powerful saint who responds to one always devoted to him (150). And the

---

40 There is likely a difficulty with Stubbs's text here. Stubbs uses Arundel 16 as his base text. But cap. 19 was excised at some point and supplied in the sixteenth century by John Jocelyn. Stubbs's reading "respondebat de Se Filium esse" is possibly erroneous, but the issue can only be resolved after full collation of the manuscripts. A contemporary version of the *Miracula* in Cambridge, Corpus Christi College 328, p. 64, reads "respondebat d<e>i filiu<m> se esse" (he answered that he was the son of God). For further discussion of Arundel 16 see below, 217–18 and notes.

miracle of healing is effected through the medium of a relic of Dunstan's – his episcopal standard. While it is unsurprising that a miracle story about Dunstan would produces a marvellous result, this miracle's use of Lanfranc as Dunstan's foil is, at a minimum, strikingly undiplomatic.

Eadmer's much sparer treatment of the same miracle in his version of the *Miracula S. Dunstani* is instructive by comparison, especially since Eadmer used Osbern's collection as a source.[41] He pares the attention to confession in the miracle story and radically reduces mention of Lanfranc, making the prior the principal in hearing confession and granting absolution. In the present context two moments in his account are worth pausing over; both deal with ethnic identity, where Eadmer's detail shows Osbern's generality to be tactical. At the height of the possession, Osbern records that the demon moves around inside the sick man "modo catelli per diversos viscerum meatus" (149) (like a little dog through the various regions of his innards). Eadmer, by contrast, uses this incident to tell a revealing story about the community:

> Cernebatur demon qui eum possidebat in uentre eius hac et illac discurrendo uagari, ut putares illum modo per os, modo per inferiores corporis partes fugam parare. Quibusdam uero qui circumstabant manus ad discursum inimici protendentibus, et quod in modum paruuli catti discurreret Francigena lingua dicentibus, ille contra qui linguae ipsius omnimodis inscius erat subridens eadem lingua similiter uerbo diminutiuo consonanter respondebat, dicens: "Non ut cattulus, sed ut catellus."[42]

> [The demon that possessed him could be seen to move in his belly running here and there, so that you might think that he was preparing to run from him, at one time through his mouth, at others through the lower parts of his body. But to those standing around stretching out their hands at the running of the demon, and saying in the French language that it ran like a little cat, he (viz. the demoniac), who knew nothing of that language, responded appropriately with a diminutive in that same language, saying with a smile, "Not like a little cat, but like a puppy."]

41 Turner and Muir, eds., *Eadmer of Canterbury*, lxix, regard Eadmer's *vita* and *miracula* of Dunstan as striking in the "way they set out to correct and supersede" Osbern's work.

42 Ibid., cap. 19, pp. 182–9, at 186.

In making the point of the story the demon's terrifying linguistic ability, Eadmer necessarily draws attention to the ethnic and linguistic divide at Christ Church: Ægelward the young English monk knew no French, and those observing him spoke no English. In highlighting the difference in languages spoken, Eadmer shines a bright light on the ethnic differences in the community that Osbern aims to elide.

There is a second moment of consequence in Eadmer's treatment which, again by contrast, points out Osbern's tactical omission. At the climax of Ægelward's possession, while the community prays in unison, an elderly monk, especially devoted to Dunstan, begs Dunstan to have mercy on the possessed man, and immediately he is healed. Unlike Osbern, Eadmer gives him a name, "Ælfuuinus" (Ælfwine), both identifying him as an Anglo-Saxon and once again pointing to the divided ethnic makeup of the Christ Church community. Osbern's vagueness (he refers to him as "quidam monachus") is tactical: in his account the monk is special only by his particular devotion to Dunstan. But Osbern provides a further detail, which fits the larger contrast in his account between speech and silence. Osbern's unnamed monk assists in the healing by touching the demoniac with an object of the saint from his own time.

For all Osbern's rhetorical skills and the carefully deployed strategy of his preface, cap. 19 shows a fissure within Osbern's writing of community. While able to write past ethnic division and ignore the difference of languages, Osbern is inadvertently clumsy in showing Lanfranc, Osbern's Norman patron, unsuccessful in his efforts to heal one of his *familia*. Eadmer clearly reacted to it by reducing Lanfranc's exposure to critique and adding social details that were comfortable from the distance of the early twelfth century.[43] But the inadvertence structuring Osbern's account of Dunstan's healing of Ægelward proceeds from the very between-ness that Osbern's writing means to leave behind. A second, telling instance of such between-ness makes an appearance in Osbern's account of Lanfranc's vision of Dunstan at the time of a grave illness (cap. 20). Meant to document Lanfranc's devotion to the saint, it shows a curious eruption of ambiguity in an otherwise disciplined performance. In this vision, when Lanfranc tries to kiss Dunstan's foot, the saint draws his foot away.

43 Turner and Muir, eds., *Eadmer of Canterbury*, lxvii, suggest dating Eadmer's *Miracula S. Dunstani* to "early in the reign of Henry I (1100–35)" and before Anselm's death (1109).

Osbern's interpretation of Dunstan's gesture – "quasi ad factum expavescens, sive Lanfranco honoris gratiam exhibens" (152) (as if horrified at the deed or to honour Lanfranc) – confirms the striking eruption of between-ness in his lengthy account of the healing of Ægelward.[44] To ensure a vigorous continuance of Dunstan's cult, Osbern had to construct an audience in that present, Norman and Anglo-Saxon, that acknowledged its single devotion to the Anglo-Saxon patron of the house. The bubbling up of Osbern's own ambivalence about that project in a way that threatened to undercut his best efforts shows the force of the very divide he meant to write over.

Osbern's efforts to include Lanfranc in this important miracle had an effect – an unflattering portrait of the archbishop – that could never have been Osbern's intention. Instead, we may read this curious miracle as a symptom of the pervading "between-ness" of Christ Church in the years following the Conquest. It can be seen, tellingly, in the book itself: London, British Library, Arundel 16, likely the earliest surviving manuscript of Osbern's text, embodies the complicated between-ness of monastic life in Christ Church, Canterbury that continued into the 1090s.[45] Several things are noteworthy about this manuscript, not least of which is a historiated initial (fol. 2r) which appears to be a portrait of Osbern himself.[46] That portrait argues Osbern's importance as a hagiographer and the value of his writings to the Christ Church community.[47] But there are other curious features of this manuscript. Teresa Webber regards its writing as "wholly in the Christ Church style of script."[48] Yet the backward-looking layout of the manuscript in traditional Anglo-Saxon long lines is at odds with its new style of script, and its ruling in drypoint as well as lead or ink points to a bifurcation of practice that makes this post-Conquest book look both

44 Compare Eadmer, *Miracula S. Dunstani*, cap. 21, p. 192, who does not interpret the gesture.

45 Gneuss and Lapidge, *Anglo-Saxon Manuscripts*, number 303, dates the manuscript to "s. xi/xii." Gameson, *Manuscripts of Early Norman England*, item 355 (p. 94), gives "xi/xii." Budney and Graham, "Dunstan as Hagiographical Subject," 87, make CCCC 328, a Winchester manuscript (Gneuss and Lapidge, *Anglo-Saxon Manuscripts*, number 94), Arundel 16's competitor for the earliest surviving manuscript witness.

46 Budney and Graham, "Dunstan as Hagiographical Subject," make a vigorous case that the portrait is not of Dunstan but of Osbern the author.

47 Arundel 16 had additional hagiographical texts: Osbern's *Vita S. Ælphegi*, his *Translatio S. Ælphegi*, and Eadmer's *Vita S. Odonis*. See Budney and Graham, "Dunstan as Hagiographical Subject," 86–7, and Gameson, *Manuscripts of Early Norman England*, 94.

48 Webber, "Script and Manuscript Production," appendix III, table 9, p. 157.

backward and forward.[49] Osbern's portrait, identifying him with his work, places him neatly in the centre of this clash of trends. The coexistence of new script style and retrograde manner of manuscript preparation offers an uneasy analogue for the juncture of custom, language, and practice in the community. There is a further oddity about Arundel 16: at some point the miracle of Ægelward's healing was lost from the manuscript, whether omitted by an uncomfortable copyist or excised by an acquisitive collector will never be known. If Lanfranc was given an opportunity by the fire to remake the very foundations of the community, the books that required supplementation and replacement are themselves mute symptoms of the slow negotiation of identity in post-Conquest Christ Church, Canterbury. Osbern's *Miracula* managed to write a community that sutured over ethnic and linguistic division. But he couldn't manage to eradicate the traces of his own between-ness.

49 Gameson, "English Manuscript Art," 110, 114–15, and appendix II, table 7, p. 142.

Bibliography

Abbreviations

AH	*Analecta Hymnica*
ANS	*Anglo-Norman Studies*
ASE	*Anglo-Saxon England*
Bede, *HE*	Colgrave and Mynors, eds., *Bede's Ecclesiastical History*
BHL	*Bibliotheca hagiographica latina antiquae et mediae aetatis*. Brussels: Bollandist Society
CCSL	Corpus Christianorum Series Latina. Turnhout: Brepols
CSASE	Cambridge Studies in Anglo-Saxon England. Cambridge: Cambridge University Press
DMLBS	Latham, *Dictionary of Medieval Latin from British Sources*
EETS	Early English Text Society
	os Original Series
	ss Supplementary Series
GL	*Grammatici Latini*, ed. Keil
HEz	Gregory, *Homiliae in Hiezechihelem*, ed. Adriaen, CCSL 142
JML	*Journal of Medieval Latin*
MGH	Monumenta Germaniae Historica
	AA — Auctores Antiquissimi
	Briefe d. dt. Kaiserzeit — Die Briefe der deutschen Kaiserzeit
	PLAC — Poetae Latini Aevi Carolini
	QQ — Quellen zur Geistesgeschichte des Mittelalters
	SS rer. Germ. — Scriptores rerum Germanicarum
OMT	Oxford Medieval Texts
PG	*Patrologiae cursus completus: series Graeca*. Ed. J.-P. Migne. Paris, 1857–66.
SC	Sources chrétiennes. Paris: Éditions du Cerf.

Reference Works

Anderson, Harald. *The Manuscripts of Statius.* Revised ed., 3 vols. Arlington, VA: Privately published, 2009.

Healey, Antonette diPaolo, with John Price Wilkin and Xin Xiang. *Dictionary of Old English Web Corpus.* Toronto: Dictionary of Old English Project, 2009.

Gameson, Richard. *The Manuscripts of Early Norman England (c. 1066–1130).* Oxford: Oxford University Press, 1999.

Gneuss, Helmut. *Handlist of Anglo-Saxon Manuscripts: A List of Manuscripts and Manuscript Fragments Written or Owned in England up to 1100.* Tempe: Arizona Center for Medieval and Renaissance Studies, 2001.

Gneuss, Helmut, and Michael Lapidge. *Anglo-Saxon Manuscripts: A Bibliographical Handlist of Manuscripts and Manuscript Fragments Written or Owned in England up to 1100.* Toronto: University of Toronto Press, 2014.

Latham, R.E., et al. *Dictionary of Medieval Latin from British Sources.* London: Oxford University Press, 1975–2013.

Lewis, Charlton T., and Charles Short. *A Latin Dictionary.* Oxford: Clarendon Press, 1879.

Prosopography of Anglo-Saxon England (PASE). http://www.pase.ac.uk/index.html.

Searle, William G. *Onomasticon Anglo-Saxonicum.* Cambridge: Cambridge University Press, 1897.

Primary Sources

Adriaen, Marcus, ed. *S. Gregorii Magni Homiliae in Hiezechihelem Prophetam.* CCSL 142. 1971.

– *S. Gregorii Magni Moralia in Iob libri I–IX.* CCSL 143. 1979.

– *S. Hieronymi presbyteri commentariorum in Esaiam libri i–xi.* CCSL 73. 1963.

Arnold, Thomas. *Symeonis monachi opera omnia. Vol. 1: Historia ecclesiæ Dunhelmensis.* Rolls Series. London: Longman, 1882.

Baker, Peter S., and Michael Lapidge, eds. *Byrhtferth's Enchiridion.* EETS ss 15. New York: Oxford University Press, 1995.

Bannister, Henry Marriott, and Anselm Hughes, eds. *Anglo-French Sequelae.* Plainsong and Medieval Music Society. London: Nashdom Abbey, 1934; repr. 1966.

Barlow, Frank, ed. *The Life of King Edward Who Rests at Westminster.* 2nd ed. Oxford: Oxford University Press, 1992.

Bates, David, ed. *Regesta Regum Anglo-Normannorum: The Acta of William I, 1066–1087.* Oxford: Clarendon Press, 1998.

Becker, Gustav, ed. *Catalogi bibliothecarum antiqui.* Bonn: Cohen and Sons, 1885.

Blake, Martin, ed. *Ælfric's De Temporibus Anni.* Anglo-Saxon Texts. Woodbridge: D.S. Brewer, 2009.

Borret, Marcel, ed. *Origène: Homélies sur Ézéchiel.* SC 352. 1989.

Bresslau, Harry, ed. *Wiponis Opera.* MGH SS rer. Germ. 61. Hanover and Leipzig: Hahnsche Buchhandlung, 1915.

Bulst, Walther, ed. *Die ältere Wormser Briefsammlung.* MGH Briefe d. dt. Kaizerzeit 3. Weimar: Hermann Bohlaus, 1949.

Campbell, A., ed. *Æthelwulf: De abbatibus.* Oxford: Clarendon Press, 1967.

– *The Chronicle of Æthelweard.* London: T. Nelson and Sons, 1962.

– *Encomium Emmae Reginae*, rev. ed. with a Supplementary Introduction by Simon Keynes. Cambridge: Cambridge University Press, 1998.

– *Frithegodi Monachi Breuiloquium Vitae Beati Wilfredi et Wulfstani Cantoris Narratio Metrica de Sancto Swithuno.* Zürich: Artemis-Verlag, 1950.

Chardonnens, László Sándor, ed. *Anglo-Saxon Prognostics, 900–100: Study and Texts.* Brill's Studies in Intellectual History 153 and Brill's Texts and Sources in Intellectual History 3. Leiden: Brill, 2007.

Chibnall, Marjorie, ed. *The Ecclesiastical History of Orderic Vitalis.* 6 vols. Oxford: Oxford University Press, 1969–80.

Clover, Helen, and Margaret Gibson, eds. and trans. *The Letters of Lanfranc Archbishop of Canterbury.* Oxford: Clarendon Press, 1979.

Colgrave, Bertram, and R.A.B. Mynors, eds. *Bede's Ecclesiastical History of the English People.* Oxford: Clarendon Press, 1969.

Cubbin, G.P., ed. *The Anglo-Saxon Chronicle: A Collaborative Edition. Vol. 6: Manuscript D.* Cambridge: D.S. Brewer, 1996.

DeGregorio, Scott, trans. *Bede: On Ezra and Nehemiah.* Translated Texts for Historians 47. Liverpool: Liverpool University Press, 2006.

de Vogüé, Adalbert, ed. *Grégoire le Grand: Dialogues.* SC 251. 1978.

Dümmler, Ernst, ed. MGH PLAC 1. Berlin: Weidmann, 1881.

Ehwald, R., ed. *Aldhelmi Opera.* MGH AA 15. Berlin: Weidmann, 1919.

Fry, Timothy, ed. and trans. *The Rule of St Benedict.* Collegeville, MN: Liturgical Press, 1981.

Gibson, Margaret, ed. "Vita Lanfranci." In *Lanfranco di Pavia e l'Europa del Secolo XI nel IX Centenario della Morte (1089–1989)*, ed. Giulio d'Onofrio, 659–715. Rome: Herder, 1993.

Giles, J.A., ed. "Vita Sancti Ecgwini." In *Vita Quorundum Anglo-Saxonum*, 349–96. London, 1852.

Glorie, Fr., ed. *S. Hieronymi Presbiteri Opera. Pars I, 4.* CCSL 75. 1964.

Green, R.P.H., ed. *Augustine: De Doctrina Christiana.* Oxford: Clarendon Press, 1995.

Greenway, Diana, ed. and trans. *Henry of Huntingdon: Historia Anglorum: The History of the English People*. Oxford: Clarendon Press, 1996.

Günzel, Beate, ed. *Ælfwine's Prayerbook: London, British Library, Cotton Titus D. XXVI + XXVII*. Henry Bradshaw Society 108. London: Henry Bradshaw Society, 1993.

Gwara, Scott, ed. *Aldhelmi Malmesbiriensis Prosa de Virginitate cum Glosa Latina atque Anglosaxonica*. CCSL 124, 124A. 2001.

Holder, Arthur, trans. *The Venerable Bede: On the Song of Songs and Selected Writings*. New York: Paulist Press, 2011.

Huemer, Johannes. *Virgilii Maronis Grammatici Opera*. Leipzig: Teubner, 1886.

Hurst, David, ed. *Bedae Venerabilis Opera. Pars II, 2*. CCSL 119. 1962.

– *Bedae Venerabilis Opera. Pars II, 2A*. CCSL 119A. 1969.

– *Bedae Venerabilis Opera. Pars II, 2B*. CCSL 119B. 1983.

Huygens, R.B.C., ed. *Apologiae duae: Gozechini epistola ad Walcherum; Burchardi, ut videtur, Abbatis Bellevallis apologia de barbis*. CCCM 62. Turnhout: Brepols, 1985.

Jones, C.W., ed. *Bedae Venerabilis Opera Pars VI: Opera didascalica 2*. CCSL 123B. 1977.

Keil, Heinrich, ed. *Grammatici Latini*. 7 vols. Leipzig: Teubner, 1857–80. With supplemental vol. 8, *Anecdota helvetica*, ed. Hermann Hagen. Leipzig: Teubner, 1870.

Kendall, C.B., ed. *Bede: De arte metrica et de schematibus et tropis*. CCSL 123A. 1975.

Kendall, Calvin B., and Faith Wallis, trans. *Bede: On the Nature of Things* and *On Times*. Translated Texts for Historians 56. Liverpool: Liverpool University Press, 2010.

Knowles, David, ed. and trans. *The Monastic Constitutions of Lanfranc*. Rev. ed. by Christopher N.L. Brooke. Oxford: Clarendon Press, 2002.

Koepke, R., ed. *Anselmi Gesta episcoporum Leodiensium*. MGH, Scriptores 7. Hanover: Hahn, 1846.

Kotzor, Günter, ed. *Das altenglische Martyrologium*. Abhandlungen der Bayerischen Akademie der Wissenschaften, phil.-hist. Kl. ns 88.1–2. 2 vols. Munich: C.H. Beck, 1981.

Laistner, M.L.W., ed. *Bedae Venerabilis Opera. Pars II, 4*. CCSL 121. 1983.

Lapidge, Michael, ed. *Byrhtferth of Ramsey: The Lives of St Oswald and St Ecgwine*. Oxford: Clarendon Press, 2000.

Lapidge, Michael, and Michael Winterbottom, eds. *Wulfstan of Winchester: The Life of St Æthelwold*. Oxford: Clarendon Press, 1991.

Lawler, Traugott, ed. *John of Garland: Parisiana poetria*. New Haven: Yale University Press, 1974.

Liebermann, Felix. "Raginald von Canterbury." *Neues Archiv der Gesellschaft für ältere deutsche Geschichtskunde* 13 (1888): 519–56.

Liuzza, R.M., ed. *Anglo-Saxon Prognostics: An Edition and Translation of Texts from London, British Library, MS Cotton Tiberius A.iii.* Anglo-Saxon Texts. Woodbridge: D.S. Brewer, 2011.

Love, Rosalind, ed. *Goscelin of St Bertin: The Hagiography of the Female Saints of Ely*. Oxford: Oxford University Press, 2004.

– *Three Eleventh-Century Anglo-Latin Saints' Lives: Vita S. Birini, Vita et Miracula S. Kenelmi, Vita S. Rumwoldi.* Oxford: Oxford University Press, 1996.

Loyen, André, ed. *Sidoine Apollinaire: Lettres*. 3 vols. Paris: Les Belles Lettres, 1970.

Manitius, Karl, ed. *Sextus Amarcius: Sermones*. MGH QQ 6. Weimar: Hermann Böhlaus, 1969.

McGurk, P., ed. *An Eleventh Century Anglo-Saxon Miscellany*. Early English Manuscripts in Facsimile 21. Copenhagen: Rosenkilde and Bagger, 1983.

Milfull, Inge B., ed. *The Hymns of the Anglo-Saxon Church*. CSASE 17. 2007.

Misset, E., and W.H.I. Weale, eds. *Analecta Liturgica*. 2 vols. Lille: Typis Societatis S. Augustini, 1888–92.

Muir, Bernard, ed. *The Exeter Anthology of Old English Poetry: An Edition of Exeter Dean and Chapter MS 3501*. 2 vols. Exeter: Exeter University Press, 1994.

Mynors, R.A.B., R.M. Thomson, and M. Winterbottom, eds. *William of Malmesbury: Gesta Regum Anglorum*. Vol. 1. Oxford: Oxford University Press, 1998.

O'Brien O'Keeffe, Katherine, ed. *The Anglo-Saxon Chronicle: A Collaborative Edition. Vol. 5: MS C*. Cambridge: D.S. Brewer, 2001.

Orchard, Nicholas, ed. *The Leofric Missal*. 2 vols. Henry Bradshaw Society 113–14. London: Boydell Press, 2002.

Peiper, Rudolf, ed. *Anicii Manlii Severini Boetii Philosophiae consolationis libri quinque*. Leipzig: Teubner, 1871.

Petschenig, Michael, ed. *Iohannis Cassiani Conlationes XXIIII*. Corpus Scriptorum Ecclesiasticorum Latinorum 13. Vienna: C. Geroldi Filium, 1886.

Polara, Giovanni, ed. *Publilii Optatiani Porfyrii carmina*. 2 vols. Turin: Paravia, 1973.

Pope, John C., ed. *The Homilies of Ælfric: A Supplementary Collection*. 2 vols. EETS os 259, 260. London: Oxford University Press, 1967–8.

Porter, David W., ed. *Excerptiones de Prisciano: The Source for Ælfric's Latin-Old English Glossary*. Anglo-Saxon Texts 4. Cambridge: D.S. Brewer, 2002.

Raine, James, ed. "Chronicle of the Archbishops of York." In *The Historians of the Church of York*. Rolls Series. London: Longman and Co., 1886.

Ramsey, Boniface, trans. *John Cassian: The Conferences*. Ancient Christian Writers 57. New York: Newman Press, 1997.

Rankin, Susan, ed. *The Winchester Troper*. Early English Church Music 50. London: Stainer and Bell, 2007.

Rau, Reinhold, ed. *Briefe des Bonifatius, Willibalds Leben des Bonifatius.* Darmstadt: Wissenschaftliche Buchgesellschaft, 1968.

Rauer, C., ed. *The Old English Martyrology.* Anglo-Saxon Texts 10. Cambridge: D.S. Brewer, 2013.

Robertson, A.J., ed. *Anglo-Saxon Charters*. 2nd ed. Cambridge: Cambridge University Press, 1956.

Schmitt, F.S., ed. *S. Anselmi Cantuariensis Archiepiscopi Opera Omnia*. Vol. 3. Edinburgh: Thomas Nelson and Sons, 1946.

Skeat, W.W., ed. *Ælfric's Lives of Saints*. 4 vols. EETS os 76, 82, 94, 114. Oxford, 1881–1900; repr. in 2 vols. London: Oxford University Press, 1966.

Stubbs, William, ed. *Memorials of Saint Dunstan*. Rolls Series 63. London: Rolls Series, 1874.

Sweet, Henry, ed. *King Alfred's West-Saxon Version of Gregory's Pastoral Care*. 2 vols. EETS os 45, 50 (1871); repr. London: Oxford University Press, 1958.

Swoboda, Anton, ed. *Odonis abbatis Cluniacensis Occupatio*. Leipzig: Teubner, 1900.

Tangl, Michael, ed. *Die Briefe des heiligen Bonifatius und Lullus.* MGH ES 1. 1916.

Thilo, Georg, and Hermann Hagen, eds. *Servii Grammatici qui feruntur in Vergilii carmina commentarii*. 3 vols. Leipzig: Teubner, 1881.

Thomson, Rodney, ed. *The Life of Gundulf Bishop of Rochester*. Toronto: Pontifical Institute of Mediaeval Studies, 1977.

Traube, Ludwig. MGH PLAC 3. Berlin: Weidmann, 1896.

Turner, Andrew J., and Bernard J. Muir, eds. and trans. *Eadmer of Canterbury: Lives and Miracles of Saints Oda, Dunstan, and Oswald*. OMT. Oxford: Clarendon Press, 2006.

Voigt, Ernst, ed. *Egberts von Lüttich: Fecunda Ratis*. Halle: Niemeyer, 1889.

Wallis, Faith. *Bede: The Reckoning of Time, Translated with Introduction, Notes and Commentary*. Translated Texts for Historians 29. Liverpool: Liverpool University Press, 1999.

– *The Calendar and the Cloister: Oxford, St John's College MS 17*. McGill University Library, Digital Collections Program, 2007.

Ward, Benedicta. *The Desert Fathers: Sayings of the Early Christian Monks*. New York: Penguin, 2003.

– *The Sayings of the Desert Fathers: The Alphabetical Collection*. Cistercian Studies Series 59. Kalamazoo, MI: Cistercian Publications, 1984.

Watkiss, Leslie, and Majorie Chibnall, eds. *The Waltham Chronicle*. Oxford: Oxford University Press, 1994.

Weber, R., ed. *Biblia Sacra iuxta Vulgatam Versionem*. Stuttgart: Deutsche Bibelgesellschaft, 1994.

Wilcox, Jonathan, ed. *Ælfric's Prefaces*. Durham Medieval Texts 9. Durham: Durham Medieval Texts, 1994.

Wilmart, André, ed. "La légende de Ste Édith en prose et verse par le moine Goscelin." *Analecta Bollandiana* 56 (1938): 5–101 and 265–307.

Winterbottom, Michael, and Michael Lapidge, eds. and trans. *The Early Lives of St Dunstan*. OMT. Oxford: Clarendon Press, 2012.

Winterbottom, Michael, and R.M. Thomson, eds. *William of Malmesbury: Gesta Pontificum Anglorum*. Oxford: Oxford University Press, 1997.

– *William of Malmesbury: Saints' Lives: Lives of SS. Wulfstan, Dunstan, Patrick, Benignus and Indract.* Oxford: Clarendon Press, 2002.

Wright, Michael, and Kathleen Loncar. "Goscelin's Legend of Edith." In *Writing the Wilton Women: Goscelin's Legend of Edith and Liber Confortatorius*, ed. Stephanie Hollis, 23–67. Turnhout: Brepols, 2004.

Zeydel, Edwin H., ed. *Ecbasis cuiusdam captivi per tropologium: Escape of a Certain Captive Told in a Figurative Manner: An Eleventh-Century Latin Beast Epic*. New York: AMS Press, 1966.

Ziolkowski, Jan M., ed. *The Cambridge Songs (Carmina Cantabrigiensia)*. New York: Garland Publishing, 1994.

Zupitza, Julius, ed. *Ælfrics Grammatik und Glossar*. Sammlung englischer Denkmäler in kritischen Ausgaben 1. Berlin: Weidmannsche Buchhandlung, 1880.

Secondary Sources

Adams, Kenneth A. "Monastery and Village at Crayke, North Yorkshire." *Yorkshire Archaeological Journal* 62 (1990): 29–50.

Baker, Jordan Timothy Ray. "'Sing to the Lord a new song': Memory, Music, Epistemology, and the Emergence of Gregorian Chant as Corporate Knowledge." MA thesis, University of Tennessee, Knoxville, 2012.

Baker, Peter S. "Byrhtferth's *Enchiridion* and the Computus in Oxford, St. John's College 17." *ASE* 10 (1982): 123–42.

– "The Old English Canon of Byrhtferth of Ramsey." *Speculum* 55 (1980): 22–37.

Balint, Bridget K. *Ordering Chaos: The Self and the Cosmos in Twelfth-Century Latin Prosimetrum*. Leiden: Brill, 2009.

Barlow, Frank. *Edward the Confessor*. Berkeley: University of California Press, 1970.

– *The English Church: 1000–1066*. 2nd ed. London: Longman, 1979.

– "Leofric and His Times." In *Leofric of Exeter*, ed. Frank Barlow et al., 1–16. Exeter: University of Exeter, 1972.

Baswell, Christopher. "Marvels of Translation and Crises of Transition in the Romances of Antiquity." In *The Cambridge Companion to Medieval Romance*, ed. Roberta Krueger, 29–44. Cambridge: Cambridge University Press, 2000.

Baxter, Stephen. "MS C of the Anglo-Saxon Chronicle and the Politics of Mid-Eleventh-Century England." *English Historical Review* 122 (2007): 1189–1227.

Beechy, Tiffany. *The Poetics of Old English*. Farnham: Ashgate, 2010.

Bethurum, Dorothy. "The Form of Ælfric's *Lives of Saints*." *Studies in Philology* 29 (1932): 515–33.

Bischoff, Bernhard, and Michael Lapidge. *Biblical Commentaries from the Canterbury School of Theodore and Hadrian*. CSASE 10. 1994.

Bischoff, Georges, and Benoît Tock, eds. *Léon IX et son temps*. Turnhout: Brepols, 2006.

Blair, John. *The Church in Anglo-Saxon Society*. Oxford: Oxford University Press, 2005.

Bodden, Mary Catherine. "Evidence for the Knowledge of Greek in Anglo-Saxon England." *ASE* 17 (1988): 217–46.

Bourgain, Pascale. "Le génitif d'interprétation en latin médiéval." *JML* 17 (2007): 300–12.

Boutemy, André. "À propos d'anthologies poétiques au XIIe siècle." *Revue belge de philologie et d'histoire* 19 (1940): 229–33.

Bredehoft, Thomas A. *Early English Metre*. Toronto: University of Toronto Press, 2005.

Brooks, Nicholas. "The Anglo-Saxon Cathedral Community, 597–1070." In *History of Canterbury Cathedral*, ed. Collinson, Ramsay, and Sparks, 1–37.

Brown, Virginia. "Lupus of Ferrières on the Metres of Boethius." In *Latin Script and Letters A.D. 400–900: Festschrift Presented to Ludwig Bieler*, ed. John J. O'Meara and Bernd Naumann, 63–79. Leiden: Brill, 1976.

Brühl, Carlrichard. "Die Sozialstruktur des deutschen Episkopats im 11. und 12. Jahrhundert." In *Le istituzioni ecclesiastiche della "societas christiana" dei secoli XI–XII: diocesi, pievi e parrocchie*, 42–56. Atti della sesta Settimana internazionale di studio, Mendola, Milano, 1–7 settembre 1974. Pubblicazioni dell'Università cattolica del Sacro Cuore, Miscellanea del Centro di studi medioevali 8, Milan, 1977.

Brunhölzl, Franz. *Histoire de la littérature latine du moyen âge. Vol. 2: De la fin de l'époque carolingienne au milieu du XIe siècle*. Trans. Henri Rochais. Turnhout: Brepols, 1996.

Budney, Mildred, and Timothy Graham. "Dunstan as Hagiographical Subject or Osbern as Author? The Scribal Portrait in an Early Copy of Osbern's *Vita Sancti Dunstani*." *Gesta* 32.2 (1993): 83–96.

Bulst, Walther. "Zur Vorgeschichte der Cambridger und anderer Sammlungen." *Historische Vierteljahrsschrift* 27 (1932): 827–31.

Cain, Christopher. "Phonology and Meter in the Old English Macaronic Verses." *Studies in Philology* 98 (2001): 273–91.

Campbell, Alistair. "Some Linguistic Features of Early Anglo-Latin Verse and Its Use of Classical Models." *Transactions of the Philological Society* 52 (1953): 1–20.

Campbell, James. "England, France, Flanders and Germany in the Reign of Ethelred II: Some Comparisons and Connections." In his *Essays in Anglo-Saxon History*, 191–207. London: Hambledon, 1986.

Carruthers, Mary J. *The Craft of Thought: Meditation, Rhetoric, and the Making of Images 400–1200*. Cambridge Studies in Medieval Literature 34. Cambridge: Cambridge University Press, 2000.

Cassidy, Frederic G. "The Anglo-Saxon Interjection." In *Bright Is the Ring of Words: Festschrift für Horst Weinstock zum 65. Geburtstag*, 45–8. Bonn: Romanistischer Verlag, 1996.

Chapman, D. "Uterque Lingua / Ægðer Gereord: Ælfric's Grammatical Vocabulary and the Winchester Tradition." *JEGP* 109 (2010): 421–55.

Christman, Angela Russell. *What Did Ezekiel See? Christian Exegesis of Ezekiel's Vision of the Chariot from Irenaeus to Gregory the Great*. Leiden: Brill, 2005.

Clark, Cecily. "People and Languages in Post-Conquest Canterbury." *Journal of Medieval History* 2 (1976): 1–33.

Clemoes, Peter. "Ælfric." In *Continuations and Beginnings: Studies in Old English Literature*, ed. E.G. Stanley, 176–209. London: Nelson, 1966.

Coleman, Janet. *Ancient and Medieval Memories: Studies in the Reconstruction of the Past*. Cambridge: Cambridge University Press, 1992.

Collinson, Patrick, Nigel Ramsay, and Margaret Sparks, eds. *A History of Canterbury Cathedral*. Oxford: Oxford University Press, 1995.

Copeland, Rita. *Rhetoric, Hermeneutics, and Translation in the Middle Ages: Academic Traditions and Vernacular Texts*. Cambridge: Cambridge University Press, 1991.

Cowdrey, H.E.J. *Lanfranc: Scholar, Monk, and Archbishop*. Oxford: Oxford University Press, 2003.

Crocker, Richard L. *The Early Medieval Sequence*. Berkeley: University of California Press, 1977.

Cross, J.E. "The Apostles in the *Old English Martyrology*." *Mediaevalia* 5 (1979): 1–59.

– "The Influence of Irish Texts and Traditions on the *Old English Martyrology*." *Proceedings of the Royal Irish Academy* 81C (1981): 173–92.

– "The *Passio S. Laurentii et aliorum*: Latin Manuscripts and the *Old English Martyrology*." *Mediaeval Studies* 45 (1983): 200–13.

Cross, J.E., ed. *Two Old English Apocrypha and Their Manuscript Source: "The Gospel of Nicodemus" and "The Avenging of the Saviour."* Cambridge: Cambridge University Press, 1996.

Cubitt, Catherine. "Monastic Memory and Identity in Early Anglo-Saxon England." In *Social Identity in Early Medieval Britain*, ed. William O. Frazer and Andrew Tyrrell, 253–76. London: Leicester University Press, 2000.

Curtius, Ernst Robert. *European Literature and the Latin Middle Ages*. Trans. Willard R. Trask. Bollingen Series 36. Princeton: Princeton UP, 1953; repr. 1990.

Davis-Secord, Jonathan. "Rhythm and Music: The Sequences of Notker Balbulus." *JML* 22 (2012): 117–48.

DeGregorio, Scott. "Affective Spirituality: Theory and Practice in Bede and Alfred the Great." *Essays in Medieval Studies* 22 (2005): 127–37.

– "Bede and Benedict of Nursia." In *Early Medieval Studies in Memory of Patrick Wormald*, ed. Stephen Baxter et al., 149–63. Burlington, VT: Ashgate, 2008.

– "Bede, the Monk, as Exegete: Evidence from the Commentary on Ezra-Nehemiah." *Revue bénédictine* 115 (2005): 343–69.

– "Bede's Commentary on Ezra and Nehemiah: A Document in Church Reform?" In *Bède le Vénérable: entre tradition et postérité*, ed. Stéphane Lebecq, Michel Perrin, and Olivier Szerwiniack, 97–107. Villeneuve d'Ascq: CEGES, 2005.

– "Bede's *In Ezram et Neemiam* and the Reform of the Northumbrian Church." *Speculum* 79 (2004): 1–25.

– "The Figure of Ezra in the Writings of Bede and the Codex Amiatinus." In *Listen, O Isles, unto Me: Studies in Medieval Word and Image in Honour of Jennifer O'Reilly*, ed. Diarmuid Scully and Elizabeth Mullins, 115–25. Cork: Cork University Press, 2011.

– "Footsteps of His Own: Bede's Commentary on Ezra-Nehemiah." In *Innovation and Tradition*, ed. DeGregorio, 143–68.

– "Literary Contexts: Cædmon's Hymn as a Center of Bede's World." In *Transformations: Bede, Cædmon's "Hymn," and the Interdisciplinary Anglo-Saxon World*, ed. Allen J. Frantzen and John Hines, 51–79. Morgantown: West Virginia University Press, 2007.

– "The Venerable Bede and Gregory the Great: Exegetical Connections, Spiritual Departures." *Early Medieval Europe* 18 (2010): 43–60.

DeGregorio, Scott, ed. *Innovation and Tradition in the Writings of the Venerable Bede*. Medieval European Studies 7. Morgantown: West Virginia University Press, 2006.

de Jong, Mayke. *In Samuel's Image: Child Oblation in the Early Medieval West.* Brill's Studies in Intellectual History 12. Leiden: Brill, 1996.

Dekker, K. "Ælfric and His Relation to the Latin Tradition." In *History of the Language Sciences*, ed. S. Auroux, E.F.K. Koerner, H.-J. Niederehe, and K. Versteegh, 2 vols, 1:625–33. Berlin: de Gruyter, 2000.

– "Pentecost and Linguistic Self-Consciousness in Anglo-Saxon England: Bede and Ælfric." *JEGP* 104 (2005): 345–72.

de Lubac, Henri. *Medieval Exegesis: The Four Senses of Scripture.* Trans. M. Sebac and E.M. Macierowski. 3 vols. Grand Rapids, MI: W.B. Eerdmans, 1998–2009.

Derolez, R. "Anglo-Saxon Glossography." In *Anglo-Saxon Glossography*, ed. Derolez, 9–42.

– "Those Things Are Difficult to Express in English ..." *English Studies* 70 (1989): 469–76.

Derolez, René, ed. *Anglo-Saxon Glossography.* Brussels: Paleis der Academiën, 1992.

Devine, A.M., and Laurence D. Stephens. *Latin Word Order: Structured Meaning and Information.* Oxford: Oxford University Press, 2006.

Dionisotti, A.C. "On Bede, Grammars, and Greek." *Revue bénédictine* 92 (1982): 111–41.

Drage, E.M. "Bishop Leofric and the Exeter Cathedral Chapter, 1050–1072: A Reassessment of the Manuscript Evidence." DPhil thesis, Oxford University, 1978.

Driver, Steven. *John Cassian and the Reading of Egyptian Monastic Culture.* Studies in Medieval History and Culture 8. New York: Routledge, 2002.

Dronke, Peter. *Verse with Prose from Petronius to Dante: The Art and Scope of the Mixed Form.* Cambridge, MA: Harvard University Press, 1994.

Dronke, Peter, Michael Lapidge, and Peter Stotz. "Die unveröffentlichen Gedichte der Cambridger Liederhandschrift (CUL Gg.5.35)." *Mittellateinisches Jahrbuch* 17 (1982): 54–95.

Eales, Richard, and Richard Sharpe, eds. *Canterbury and the Norman Conquest: Churches, Saints, and Scholars, 1066–1109.* London: Hambledon Press, 1995.

Fernie, Eric. "Edward the Confessor's Westminster Abbey." In *Edward the Confessor: The Man and the Legend*, ed. Richard Mortimer, 139–50. Woodbridge: Boydell, 2009.

Fleckenstein, Josef. *Die Hofkappelle der deutschen Könige.* 2 vols. Stuttgart: Hierseman, 1959–66.

Fleming, Damian. "*Jesus*, that is *hælend*: Hebrew Names and the Vernacular Savior in Anglo-Saxon England." *JEGP* 112 (2013): 26–47.

– "*Rex regum et cyninga cyning:* 'Speaking Hebrew' in Cynewulf's *Elene.*" In *Old English Literature and the Old Testament*, ed. Michael Fox and Manish Sharma, 229–52. Toronto: University of Toronto Press, 2012.

Flores, E., and G. Polara. "Specimina di analisi applicate a strutture di 'Versspielerei' latina." *Rendiconti dell'Accademia di archeologia, lettere e belle arti di Napoli* 44 (1969): 111–36.

Foot, Sarah. "Anglo-Saxon 'Purgatory.'" In *The Church, the Afterlife, and the Fate of the Soul*, ed. Peter Clarke and Tony Claydon, 87–96. Studies in Church History 45. Woodbridge: Boydell, 2009.

– *Monastic Life in Anglo-Saxon England, c. 600–900.* Cambridge: Cambridge University Press, 2006.

Gameson, Richard. "English Manuscript Art in the Late Eleventh Century: Canterbury and Its Context." In *Canterbury and the Norman Conquest*, ed. Eales and Sharpe, 95–144.

– "The Origin of the Exeter Book of Old English Poetry." *ASE* 25 (1996): 135–85.

Garnett, George. "'Franci and Angli': The Legal Distinctions between Peoples after the Conquest." *ANS* 8 (1985): 109–37.

Garrison, Mary. "Alcuin and Tibullus." In *Poesía Latina Medieval (siglos V–XV): Actas del IV Congreso del "Internationales Mittellateinerkomitee."* Ed. Manuel C. Díaz y Díaz and José M. Díaz de Bustamante, 749–59. Florence: SISMEL, 2005.

– "The Emergence of Carolingian Latin Literature and the Court of Charlemagne (780–814)." In *Carolingian Culture: Emulation and Innovation*, ed. Rosamond McKitterick, 111–40. Cambridge: Cambridge University Press, 1994.

– "The English and the Irish at the Court of Charlemagne." In *Karl der Grosse und sein Nachtwirken: 1200 Jahre Kultur und Wissenschaft in Europa. Band I. Wissen und Weltbild*, ed. P. Butzer, M. Kerner, and W. Oberschelp, 97–123. Turnhout: Brepols, 1997.

– "The Social World of Alcuin: Nicknames at York and at the Carolingian Court." In *Alcuin of York: Scholar at the Carolingian Court*, ed. L.A.J.R. Houwen and A.A. MacDonald, 59–79. Germania Latina 3. Groningen: Egbert Forsten, 1998.

Gem, Richard. "The Romanesque Rebuilding of Westminster Abbey." *ANS* 3 (1981): 33–60, 203–7.

Gerould, G.H. "Abbot Ælfric's Rhythmic Prose." *Modern Philology* 22 (1925): 353–66.

Giandrea, Mary Frances. *Episcopal Culture in Late Anglo-Saxon England.* Woodbridge: Boydell and Brewer, 2007.

Gibson, Margaret. "Normans and Angevins, 1070–1220." In *A History of Canterbury Cathedral*, ed. Collinson, Ramsay, and Sparks, 38–68.

Glauche, Günter. *Schullektüre im Mittelalter: Entstehung und Wandlungen des Lektürekanons bis 1200 nach den Quellen dargestellt*. Munich: Arbeo-Gesellschaft, 1970.

Gneuss, Helmut. "*Anglicae linguae interpretatio*: Language Contact, Lexical Borrowing, and Glossing in Anglo-Saxon England." In his *Language and History in Early England*, 109–48. Aldershot: Ashgate, 1996.

– *Hymnar und Hymnen im englischen Mittelalter*. Tübingen: Max Niemeyer, 1968.

– "The Study of Language in Anglo-Saxon England." *Bulletin of the John Rylands Library* 72 (1990): 1–32.

Godden, Malcolm R. "Ælfric's Changing Vocabulary." *English Studies* 61 (1980): 206–23.

– "Glosses to the *Consolation of Philosophy* in Late Anglo-Saxon England: Their Origins and Their Uses." In *Rethinking and Recontextualizing Glosses: New Perspectives in the Study of Late Anglo-Saxon Glossography*, ed. P. Lendinara, L. Lazzari, and C. Di Sciacca, 67–91. Textes et études du moyen âge 54. Porto: Fédération international des Instituts d'études médiévales, 2011.

– "Literary Language." In *The Cambridge Encyclopedia to the English Language, Vol. 1: The Beginnings to 1066*, ed. Richard M. Hogg, 515. Cambridge: Cambridge University Press, 1992.

Godman, Peter, ed. *Alcuin: The Bishops, Kings, and Saints of York*. Oxford: Clarendon Press, 1982.

– *Poetry of the Carolingian Renaissance*. London: Duckworths, 1985.

– *Poets and Emperors: Frankish Politics and Carolingian Poetry*. Oxford: Clarendon Press, 1987.

Gretsch, Mechthild. *Ælfric and the Cult of Saints in Late Anglo-Saxon England*. CSASE 34. 2005.

– "Ælfric, Language, and Winchester." In *A Companion to Ælfric*, ed. Magennis and Swan, 109–37.

– "Glosses." In *The Wiley-Blackwell Encyclopedia of Anglo-Saxon England*, ed. Lapidge et al., 214–15.

– *The Intellectual Foundations of the English Benedictine Reform*. CSASE 25. 1999.

– "The Junius Psalter Gloss: Its Historical and Cultural Context." *ASE* 29 (2000): 85–121.

– "Literacy and the Uses of the Vernacular." In *The Cambridge Companion to Old English Literature*, ed. M. Godden and M. Lapidge, 273–94. 2nd ed. Cambridge: Cambridge University Press, 2013.

– "The Roman Psalter, Its Old English Glosses and the English Benedictine Reform." In *The Liturgy of the Late Anglo-Saxon Church*, ed. H. Gittos and M.B. Bedingfield, 13–28. Henry Bradshaw Society Subsidia 5. London: Boydell, 2005.

Gwara, Scott. "Canterbury Affiliations of London, British Library MS Royal 7 D. XXIV and Brussels, Bibliothèque royale MS 1650 (Aldhelm's *Prosa de virginitate*)." *Romanobarbarica* 14 (1997): 359–74.

– "Three Acrostic Poems by Abbo of Fleury." *JML* 2 (1992): 203–35.

Hall, Thomas N. "Ælfric as Pedagogue." In *A Companion to Ælfric*, ed. Magennis and Swan, 193–216.

Haubrichs, Wolfgang. "Volkssprache und volkssprachige Literaturen im Lotharingischen Zwischenreich (9–11 Jh)." In *Lotharingia: Eine Europäische Kernlandschaft um das Jahr 1000 / une région au centre de l'Europe autour de l'an mil*, ed. Hans-Walter Herrmann and Reinhard Schneider, 181–244. Saarbrücken: Kommissionsverlag, 1995.

– "Von *pêle-mêle* zum *vis-à-vis*: Sprachinseln, Bilingualität und Sprachgrenzen zwischen Maas und Rhein in Mittelalter und Neuzeit." In *Mehrsprachigkeit im Mittelalter*, ed. Michael Baldzuhn and Christine Putzo, 69–107. Berlin: De Gruyter, 2011.

Haye, Thomas. "*Nemo Mecenas, Nemo Modo Cesar*: Die Idee der Literaturförderung in der lateinischen Dichtung des hohen Mittelalters." *Classica et Mediaevalia* 55 (2004): 203–27.

Henderson, Christopher G., and Paul T. Bidwell. "The Saxon Minster at Exeter." In *The Early Church in Western Britain and Ireland: Studies Presented to C.A. Ralegh Radford*, ed. Susan M. Pearce, 145–75. BAR British Series 102. Oxford, BAR, 1982.

Hexter, Ralph J., and David Townsend, eds. *The Oxford Handbook of Medieval Latin Literature*. Oxford: Oxford University Press, 2012.

Hiley, David. "Changes in the English Chant Repertories in the Eleventh Century As Reflected in the Winchester Sequences." *ANS* 16 (1994): 136–54.

– "The Repertory of Sequences at Winchester." In *Essays on Medieval Music in Honor of David G. Hughes*, ed. Michael E. Smith, 153–93. Isham Library Papers 4. Cambridge, MA: Harvard University Press, 1995.

– "Thurstan of Caen and Plainchant at Glastonbury: Musicological Reflections on the Norman Conquest." *Proceedings of the British Academy* 72 (1986): 57–90.

Hill, Joyce. "Ælfric: His Life and Works." In *A Companion to Ælfric*, ed. Magennis and Swan, 35–65.

– "Ælfric's Grammatical Triad." In *Form and Content of Instruction in Anglo-Saxon England in the Light of Contemporary Manuscript Evidence*, ed. Patrizia Lendinara, Loredana Lazzari, and Maria Amalia D'Aronco, 285–307. Turnhout, Brepols, 2007.

– "Ælfric's Use of Etymologies." *ASE* 17 (1988): 35–44.

– "Anglo-Saxon Scholarship and Viking Raids: The Exeter Book Contextualised." *Filoloski pregled* 25 (1998): 9–28.

– "Two Anglo-Saxon Bishops at Work: Wulfstan, Leofric and Cambridge, Corpus Christi College MS 190." In *Patterns of Episcopal Power: Bishops in Tenth and Eleventh Century Western Europe*, ed. Ludger Körntgen and Dominik Waßenhoven, 145–61. Berlin: de Gruyter, 2011.

Hiltunen, Risto. "*Eala, geferan and gode wyrhtan*: On Interjections in Old English." In *Inside Old English: Essays in Honour of Bruce Mitchell*, ed. John Walmsley, 91–116. Malden, MA: Blackwell, 2006.

Hodgson, John Crawford. *A History of Northumberland. Vol. VI*. Newcastle-upon-Tyne: Andrew Reid, 1902.

Holschneider, Andreas. *Die Organa von Winchester: Studien zum ältesten Repertoire polyphoner Musik*. Hildesheim: Georg Olms, 1968.

Howlett, D.R. "The Provenance, Date, and Structure of *De abbatibus*." *Archaeologia Aeliana* ser. 5, 3 (1975): 121–30.

Huemer, Johann. "Zu Walahfrid Strabo." *Neues Archiv der Gesellschaft für ältere deutsche Geschichtskunde* 10 (1885): 166–9.

Irvine, Martin. *The Making of Textual Culture: "Grammatica" and Literary Theory, 350–1100*. Cambridge: Cambridge University Press, 1994.

Jaeger, C. Stephen. *The Envy of Angels: Cathedral Schools and Medieval Europe, 950–1200*. Philadelphia: University of Pennsylvania Press, 1993.

– *The Origins of Courtliness: Civilizing Trends and the Formation of Courtly Ideals, 939–1210*. Philadelphia: University of Pennsylvania Press, 1985.

Jolly, Karen Louise. *Popular Religion in Late Anglo-Saxon England*. Chapel Hill: University of North Carolina Press, 1996.

Jones, Charles W. "A Legend of St. Pachomius." *Speculum* 18 (1943): 198–210.

Jones, Christopher A. "*Meatim sed et rustica*: Ælfric of Eynsham as a Medieval Latin Author." *JML* 8 (1998): 1–57.

Justice, Steven. "Who Stole Robertson?" *PMLA* 124 (2009): 609–15.

Kamphausen, Hans Joachim. *Traum und Vision in der lateinischen Poesie der Karolingerzeit*. Frankfurt: Peter Lang, 1975.

Kardong, Terrance G. *Benedict's Rule: A Translation and Commentary*. Collegeville, MN: Liturgical Press, 1996.

Karkov, Catherine E. "The Mother's Tongue and the Father's Prose." *Parallax* 18 (2012): 27–37.

Keefer, Sarah Larratt, and David R. Burrows. "Hebrew and the *Hebraicum* in Late Anglo-Saxon England." *ASE* 19 (1990): 67–80.

Kerlouégan, François. "Une mode stylistique dans la prose latine des pays celtiques." *Études celtiques* 13.1 (1972): 275–97.

Keynes, Simon. "Giso, Bishop of Wells (1061–88)." *ANS* 19 (1997): 203–71.
– "Regenbald the Chancellor (sic)." *ANS* 10 (1988): 185–222.
Klopsch, Paul. *Einführung in die mittellateinische Verslehre*. Darmstadt: Wissenschaftliche Buchgesellschaft, 1972.
Klukas, Arnold William. "The Architectural Implications of the *Decreta Lanfranci*." *ANS* 6 (1983): 136–71.
Knowles, David. *The Monastic Order in England*. 2nd ed. Cambridge: Cambridge University Press, 1966.
Koopmans, Rachel. *Wonderful to Relate: Miracle Stories and Miracle Collecting in High Medieval England*. Philadelphia: University of Pennsylvania Press, 2011.
Kuhn, S.M. "The Dialect of the Corpus *Glossary*." *PMLA* 54 (1939): 1–19.
– "Synonyms in the Old English Bede." *JEGP* 46 (1947): 168–76.
Kupper, Jean-Louis. *Liège et l'église imperiale, XIe–Xiie siècles*. Paris: Belles Lettres, 1981.
Laistner, M.L.W. "The Library of the Venerable Bede." In *Bede, His Life, Times, and Writings*, ed. A. Hamilton Thompson, 237–66. Oxford: Clarendon Press, 1935.
Lapidge, Michael. "Aediluulf and the School of York." In his *Anglo-Latin Literature, 600–899*, 381–98.
– "Aldhelm's Latin Poetry and Old English Verse." In his *Anglo-Latin Literature, 600–899*, 247–69.
– *Anglo-Latin Literature, 600–899*. London: Hambledon Press, 1996.
– *Anglo-Latin Literature, 900–1066*. London: Hambledon Press, 1993.
– *The Anglo-Saxon Library*. Oxford: Oxford University Press, 2006.
– "The Authorship of the Adonic Verses 'ad Fidolium' Attributed to Columbanus." *Studi medievali* 3rd ser. 18 (1977): 815–80.
– "Æthelwold as Teacher and Scholar." In his *Anglo-Latin Literature, 900–1066*, 183–211.
– "B. and the *Vita S. Dunstani*." In his *Anglo-Latin Literature, 900–1066*, 279–91.
– "Byrhtferth and *Vita S. Ecgwini*." In his *Anglo-Latin Literature, 900–1066*, 293–315.
– "Byrhtferth at Work." In *Words and Works: Studies in Medieval English Language and Literature in Honour of Fred C. Robinson*, ed. Peter S. Baker and Nicholas Howe, 25–43. Toronto: University of Toronto Press, 1998.
– *The Cult of St Swithun*. Winchester Studies 4.ii. Oxford: Clarendon Press, 2003.
– "Ealdred of York and MS. Cotton Vitellius E.XII." In his *Anglo-Latin Literature, 900–1066*, 453–67.

– "The Hermeneutic Style in Tenth-Century Anglo-Latin Literature." In his *Anglo-Latin Literature 900–1066*, 105–49.

– "Old English Glossography: The Latin Context." In *Anglo-Saxon Glossography*, ed. Derolez, 43–57.

– "Oswald the Younger." In *The Wiley-Blackwell Encyclopedia of Anglo-Saxon England*, ed. Lapidge et al., 349.

– "Poeticism in Pre-Conqust Anglo-Latin Prose." In *Aspects of the Language of Latin Prose*, ed. Tobias Reinhardt, Michael Lapidge, and J.N. Adams, 321–38. Proceedings of the British Academy 129. Oxford: Oxford University Press, 2005.

– "The School of Theodore and Hadrian." In his *Anglo-Latin Literature, 600–899*, 141–68.

– "The Study of Latin Texts in Late Anglo-Saxon England." In his *Anglo-Latin Literature, 600–899*, 453–98.

– "Tenth-Century Anglo-Latin Verse Hagiography." *Mittellateinisches Jahrbuch* 24/25 (1989–90): 249–60.

– "A Tenth-Century Metrical Calendar from Ramsey." In his *Anglo-Latin Literature: 900–1066*, 343–86.

– "Three Latin Poems from Æthelwold's School at Winchester." In his *Anglo-Latin Literature: 900–1066*, 225–77.

– "Versifying the Bible in the Middle Ages." In *The Text in the Community: Essays on Medieval Works, Manuscripts, Authors, and Readers*, ed. Jill Mann and Maura Nolan, 11–40. Notre Dame: University of Notre Dame Press, 2006.

Lapidge, Michael, and Michael Herren. *Aldhelm: The Prose Works.* Cambridge: Brewer, 1979; repr. Woodbridge, 2009.

Lapidge, Michael, and James Rosier. *Aldhelm: The Poetic Works.* Cambridge: Brewer, 1985.

Lapidge, Michael, John Blair, Simon Keynes, and Donald Scragg, eds. *The Wiley-Blackwell Encyclopedia of Anglo-Saxon England.* 2nd ed. Chichester: Wiley-Blackwell, 2014.

Law, Vivien. "Anglo-Saxon England: Ælfric's *Excerptiones de arte grammatica anglice*." *Histoire Épistémologie Langage* 9 (1987): 47–71.

– *Wisdom, Authority and Grammar in the Seventh Century: Decoding Virgilius Maro Grammaticus.* Cambridge: Cambridge University Press, 1995.

Leclercq, Jean. *The Love of Learning and the Desire for God: A Study of Monastic Culture.* Trans. Catherine Misrahi. 3rd ed. New York: Fordham University Press, 1982.

Lehmann, Paul. "Ein neuentdecktes Werk eines angelsächsischen Grammatikers vorkarolingischer Zeit." *Historische Vierteljahrschrift* 26 (1931): 738–56.

– "Die Grammatik aus Aldhelms Kreise." *Historische Vierteljahrschrift* 27 (1932): 758–71.

Lendinara, P. "Anglo-Saxon Glosses and Glossaries: An Introduction." In her *Anglo-Saxon Glosses and Glossaries*, item 1. Aldershot: Ashgate, 1999.

– "Contextualised Lexicography." In *Latin Learning and English Lore: Studies in Anglo-Saxon Literature for Michael Lapidge*, ed. Katherine O'Brien O'Keeffe and Andy Orchard, 2 vols., 2:108–31. Toronto: University of Toronto Press, 2005.

– "Glossaries." In *The Wiley-Blackwell Encyclopedia of Anglo-Saxon England*, ed. Lapidge et al., 212–14.

– "Glosse in volgare e in latino nei codici anglosassoni." *Settimane di studio della fondazione centro italiano di studi sull'alto medioevo* 59 (2012): 945–92.

Leumann, Manu, J.B. Hofmann, and Anton Szantyr. *Lateinische Grammatik. Vol. 2: Lateinische Syntax und Stilistik*. Munich: C.H. Beck, 1965.

Lewald, Ursula. "Die Ezzonen: Das Schicksal eines rheinischen Fürstengeschlechts." *Rheinische Vierteljahrsblätter* 43 (1979): 120–68.

Lewis, C.P. "The French in England before the Norman Conquest." *ANS* 17 (1995): 123–44.

Licence, Tom. "History and Hagiography in the Late Eleventh Century: The Life and Work of Herman the Archdeacon, Monk of Bury St Edmunds." *English Historical Review* 124 (2009): 516–44.

Liuzza, Roy M. "Anglo-Saxon Prognostics in Context: A Survey and Handlist of Manuscripts." *ASE* 30 (2001): 181–230.

– "In Measure, Number, and Weight: Writing Science." *The Cambridge History of Early Medieval English Literature*, ed. Clare Lees, 475–98. Cambridge: Cambridge University Press, 2013.

Lockett, Leslie. "The Composition and Transmission of a Fifteenth-Century Latin Retrograde Sequence Text from Deventer." *Tijdschrift van de Vereniging voor Nederlandse Muziekgeschiedenis* 53 (2003): 105–50.

Löfstedt, Einar. *Late Latin*. Oslo: Aschehoug, 1959.

Lynch, Kevin M. "The Venerable Bede's Knowledge of Greek." *Traditio* 39 (1983): 432–39.

Magennis, Hugh, and Mary Swan, eds. *A Companion to Ælfric*. Leiden: Brill, 2009.

Mantello, F.A.C., and A.G. Rigg, eds. *Medieval Latin: An Introduction and Bibliographic Guide*. Washington, DC: Catholic University of America Press, 1996.

Marenbon, John. "Les sources du vocabulaire d'Aldhelm." *Archivum Latinitatis Medii Aevi* (*Bulletin du Cange*) 41 (1979): 75–90.

Markus, R.A. *Signs and Meaning: World and Text in Ancient Christianity*. Liverpool: Liverpool University Press, 1996.

Marouzeau, J. *L'ordre des mots dans la phrase latine*. Paris: E. Champion, 1922.

McClure, Joan. "Gregory the Great: Exegesis and Audience." DPhil. thesis, Oxford University, 1979.

McDougall, D. and I. McDougall. "Some Notes on Notes on Glosses in the *Dictionary of Old English*." In *Anglo-Saxon Glossography*, ed. Derolez, 115–38.

Menzer, Melinda J. "Ælfric's English *Grammar*." *JEGP* 103 (2004): 106–24.

– "Ælfric's *Grammar*: Solving the Problem of the English-Language Text." *Neophilologus* 83 (1999): 637–52.

Meyvaert, P. "The Date of Gregory the Great's Commentaries on the Canticle of Canticles and on I Kings." *Sacris erudiri* 23 (1978–9): 191–216.

Miles, Brent. "The *Carmina rhythmica* of Æthilwald: Edition, Translation, and Commentary." *JML* 14 (2004): 73–117.

Miles, Richard. "The *Anthologia Latina* and the Creation of Secular Space in Vandal Carthage." *Antiquité tardive* 13 (2005): 305–20.

Mitchell, Bruce. "The Relation between Old English Alliterative Verse and Ælfric's Alliterative Prose." In *Latin Learning and English Lore: Studies in Anglo-Saxon Literature for Michael Lapidge*, ed. Andy Orchard and Katherine O'Brien O'Keeffe, 2 vols., 2:349–62. Toronto: University of Toronto Press, 2005.

Mitchell, Bruce, and F.C. Robinson. *A Guide to Old English*. 8th ed. Chichester: Wiley-Blackwell, 2012.

Munk Olsen, Birger. *L'étude des auteurs classiques latins aux XIe et XIIe siècles*, vol. 2.2. Paris: Éditions du Centre National de la Recherche Scientifique, 1985.

– "The Production of the Classics in the Eleventh and Twelfth Centuries." In *Medieval Manuscripts of the Latin Classics: Production and Use*, ed. Claudine A. Chavannes-Mazel and Margaret M. Smith, 1–17. London and Los Altos Hills, CA: Anderson-Lovelace, Red Gull Press, 1996.

Nees, Lawrence. "Ultán the Scribe." *ASE* 22 (1993): 127–46.

Nelson, Janet L. "Parents, Children and the Church in the Earlier Middle Ages." *The Church and Childhood: Papers Read at the 1993 Summer Meeting and the 1994 Winter Meeting of the Ecclesiastical History Society*, ed. Diana Wood, 81–114. Studies in Church History 31. Oxford: Blackwell, 1994.

– "The Rites of the Conqueror." *ANS* 4 (1981): 117–32, 210–21.

Newlands, Carole E. *Statius, Poet between Rome and Naples*. London: Bristol Classical Press, 2012.

Nichols, Ann Eljenholm. "Ælfric and the Brief Style." *JEGP* 70 (1971): 1–12.

Niedermann, Max. "Les dérivés en ōsus dans les Hisperica Famina." *Bulletin du Cange* 23, fasc. 2 (1953): 75–101.

Norberg, Dag. *An Introduction to the Study of Medieval Latin Versification*. Trans. Grant C. Roti and Jacqueline de la Chapelle Skubly, ed. Jan Ziolkowski. Washington, DC: Catholic University of America Press, 2004.

Norden, Eduard. *Die antike Kunstprosa: vom VI. Jahrhundert v. Chr. bis in die Zeit der Renaissance*. 2nd ed. 2 vols. Berlin and Leipzig: Teubner, 1909.

O'Brien O'Keeffe, Katherine. *Stealing Obedience: Narratives of Agency and Identity in Later Anglo-Saxon England*. Toronto: University of Toronto Press, 2012.

O'Donnell, Thomas, Matthew Townend, and Elizabeth M. Tyler. "European Literature and Eleventh-Century England." In *The Cambridge History of Early Medieval English Literature*, ed. Clare A. Lees, 607–36. Cambridge: Cambridge University Press, 2013.

Orchard, Andy. "After Aldhelm: The Teaching and Transmission of the Anglo-Latin Hexameter." *JML* 2 (1992): 96–133.

– "The Literary Background of the *Encomium Emmae Reginae*." *JML* 11 (2001): 156–83.

– "Old Sources, New Resources: Finding the Right Formula for Boniface." *ASE* 30 (2001): 15–38.

– *The Poetic Art of Aldhelm*. CSASE 8. 1994.

Parisse, Michel. "L'évêque d'Empire au XIe siècle. L'exemple lorrain." *Cahiers de civilisation médiévale, Xe–XIIe siècles* 27 (1984): 95–105.

– "Lotharingia." In *The New Cambridge Medieval History*, vol. 3, *c.900–c.1024*, ed. Timothy Reuter, 312. Cambridge: Cambridge University Press, 1999.

Pfaff, Richard W. "Lanfranc's Supposed Purge of the Anglo-Saxon Calendar." In *Warriors and Churchmen in the High Middle Ages*, ed. Timothy Reuter, 95–108. London and Rio Grande, OH: Hambledon Press, 1992.

Pohl, Walter. "The Construction of Communities and the Persistence of Paradox: An Introduction." In *The Construction of Communities in the Early Middle Ages: Texts, Resources and Artefacts*, ed. Richard Corradini, Max Diesenberger, and Helmut Reimitz, 1–15. Leiden: Brill, 2003.

Powell, G.F. "Hyperbaton and Register in Cicero." In *Colloquial and Literary Latin*, ed. E. Dickey and A. Chahoud, 163–85. Cambridge: Cambridge University Press, 2010.

Prinz, Otto. "Zum Einfluss des Griechischen auf den Wortschatz des Mittelalters." In *Festschrift Bernhard Bischoff zu seinem 65. Geburtstag*, ed. J. Autenrieth and F. Brunhölzl, 1–15. Stuttgart: Anton Hiersemann, 1971.

Pulsiano, P. "A Proposal for a Collective Edition of the Old English Glossed Psalters." In *Anglo-Saxon Glossography*, ed. Derolez, 167–87.

Ramsay, Nigel, and Margaret Sparks. "The Cult of St Dunstan at Christ Church, Canterbury." In *St Dunstan: His Life, Times and Cult*, ed. Nigel Ramsay, Margaret Sparks, and Tim Tatton-Brown, 311–23. Woodbridge: Boydell Press, 1992.

Rankin, Susan. "From Memory to Written Record: Musical Notation in Manuscripts from Exeter." *ASE* 13 (1984): 97–112.

– "Making the Liturgy: Winchester Scribes and Their Books." In *The Liturgy of the Late Anglo-Saxon Church*, ed. Helen Gittos and M. Bradford Bedingfield, 29–52. London: Henry Bradshaw Society, 2005.

– "Neumatic Notations in Anglo-Saxon England." In *Musicologie médiévale: Notations et séquences*, ed. Michel Hugo, 129–44. Paris: Champion, 1987.

Rauer, C. "Errors and Textual Problems in the *Old English Martyrology*." *Neophilologus* 97 (2013): 147–64.

– "Old English *blanca* in the *Old English Martyrology*." *Notes and Queries* 55 (2008): 396–9.

– "Pelagia's Cloak in the *Old English Martyrology*." *Notes and Queries* 57 (2010): 3–6.

Raven, D.S. *Latin Metre*. London: Bristol Classical Press, 1998.

Ray, Roger. "Who Did Bede Think He Was?" In *Innovation and Tradition*, ed. DeGregorio, 11–35.

Reeve, M.D. "Statius." In *Texts and Transmission: A Survey of the Latin Classics*, ed. L.D. Reynolds, 394–7. Oxford: Clarendon Press, 1993.

Renardy, Christine. "Les écoles liégeoises du IXe au XIIe siècles: grandes lignes de leur evolution." *Revue belge de philologie et d'histoire* 57 (1979): 309–28.

Reuter, Timothy. "The 'Imperial Church System' of the Ottonian and Salian Rulers: A Reconsideration." In his *Medieval Polities and Modern Mentalities*, ed. Janet L. Nelson, 325–54. Cambridge: Cambridge University Press, 2006.

Riché, Pierre. *Les écoles et l'enseignement dans l'Occident chrétien de la fin du Ve siècle au milieu du XIe siècle*. Paris: Aubier Montaigne, 1979.

Ridyard, S.J. "*Condigna veneratio*: Post-Conquest Attitudes to the Saints of the Anglo-Saxons." *ANS* 9 (1986): 179–206.

Rigg, A.G. "Henry of Huntingdon's Metrical Experiments." *JML* 1 (1991): 60–72.

– *A History of Anglo-Latin Literature, 1066–1422*. Cambridge: Cambridge University Press, 1992.

– "Medieval Latin Poetic Anthologies (I)." *Mediaeval Studies* 39 (1977): 281–330.

Rigg, A.G., and G.R. Wieland. "A Canterbury Classbook of the Mid-Eleventh Century (the 'Cambridge Songs' Manuscript)." *ASE* 4 (1975): 113–30.

Robertson, Duncan. *Lectio Divina: The Medieval Experience of Reading*. Cistercian Studies Series 238. Collegeville, MN: Liturgical Press, 2011.

Rosé, Isabelle. *Construire une société seigneuriale: itinéraire et ecclésiologie de l'abbé Odon de Cluny*. Turnhout: Brepols, 2008.

Rowley, Sharon M. *The Old English Version of Bede's Historia ecclesiastica*. Anglo-Saxon Studies 16. Cambridge: D.S. Brewer, 2011.

Rubenstein, Jay. "The Life and Writings of Osbern of Canterbury." In *Canterbury and the Norman Conquest*, ed. Eales and Sharpe, 27–40.

Ruff, Carin. "The Perception of Difficulty in Aldhelm's Prose." In *Insignis Sophiae Arcator: Medieval Latin Studies in Honour of Michael Herren on His 65th Birthday*, ed. Gernot R. Wieland, Carin Ruff, and Ross G. Arthur, 165–77. Publications of The Journal of Medieval Latin 6. Turnhout: Brepols, 2006.

– "The Place of Metrics in Anglo-Saxon Latin Education: Aldhelm and Bede." *JEGP* 104 (2005): 149–70.

Rusche, Philip G. "The Cleopatra Glossaries: An Edition with Commentary on the Glosses and Their Sources." PhD dissertation, Yale University, 1996.

– "Dry-Point Glosses to Aldhelm's *De laudibus uirginitatis* in Beinecke 401." *ASE* 23 (1994): 195–213.

– "Isidore's *Etymologiae* and the Canterbury Aldhelm Scholia." *JEGP* 104 (2005): 437–55.

– "The *Old English Martyrology* and the Canterbury Aldhelm Scholia" (forthcoming).

Sauer, Hans. "Ælfric and Emotion." *Poetica* 66 (2006): 37–52.

– "How the Anglo-Saxons Expressed Their Emotions with the Help of Interjections." *Brno Studies in English* 35 (2009): 167–83.

– "Interjection, Emotion, Grammar, and Literature." In *Historical Englishes in Varieties of Texts and Contexts*, ed. Masachiyo Amano, Michiko Ogura, and Masayuki Ohkado, 389–93. Bern: Peter Lang, 2008.

– "Language and Culture: How Anglo-Saxon Glossators Adapted Latin Words and Their World." *JML* 18 (2006): 437–68.

Schaller, Dieter. "Vortrags- und Zirkulardichtung am Hof Karls des Großen." *Mittellateinisches Jahrbuch* 6 (1970). Repr. in his *Studien zur lateinischen Dichtung des Frühmittelalters*, 87–109. Stuttgart: Anton Hiersemann, 1995.

Schmidt, Paul. "Heinrich III: Das Bild des Herrschers in der Literatur seiner Zeit." *Deutsches Archiv für Erforschung des Mittelalters* 39 (1983): 582–90.

Schneider, Jens. "Latein und Althochdeutsch in der Cambridger Liedersammlung: De Henrico, Clericus et Nonna." In *Volkssprachig-lateinische Mischtexte und Textensembles in der althochdeutschen und altenglischen Überlieferung*, ed. Rolf Bermann. Heidelberg: Winter, 2003.

Scholz, Bernhard W. "Eadmer's Life of Bregwine, Archbishop of Canterbury, 761–764." *Traditio* 22 (1966): 127–48.

Searle, Eleanor. "Women and the Legitimisation of Succession at the Norman Conquest." *ANS* 3 (1981): 159–70.

Sharpe, Richard. "The Varieties of Bede's Prose." In *Aspects of the Language of Latin Prose*, ed. Tobias Reinhardt, Michael Lapidge, and J.N. Adams, 339–56. Oxford: Oxford University Press for the British Academy, 2005.

Short, Ian. "Patrons and Polyglots: French Literature in Twelfth-Century England." *ANS* 14 (1991): 229–49.

– "*Tam Angli quam Franci*: Self-Definition in Anglo-Norman England." *ANS* 18 (1996): 153–75.

Sisam, Kenneth. "The Order of Ælfric's Early Books." In his *Studies in the History of Old English Literature*. Oxford: Clarendon Press, 1953.

Smalley, Beryl. *The Study of the Bible in the Middle Ages.* Notre Dame, IN: Notre Dame University Press, 1964.

Southern, R.W. "The Place of England in the Twelfth Century Renaissance." In his *Medieval Humanism and Other Studies*, 158–80. Oxford: Basil Blackwell, 1970.

– *Saint Anselm and His Biographer: A Study of Monastic Life and Thought, 1059–c. 1130*. Cambridge: Cambridge University Press, 1963.

Spallone, Maddalena. "Il Par. lat. 10318 (Salmasiano): dal manoscritto alto-medioevale ad una raccolta enciclopedica tardo-antica." *Italia medioevale e umanistica* 25 (1982): 36–51.

Stafford, Pauline. "Archbishop Ealdred and the D Chronicle." In *Normandy and Its Neighbours, 900–1250: Essays for David Bates*, ed. David Crouch and Kathleen Thompson, 135–56. Turnhout: Brepols, 2011.

Stephenson, Rebecca. "Ælfric of Eynsham and Hermeneutic Latin: *Meatim sed et rustica* Reconsidered." *JML* 16 (2006): 111–41.

– "Byrhtferth's *Enchiridion*: The Effectiveness of Hermeneutic Latin." In *Conceptualizing Multilingualism in England, c.800–c.1250*, ed. Elizabeth M. Tyler, 121–43. Turnhout: Brepols, 2011.

– "Deliberate Obfuscation: The Purpose of Hard Words and Difficult Syntax in the Literature of Anglo-Saxon England." PhD dissertation, University of Notre Dame, 2004.

– *Politics of Language: Byrhtferth, Ælfric, and the Multilingual Identity of the Benedictine Reform.* Toronto: University of Toronto Press, 2015.

– "Scapegoating the Secular Clergy: The Hermeneutic Style as a Form of Monastic Self-Definition." *ASE* 38 (2009): 101–35.

Swan, Mary, and Elaine Treharne, eds. *Rewriting Old English in the Twelfth Century*. Cambridge: Cambridge University Press, 2000.

Szarmach, Paul E. "Bede on Aldhelm: *Nitidus sermone*." *American Notes & Queries* 9 (1971): 375–7.

Taylor, H.M. "The Architectural Interest of Æthelwulf's 'De abbatibus.'" *ASE* 3 (1974): 163–73.

Thacker, Alan. "Bede's Ideal of Reform." In *Ideal and Reality in Frankish and Anglo-Saxon Society: Studies Presented to J.M. Wallace-Hadrill*, ed. Patrick Wormald, Donald Bullough, and Roger Collins, 130–53. Oxford: Basil Blackwell, 1983.

– "Monks, Preaching and Pastoral Care." In *Pastoral Care before the Parish*, ed. John Blair and Richard Sharpe, 137–70. Leicester: Leicester University Press, 1992.

Thiel, Matthias. *Grundlagen und Gestalt der Hebräischkenntnisse des frühen Mittelalters*. Biblioteca degli Studi Medievali 4. Spoleto: Centro Italiano di Studi sull'alto Medioevo, 1973.

Thijs, C.B. "Wærferth's Translation of the *Dialogi* of Gregory the Great." PhD dissertation, University of Leeds, 2003.

Thomson, R.M. "England and the Twelfth-Century Renaissance." *Past and Present* 101 (1983): 2–21.

– "The Norman Conquest and English Libraries." In his *England and the Twelfth-Century Renaissance*, item XVIII, 27–40. Aldershot: Variorum, 1998.

– "The Place of Germany in the Twelfth-Century Renaissance." In *Manuscripts and Monastic Culture: Reform and Renewal in Twelfth-Century Germany*, ed. A. Beach, 19–42. Turnhout: Brepols, 2007.

Thornbury, Emily V. "Aldhelm's Rejection of the Muses and the Mechanics of Poetic Inspiration in Early Anglo-Saxon England." *ASE* 36 (2007): 71–92.

– *Becoming a Poet in Anglo-Saxon England*. Cambridge Studies in Medieval Literature 88. Cambridge: Cambridge University Press, 2014.

Tilliette, Jean-Yves. "*Troiae ab oris*: Aspects de la revolution poétique de la seconde moitié du XIe siècle." *Latomus* 58 (1999): 405–31.

Townsend, David. "Anglo-Latin Hagiography and the Anglo-Norman Transition." *Exemplaria* 3.2 (1991): 385–433.

– "Latinities, 893–1143." In *The Cambridge History of Early Medieval English Literature*, ed. Clare A. Lees, 530–53. Cambridge: Cambridge University Press, 2013.

Traube, Ludwig. *Karolingische Dichtungen*. Berlin: Weidmannsche Buchhandlung, 1888.

Treharne, Elaine. "Bishops and Their Texts in the Later Eleventh Century: Worcester and Exeter." In *Essays in Manuscript Geography: Vernacular Manuscripts of the English West Midlands from the Conquest to the Sixteenth Century*, ed. Wendy Scase, 13–28. Turnhout: Brepols, 2007.

– "Categorization, Periodization: The Silence of (the) English in the Twelfth Century." *New Medieval Literatures* 8 (2006): 247–73.

– *Living through Conquest: The Politics of Early English, 1020–1220*. Oxford: Oxford University Press, 2012.
– "Producing a Library in Late Anglo-Saxon England: Exeter, 1050–72." *Review of English Studies* 54 (2003): 155–72.
– "The Production and Use of English Manuscripts 1060–1220." www.le.ac.uk/ee/em1060to1220.
Tyler, Elizabeth M. "Crossing Conquests: Polyglot Royal Women and Literary Culture in Eleventh-Century England." In *Conceptualizing Multilingualism in England: c.800–c.1250*, ed. Elizabeth M. Tyler, 171–96. Turnhout: Brepols, 2011.
– *England in Europe: English Royal Women and Literary Patronage, c.1000–c.1150*. Toronto: University of Toronto Press, forthcoming.
– "Fictions of Family: The *Encomium Emmae Reginae* and Virgil's *Aeneid*." *Viator* 36 (2005): 149–79.
– "From Old English to Old French." In *Language and Culture in Medieval Britain: The French of England, c.1100–c.1500*, ed. Jocelyn Wogan-Browne et al., 164–78. Woodbridge: York Medieval Press, in association with Boydell and Brewer, 2009.
– "Talking about History in Eleventh-Century England: The *Encomium Emmae Reginae* and the Court of Harthacnut." *Early Medieval Europe* 13 (2005): 359–83.
– "The *Vita Ædwardi*: The Politics of Poetry at Wilton Abbey." *ANS* 31 (2009): 135–56.
Ullman, B.L. "Latin Word-Order." *Classical Journal* 14 (1918): 154–85.
von den Steinen, Wolfram. "Die Anfänge der Sequenzendichtung." *Zeitschrift für Schweizerische Kirchengeschichte* 40 (1946): 190–212, 241–68; 41 (1947): 19–48, 122–62.
– *Notker der Dichter und seine geistige Welt*. 2 vols. Bern: A. Francke, 1948.
Waite, G.G. "The Vocabulary of the Old English Version of Bede's *Historia ecclesiastica*." PhD dissertation, University of Toronto, 1984.
Wallis, Faith. "Background Essay: St John's College 17 as a Computus Manuscript." In *The Calendar and the Cloister: Oxford, St John's College MS 17*. 2007. McGill University Library. Digital Collections Program. http://digital.library.mcgill.ca/ms-17.
– "Bede and Science." In *The Cambridge Companion to Bede*, ed. DeGregorio, 113–26.
– "Cædmon's Created World and the Monastic Encyclopedia." In *Cædmon's Hymn and Material Culture in the World of Bede*, ed. Allen J. Frantzen and

John Hines, 80–110. Medieval European Studies 7. Morgantown: West Virgina University Press, 2007.

Webber, Teresa. *Scribes and Scholars at Salisbury Cathedral, c. 1075–c. 1120*. Oxford: Clarendon Press, 1992.

– "Script and Manuscript Production at Christ Church, Canterbury, after the Norman Conquest." In *Canterbury and the Norman Conquest*, ed. Eales and Sharpe, 145–58.

Weise, Oscar. *Die griechischen Wörter im Latein*. Leipzig, 1882.

Wetherbee, Winthrop. "From Late Antiquity to the Twelfth Century." In *The Cambridge History of Literary Criticism. Vol. 2: The Middle Ages*, ed. Alastair Minnis and Ian Johnson, 99–144. Cambridge: Cambridge University Press, 2005.

Wieland, G.R. "The Glossed Manuscript: Classbook or Library Book?" *ASE* 14 (1985): 153–73.

Wilson, R.M. "The Provenance of the Vespasian Psalter Gloss: The Linguistic Evidence." In *The Anglo-Saxons: Studies in Some Aspects of Their History and Culture Presented to Bruce Dickins*, ed. P. Clemoes, 292–310. London: Bowes and Bowes, 1959.

Winterbottom, Michael. "Aldhelm's Prose Style and Its Origins." *ASE* 6 (1977): 39–76.

– "The Style of Æthelweard." *Medium Ævum* 36 (1967): 109–18.

Wolfram, Herwig. *Conrad II: 900–1039*. Trans. Denise Kaiser. University Park: Pennsylvania State University Press, 2006.

Wood, Ian. "Monasteries and the Geography of Power in the Age of Bede." *Northern History* 45 (2008): 11–25.

Wormald, Patrick. "Æthelwold and His Continental Counterparts: Contact, Comparison, Contrast." In *Bishop Æthelwold*, ed. Yorke, 13–42.

Yorke, Barbara, ed. *Bishop Æthelwold: His Career and Influence*. Woodbridge: Boydell Press, 1988.

Zetzel, James E.G. *Marginal Scholarship and Textual Deviance: The Commentum Cornuti and the Early Scholia on Persius*. Bulletin of the Institute of Classical Studies Supplement 84. London: Institute of Classical Studies, School of Advanced Study, University of London, 2005.

Index of Manuscripts

General Index

Toronto Anglo-Saxon Series

1 *Preaching the Converted: The Style and Rhetoric of the Vercelli Book Homilies*, Samantha Zacher
2 *Say What I Am Called: The Old English Riddles of the Exeter Book and the Anglo-Latin Riddle Tradition*, Dieter Bitterli
3 *The Aesthetics of Nostalgia: Historical Representation in Anglo-Saxon Verse*, Renée Trilling
4 *New Readings in the Vercelli Book*, edited by Samantha Zacher and Andy Orchard
5 *Authors, Audiences, and Old English Verse*, Thomas A. Bredehoft
6 *On Aesthetics in* Beowulf *and Other Old English Poems*, edited by John M. Hill
7 *Old English Metre: An Introduction*, Jun Terasawa
8 *Anglo-Saxon Psychologies in the Vernacular and Latin Traditions*, Leslie Lockett
9 *The Body Legal in Barbarian Law*, Lisi Oliver
10 *Old English Literature and the Old Testament*, edited by Michael Fox and Manish Sharma
11 *Stealing Obedience: Narratives of Agency and Identity in Later Anglo-Saxon England*, Katherine O'Brien O'Keeffe
12 *Traditional Subjectivities: The Old English Poetics of Mentality*, Britt Mize
13 *Land and Book: Literature and Land Tenure in Anglo-Saxon England*, Scott T. Smith
14 *Writing Women Saints in Anglo-Saxon England*, edited by Paul E. Szarmach
15 *Anglo-Saxon Manuscripts: A Bibliographical Handlist of Manuscripts and Manuscript Fragments Written or Owned in England up to 1100*, Helmut Gneuss and Michael Lapidge

16 *The King's Body: Burial and Succession in Anglo-Saxon England*, Nicole Marafioti
17 *From Lawmen to Plowmen: Anglo-Saxon Legal Tradition and the School of Langland*, Stephen Yeager
18 *The Politics of Language: Byrhtferth, Ælfric, and the Multilingual Identity of the Benedictine Reform*, Rebecca Stephenson
19 *Weaving Words and Binding Bodies: The Poetics of Human Experience in Old English Literature*, Megan Cavell
20 *Joinings: Compound Words in Old English Literature*, Jonathan Davis-Secord
21 *Imagining the Jew in Anglo-Saxon Literature and Culture*, edited by Samantha Zacher
22 *Latinity and Identity in Anglo-Saxon Literature*, edited by Rebecca Stephenson and Emily V. Thornbury

www.ingramcontent.com/pod-product-compliance
Lightning Source LLC
LaVergne TN
LVHW090155080826

844660LV00013B/824/J

* 9 7 8 1 4 4 2 6 3 7 5 8 0 *